INDIANA GOTHIC

A STORY OF ADULTERY
AND MURDER IN
AN AMERICAN FAMILY

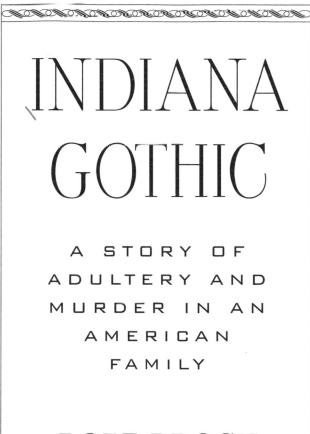

INDIANA GOTHIC

A STORY OF ADULTERY AND MURDER IN AN AMERICAN FAMILY

POPE BROCK

NAN A. TALESE

DOUBLEDAY

New York London Toronto

Sydney Auckland

PUBLISHED BY NAN A. TALESE
an imprint of Doubleday
a division of Random House, Inc.
1540 Broadway, New York, New York 10036

DOUBLEDAY is a trademark of Doubleday, a division of
Random House, Inc.

Book design by Marysarah Quinn

Library of Congress Cataloging-in-Publication Data
Brock, Pope.
Indiana gothic: a story of adultery and murder in an
American family / Pope Brock. — 1st ed. in the U.S.A.
        p.   cm.
        I. Title.
     PS3552.R59I53   1999
813'.54—dc21   98-41736
              CIP

ISBN 0-385-48509-3

1   3   5   7   9   10   8   6   4   2

First Edition

FOR SUSAN

NOTE TO THE READER

The story you are about to read lay buried in my family for a long time. It concerns the true circumstances of the death of my great-grandfather, Ham Dillon, and it was kept secret from most of us, his descendants, for nearly eighty years.

Looking back, I can see that this episode contributed its share to what my sister calls "the rigid and desperate decorum" that pervaded our lives as we were growing up. There was a whiff of sourceless shame in our house, a relentless emphasis on good behavior even stronger than the usual strictures of growing up Christian in the fifties. It was as though the family was bent on making sure that nothing untoward would ever happen again.

In the mid-eighties my great-aunt Ruth—she was nearly as old as the century then, and settling accounts before passing on— finally dropped some clues to this scandal that had shadowed us all. But it wasn't until 1994 that a cousin of mine, Michal Yanson, had the wit and enterprise to write the local library in Washington, Indiana, to see if there were any records of this tale. The result was a handful of newspaper clippings from microfilm.

Over the next couple of years I made three trips out to Indiana, where I found a trove of other press coverage. The transcript of the trial was missing, lost in the usual courthouse fire, though I did find a few charred documents relating to the case. I immersed myself in research on the time and place.

What follows then is a true story, reconstructed. No plot points have been jiggered to make it a better tale. However, much of the record was fragmentary, of course—including the courtroom testimony—or missing altogether. Ultimately the facts formed a line of buoys in a sea of my own imagination.

"I drove all night. . . . I could see myself in the windshield. My face. My eyes. I studied my face. Studied everything about it. As though I was looking at another man. As though I could see his whole race behind him. . . . And then his face changed. His face became his father's face. Same bones. Same eyes. Same nose. Same breath. And his father's face changed to his Grandfather's face. And it went on like that. Changing. Clear on back to faces I'd never seen before but still recognized."

—SAM SHEPARD,
Buried Child

PROLOGUE

JOLTING ALONG in his buggy through the freezing night, gripping the seat with his free hand, Dr. MacGregor Porter could see the bonfire from the road. It was a mile or more off, up a slight rise of hill, but he could make out the lick and leap of the flames plain enough, see the dark and shifting figures. He knew what they were doing and why. Hell, he'd advised it. That day a patient of his who lived there, nice woman, had died of cancer. Now the family was burning her bedroom furniture and her clothes.

Yea, *man is born to trouble as the sparks fly upward,* the doctor said to himself. He was a compact individual, with wry eyes and a bandito's mustache, bundled up as snug as he could get against the cold. Coasting onto a smoother stretch of road, he snapped the reins on the horse's flank and picked up speed. He was on his way to another farmhouse now, on another hurry-up call. A boy with

1

a cough this time. Could mean anything. Maybe just a cold. Maybe TB.

He blew out a breath and looked up at the great splatter of stars overhead, and at the moon half slipped into the pocket of the sky. The whole firmament seemed to be catching its light from the snow, which lay smooth and undisturbed in every direction, mile after mile—and flat mostly, with a few rolling hills that kept losing their initiative. As he rode along, resting his boots on a heated brick wrapped in rags, Dr. Porter could pick out a weathered farmhouse here and there in the distance, a barn, ribbons of fence. Along the western horizon he could see a long sketch of bare trees and nearby them, like a crack in the porcelain, a dark creek running toward the White River, which marked the county line.

It was called the Pocket, this rich wedge of land in southwestern Indiana, and it was farming soil as fine as any in the nation. Come summer, these fields would turn to kingdoms of corn and wheat and cattle, a good hundred thousand acres here in Daviess County alone, tended by farmers and their families who devoted their lives to work and worship and not a whole lot else.

Dr. Porter believed there were a few who overdid it. When it came to religion, in particular, he could name several people he thought should cut down their dosage. Starting with these temperance crusaders: right in the village of Elnora, where he lived, they had already managed to ban saloons in the referendum of '04, and now they were taking the fight to the town of Washington, the county seat, and some of them didn't put any bounds on what they would do in the name of the cause. Every once in a while another tavern would explode in a fireball, usually in the middle of the night, showering glass and flaming debris all over the street—not often, but just enough to keep a man's buttocks a little tight on the barstool.

The temperance nuts weren't the worst of it. Vigilante groups were springing up now too, through the nation's South and Midwest, full of their own ideas of how everybody should behave. Around Elnora one of these ragtag posses had been operating lately—some wearing hoods, some bank-robber kerchiefs, only a couple ever identified—galloping through the night every once in a while with torches held high, burning crops and beating up Catholics. Maybe they'd give some fellow who'd been lifting his hand against his wife a taste of his own medicine. You could never predict what these birds wouldn't like.

Of course, most people around here weren't this way. They weren't fanatics, just deep-down Christians who clung to the Bible as their solace and their code. Even so, Dr. Porter had noticed how most of these regular citizens seemed to put up with the bombers and night riders. Nobody ever really organized or fought back. Mulling that little puzzle over, with the detached air of a medical man, Dr. Porter had concluded that in a place like the Pocket, so steeped in old-time morality, where flagrant sinners could be marked with the flaming brand of outcasts—well, a few abscesses on the body religious were the kind of thing you had to expect. Although some families just mixed a pinch of morality in a bucket of ignorance. A lot of Protestant children actually had it in their heads that someday the Pope might show up, lead them all out of town like the Pied Piper, and drown them in the river.

Dr. Porter slowed down, peering along the rail fence by the roadside for the turn-up to the Hale house. He was four or five miles southeast of Elnora now, on a route he'd ridden a couple thousand times in his life, but he'd never actually been to this place before. It was a little runt of a farm, maybe twenty-five acres, squeezed in between some much grander holdings. The Hales had just bought it that past fall. Before that, the land had been owned by some kind of fundamentalist family who didn't believe in doctors.

Creaking along slowly now, over frozen mud and gravel up the snaking drive, he looked ahead for the house. He drove through a twist of trees and there it was, a dark hulk, sharp-bladed, against the night sky. Two upended rectangles of light threw a minor glow onto the front porch.

Dr. Porter came to a stop and climbed down from his rig, then reached back in for his bag. Hugging his greatcoat tight against the wind, he hollowly mounted the steps to the front door. It was flung open before he could knock.

He was in a hallway now, slashed by a great shadow, the door closed behind him. A woman was talking. She probably thought she was telling him something, but all he caught was her fear. Off to the left, he noticed there were two other people in the parlor, her daughters most likely: one, a plump child of six or so, lay on her belly on the carpet with a stereoscope pressed against her face like opera glasses, idly kicking her legs; the other, a girl in her mid-teens with a waterfall of dark hair, stood against the wall, wedged between the edge of the piano and the window, gazing directly at the doctor with a look he couldn't read.

He glanced back to find that the woman had already turned and was heading up the stairs. He followed. In a moment they were standing in a dim sickroom, lit by three or four sulfur candles placed here and there, reeking with disinfectant. The boy, Arthur Hale, about ten years old, lay in a moon-stained bed by the window fighting to breathe.

Another huge cough, grinding up from deep in his chest, brought the child halfway to a sitting position, and then he fell back again on his pillow. The doctor blew out two of the candles, forced the window open wider, and then, dragging a chair to the bedside, opened his bag and began rifling through it. At the same time he pushed a wastebasket closer with his foot.

Now it was too damn dark. "Can you light that?" he asked the mother, and poked a thumb at the kerosene lamp on the bedtable. Fetching matches from the mantelpiece, Mrs. Hale struck one and applied it to the wick.

In the bloom of light Dr. Porter could see the boy's face

clearly now; it was a mottled white and blue. A sucking noise came from his windpipe.

Sliding his index finger into Arthur's mouth and reaching deep, the doctor drew out a long gray eel of phlegm, pulled it free and slung it into the trash can. The boy snatched a tremendous breath. Then Dr. Porter touched the homemade poultice on Arthur's chest—it was cooling off—and glanced at the bedtable. Nothing on it but a bottle of Foley's Honey and Tar Cough Syrup. Might as well give the boy glue.

With a half-turn of his head, the doctor told Mrs. Hale to go down to the kitchen and heat up some onions for another poultice. When he called to her again—he had some other instruction to add—she had reached the bedroom door, and for the first time, in the light from the hallway, he got a good look at her face.

She had the eyes of a cornered animal, but God almighty, what a handsome woman.

Mrs. Hale was poised listening to him; then she was gone. A moment later Dr. Porter pulled his eyes from the doorway and returned his attention to the boy.

"You been vomiting, son?" he asked as he searched for something in his bag. The boy rocked his head no.

Sloshing a little whiskey into a glass from the flask he carried, Dr. Porter crumbled in a bit of rock sugar and gave it a quick stir with his house key. (Whatever else he gave his patients, they all got whiskey.) He brought the glass to Arthur's lips.

But Mrs. Hale continued to float in his mind's eye. There were a few iron gleams in her auburn hair now, but she had the kind of looks that last—those wide gray eyes and prime bones. He was trying to remember what he knew about her.

She had a sister, that was it: Maggie, the one who married Ham Dillon. They lived not more than a mile away. But the Dillons had a first-class farm, one of the finest around, and Ham himself was one of the leading lights of the county.

It was peculiar, all right. Here was the older sister, a real belle of the ball, stuck off in this little hog wallow, living in Maggie's shadow more or less.

Where was Mr. Hale anyhow?

Briskly the doctor kept working away on Arthur, who was breathing better now. With daubs of skunk grease—a sort of light yellow cold cream, a good inhalant, supplied to him by a local trapper—he streaked the boy's throat and chest while making low, soothing sounds. But his mind lingered on the mother.

Then he was jarred by piano music suddenly rising up from downstairs, aching and rippling, a deathbed farewell to love. For an instant he felt as if he'd been caught at something. Must be that older girl playing. What was it? Chopin. Even Dr. Porter, whose taste in music ran more toward Civil War tunes and coon songs, knew Chopin when he heard it. His wife played the same thing. Nobody knew quite why, but that fellow's music seemed to have crystallized some great, romantic yearning in the air. It had found its way into practically every piano bench in the United States.

Borne along by the foaming piano downstairs, Dr. Porter thought again of Mrs. Hale. He thought of her long body, of the delicate blue veins that traced the back of the hand he'd seen at her throat. She looked strong, though. He pictured those translucent hands of hers in the sharp grip of passion.

A wracking cough from Arthur brought him to.

DOWN IN THE KITCHEN Allie Hale, a long knife in her hand, was savaging an onion on the cutting board. The music from the parlor she barely heard. Allie was caught in her own electric anxiety, and under her knife the onion turned to dozens, hundreds of little pieces.

She had good reason to worry. Any illness could be frightening, and infections were always running around loose. People died all the time of the littlest things. Last fall twelve-year-old Mamie Bowers over in Odon had come home with a squiggle of blood on her elbow, and the next week she was dead.

But farm people lived with the fear and the fatalities, and they didn't come apart. Something else was pushing Allie to the ragged edge of hysteria. As she worked at the cutting board, she was trying to figure out what it was.

If he dies, it's a judgment on me.

She paused with the knife in mid-stroke. It was there in the Bible, that bit about the sins of the father being visited on the children. It must apply to mothers too.

The baby woke up and began to whimper. The littlest, Lewis: he was tucked into a homemade wooden cradle with PIERCE'S ALL-RIO COFFEE embossed on the side, set beside the glowing stove to help keep him warm. At the sound of his cries Big Jack, the dog, heaved himself up from the corner by the woodbox and plodded over to investigate. With great care he sniffed all around the baby's head, then looked over at Allie, his eyes empty of news.

The Lord would never do that, Allie thought, as she reattacked the onion. Kill a child like that? No. It was impossible. Then she thought of Maggie, her younger sister—so easy to resent now, with her big house, her prying solicitude. She remembered Maggie's presents from last Christmas, delivered with that remark that the Hale children sure looked ready for some good warm clothes. And her pies. Gooseberry, blackberry, cherry, plum: Maggie made the most wonderful pies around, everybody said so, with crust that crumbled like— *Nothing has crumbled so magnificently since the Roman Empire,* that's what their father had said one night years ago, in the mellow throes of a good Bordeaux. And Maggie sitting there silent with that glint of triumph in her eyes. That's what her pies were, little golden-brown acts of triumph with fork holes to let the steam out. Especially when she brought one by these days for Allie and her family, the overworked Hales who were having such a rough time. Allie rarely telephoned her these days, but Maggie still kept it up, still turned up sometimes, at galling moments, uninvited.

And yet she could never dislike Maggie for long. You couldn't deeply dislike someone you had betrayed; you didn't have the right, or that's the way it seemed. Of course, you couldn't love the person either, or even like her much. Every sisterly emotion held suspended: that was Allie now. Except for those moments when terror touched her, as light as a kiss, that Maggie would find out what she'd done.

With a wooden spoon Allie shoved the smoking bits of onion around in a skillet. Leaving them sizzling, she crossed to the kitchen table, pulled a square of red flannel out of a drawer, and spread it out flat. Then she returned to the skillet, grasped the handle with a dishcloth, walked back over, and scraped the steaming mound of onions onto the flannel. With quick strokes she smoothed them out with the spoon, folded the red cloth over and then, snatching it up, darted for the stairs. Chopin and onions wafted through the house.

"It's croup, Mrs. Hale," the doctor said, the moment she entered Arthur's room. "He's a sick boy, but he's going to make it. I mean to say, it's not whooping cough, it's just . . ." He paused, gazing at her, then added idiotically: "croup."

Together they taped the poultice onto Arthur's chest—it was so hot the first touch made the boy cry out—while Allie kissed his forehead, smoothed his hair. From downstairs they heard the baby erupt with a great howl. The music broke off. There was the sound of running feet.

Soon after, Dr. Porter and Allie were downstairs again in the hall, he reassuring, she grateful, he taking his overcoat down from a peg (and swearing to himself he'd be back in church next Sunday). Louise was standing in the parlor with her back to him now, holding and patting Lewis, whose moonface loomed up over her shoulder. His eyes were fixed on the doctor. The baby looked old and infinitely troubled.

As he reached down for his bag, Dr. Porter felt a tug at his coat. It was the six-year-old. She was holding up the stereoscope.

"Look," she said.

He did (stepping into the parlor where the light was better), and brought to his eyes a vast lavender wonderland, an Arabian dream: it was every possible shade of purple, a marvelously tinted photograph of mosques and minarets, minutely etched, rising up behind some sort of main street where he could make out bearded merchants in their stalls and a woman swathed in a long cloak. The three-dimensional effect was really extraordinary, he thought. He hadn't looked at a stereoscope in years.

It was the figure of the woman that held his attention most. As far away as she was standing—she was really just one small element in the scheme of the picture—she was the only one facing the camera, gazing with a taut pride that seemed to say: *Everything you see here, this whole luminous kingdom, belongs to me.*

Just then came the crunch of buggy wheels approaching the house, and the sound of a horse clopping to a stop. Allie went to the parlor window and looked out. The buggy had pulled in under the eave of the barn, where it was dark, but the lightspill from the house was enough to show her that it was Maggie climbing down, Maggie reaching back to pluck something off the seat. As Allie expected, it was the hamper her sister used for carrying pies.

PART ONE

O, it scts my heart a-clickin' like the

tickin' of a clock,

When the frost is on the punkin and the

fodder's in the shock.

—JAMES WHITCOMB RILEY

1

TIME WAS, thousands of Shawnee were spread along the White River in western Indiana, under the command of Tecumseh, their great chief. Tecumseh's scorching hatred for the white man was regarded—by white men anyway—as borderline crazy. He and his warriors were such ferocious fighters, it seemed to take an ungodly amount of time to get them out of there.

Even after the Shawnee were finally driven out, though, around 1811, you couldn't say that western Indiana fully belonged to the white man. Or if you did say it, you might get an argument. Some thought it belonged more to the owls.

Throughout the northern reaches of Daviess County in particular, the forests and open fields were full of owls, infested with them. Screech owls, barred owls, owls with ears like rabbits, owls which seemed to have no ears at all—*whoop, toot, chirrr,* the racket they made was like monkeys sometimes, coming from all sides, even during daylight. But after dark, that's when you really heard it, because that's when they were hungry.

Every night thousands of owls would be diving and striking in the great oak forests of Daviess County, or perched on moonlit branches eating insects and mice—always the head first. Even when more and more settlers came, on into 1850, 1875, and drained the fields and cut down trees and built homes, that didn't bother these birds. They started treating the new barnyards like free-lunch joints featuring baby chicks, kittens, even full-grown cats. There were farm children who would remember for the rest of their lives the sight of a favorite pet rising suddenly into the sky, attached to the underside of some owl.

So it was perfectly natural that when the first Dillons arrived in the area in the mid-1800s, pushing westward from Tennessee, and homesteaded on the edge of these woods, they found that the nearest community was called Owltown, the surrounding flatlands were known as Owl Prairie, and the owl generally had seized the local imagination to a powerful degree. Somebody re-marked that it seemed like Hallowe'en all year round.

It was here in Owltown, Indiana, that Wesley Dillon was born in May 1844. He was a gaunt youth who grew up like most of his neighbors, his face to the stale wind, plowing, clearing brush, forcing a living out of the soil. (As the pioneers who got this far liked to say, "The cowards never started, and the weak died along the way.") Wesley got married young to a local farm girl named Evangeline Arford, and after that he and his bride set up on a 120-acre tract of farmland given to them by Wesley's father. The couple worked and went to church, expanded their holdings to 205 acres, and had five sons. They put up a big brick farmhouse. Then typhoid fever killed Wesley at the age of thirty-eight. His widow was twenty-eight, left with the five boys to raise.

Around Owltown, Evangeline Dillon and those sons of hers turned into quite a topic of conversation. Customers who ran into each other at the feed and seed; the men who gathered at the grocery late at night to swap stories and eat cheese by the light of a big kerosene lamp on the counter; the women in the sewing circle; the idlers holding up the front of the post office—sooner or later just about everyone had something to say about Evangeline and those mite-sized boys, the prevailing view being that she'd never make a go of it on that farm. Of course, her neighbors, the women especially, had pitched in early on, even back when Wesley was failing. On the night he died, three or four of them were out in the yard under a big catalpa tree, taking turns stirring a kettle of apple butter over a hickory fire, and keeping their voices low the whole time so as not to trouble him. The fat fragrance of sugared apples had come rolling and spreading through the late summer air, till it finally filtered into the bedroom where Wesley lay, all hot and hollowed out from the typhoid. He turned his head toward the smell. Later on, when asked how her husband had met his Maker, Evangeline just said he died hungry.

That was Evangeline: very closemouthed. Even on his death-bed, she didn't tell Wesley she loved him until he was delirious.

In the months following his death, the neighbors continued to do what they could. They brought over baskets of food and helped with the washing. But there was only so much neighborliness could accomplish. Sooner or later, people said—unless she stopped turning up her nose at a certain party, or some stranger with a strong back turned up—Evangeline was going to have to sell out and move on, the Lord knew where.

But Mrs. Dillon had a grit beyond the ordinary. The day she realized this she was standing in the kitchen a few months after Wesley died. She was wearing her overshoes (in winter the kitchen floor never did get warm) and toasting diapers on the stove. First one side, then the other: she would flip them like flapjacks, then loft them, lightly smoking, into a wicker basket. The two oldest boys were outdoors—Walter was gathering wood, and William was pouring a kettle of boiling water on the outside pump to get the ice off. The three littlest, including the baby, were clustered around the fire in the parlor. So she was all alone.

There weren't any choiring angels involved, but she did say later it came on her like a visitation. She wasn't just going to keep the farm. *She was going to put all five boys through college.* In the context of that time and place—Owltown, 1882—this was like deciding you were going to raise five kings.

From that day on she dedicated herself to their advancement. (She never let them forget it either. If she martyred herself to her children, as some people said, it was with a martyr's egotism.)

First she set out to save the property. She tried out two or three different hired men, one after another, fired them, kept looking. Her optimism took on a bitter edge. She pelted her sons with maxims and homilies, most of which involved money. *Use it up, wear it out, make it do, or do without.* . . .

She made them jump too. "Run and get me this," she'd say, and "run and get me that." Each boy had his assigned chores, and if she caught one of them sloughing off, he'd have to go out and cut a switch off a peach tree, and then bring it back in, and she'd use it.

Yet there were other times—as they struggled over their homework in the evenings, or when they stood with their hymnals in church, as straight as a row of candles, all of them with those black-Irish good looks they'd picked up from Wesley—times like these when she would look at them and feel her heart shift in her chest. It wasn't entirely pleasant, this contradictory surge of humility and pride; still, though she never told them outright, she knew well enough what that feeling was.

Finally Evangeline took on a hired man who worked out all right. This was Ed Watkins, a thirty-seven-year-old itinerant from Missouri. What she saw in him in the first place, nobody ever did figure out. He was an unpromising lump of God's clay, a tall, weak-eyed, scrawny-necked individual with hay-colored hair that rose and parted like a courtyard fountain; the morning he first crossed the front yard toward the Dillon house, his loose-soled shoes lapped up dust with every step. Mrs. Dillon kept her hand on the knob as she eyed him doubtfully from the doorway.

"What do you want?" she asked, once he'd told her his name.

He was peering past her inside, in a molelike manner, as if he'd never seen a house before.

She asked again, sharply now. He said he was looking for work.

"What can you do?"

He thought that one over. "Farm?" he said.

Evangeline decided to give him a meal before sending him on his way—just out of Christian charity, she said later—but once she had, she discovered that this gawk wasn't so much half-witted as he was drained from hunger. After his second piece of lemon pie he perked up. He looked around the kitchen with passable alertness. Asked questions about the spring planting she had underway that couldn't have come from an ignoramus. So she gave him a trial.

She soon found that Ed Watkins—though he was and always would be invincibly naive; years of rambling had done nothing to change that—had collected a sort of mental toolbox all his own. Ed knew some interesting things, like how to make a hen squawk from ten feet away without throwing a rock at it. He had also doggedly studied whatever books fell into his hands in the course of his travels, everything from a butterfly manual to a volume of English words with Latin roots, so that once in a while he would emit a surprising fact or string of syllables.

Still, he wasn't any fireball. Early on he used to stand there like a road sign every morning till Mrs. Dillon had given him the day's instructions in detail. But Evangeline knocked him into shape pretty quickly, just as she had her boys, and once Ed realized he was expected to make a few decisions himself, he began to take to it.

The boys treated him like a sort of idiot cousin; they made fun of him, but mostly behind his back. Then gradually they started asking him questions about this and that. After all, the farthest they had ever traveled was eighteen miles south to Washington, Indiana, the county seat, whereas Ed had been in four different states of the union and fought a forest fire and seen a trestle.

One afternoon in the summer of '88—Ed had been on the place now a couple of years—one of the boys came bursting out the back door looking for him. It was Albert Hamlet, the ten-year-old; Ham, he was called. He had a straw hat jammed over his ears because his mother had just given him a haircut.

He dodged around the house, looking here and there, and finally found Ed sitting on a shaded stump out behind the barn, castrating piglets. Like most farm jobs, this one kept coming around like a wheel: any male pigs not set aside for breeding always got the knife before they were a month old. They grew faster that way. Not to mention the fact that a three-hundred-pound boar with a hard-on was meaner than a mad bull.

"Ed," said Ham, still breathing hard, "I got a question for you."

He had to shout it. His older brother Walter was standing in front of Ed with a squalling piglet upside down against his body. Now Walter made a wincing face as Ed, after adjusting his spectacles, went to work with his blade. Squeezing the pig's scrotum, he made quick cuts, one on each side, to free the testes, then sliced them off clean with a stroke.

"How can I help you, son?" said Ed.

Tha-dunk went the nuts, into the bucket.

Posing a wild hypothetical the way boys often do—with the air of grimly preparing for life—Ham asked if something he'd read was true: that if you were riding a horse away from a forest fire, galloping as fast as you could go, and the fire was gaining on you anyway, and you were just about done for, could you jump off and shoot your horse, and then slice open his belly and pull the guts out and climb inside and stay there safe until the fire passed? Would that work?

Ed gave the piglet's crotch wound a quick swab with alcohol as he gravely considered the question, then released the animal, which went fleeing around the corner of the barn in a burst of squeals.

"Well," said Ed finally, scratching his throat with a spidery hand, "before I got to cutting up a perfectly good horse and, as you might say, invaginating myself, I'd probably want to know this: why is this here fire after me?"

Ham didn't understand.

"Have I done something to aggravate the Lord?" Ed said, wiping the blade of his knife with a rough rag. "That's the question. Because if I have, there is no horse's belly in the world that's going to save me. You all know the story of Jonah, don't you? There's a man tried to hide in a whole damn whale and he couldn't do it."

"Have you ever seen a whale?" asked Ham.

"Listen, the things I've seen—boy, I don't even want to get into some of the things I've seen," Ed replied. "The point is, Has God lit that fire because of you? 'Cause if He has, that's all, friend. You're done like a baked potato. But on the other hand, if this fire's not after you, if this fire's maybe a message to somebody else and you just happened to wander into the middle of the transmission, well then, that's something else entirely. I'd say you got a pretty good chance."

"So how can you tell if a fire's after you?"

"You can't never tell," said Ed promptly. "God keeps a warehouse full of secrets, and that's just one of them. The best you can do," he said, interrupting Ham's protest, "is to live a good Christian life. Love God, honor your parents, and work hard," he added comprehensively. A gust of wind stirred his hair, and the sun blazed off his spectacles. "Beware the temptress, boys," Ed said. "Remember that one. Always keep down the demon of lust. It's damned a lot of good men to everlasting perdition, and where does it all start? With a shimmy, with a shake. With the world-famous Salome dance with hootchy-cootchy music accompaniment." (Over the years the rhetoric of preachers and of carnival barkers, often similar anyhow, had gotten a little muddled in his mind.) "I don't refer," said Ed, "to paragons like your ma, who are the wingless angels of this life. I mean the other type of female, who will put you on the greasy road to hell if you don't look out, and it's up to you, for the sake of your ma, to avoid the vile and sinful way and go the other."

He might have continued in this vein, but just then Walter came staggering up with another piglet that was furious with fear.

"Listen, Booger," cried Walter, in extremis with the pig, "why don't you give us a hand here?"

In a flash Ham was gone around the side of the barn.

His quick feet dug in the road as he sprinted shoeless out toward the wheat fields. At last he came alongside a small pasture with a few cows grazing and slowed up. He trotted over to the fence and rested his arms on the sun-warmed wood. Cows, two or three, gazed back at him. One wouldn't, so Ham dug around in the dust for a small stone and flung it, catching the animal on the flank. It heaved into a heavy trot, then came to a stop after a couple of steps with its bony butt pointed at him. The boy sighed.

There was another gust of wind. It had been kicking up all day, off and on, the kind that just blew the heat around. From his perch on the fence Ham watched the acres of wheat bending and shifting just beyond the strip of pasture. A puff of wind struck a pocket of grain, turning it dark as a catcher's mitt, and skidded across the whole field. The next breeze caught his hat and sent it sailing. It went sliding and rolling and finally vanished deep in the wheat. Ham kept clinging to the rail, a cabin boy with his face to the sea.

NONE OF THE DILLON BOYS exactly hid their light under a bushel. But of the five of them it was always Ham, the middle one, who had the most spark.

Even as a boy he knew he had those wounded good looks. And he was a quick-change artist of mood—quiet and self-absorbed one moment, gregarious the next—a youngster whose nature was balanced on a knife blade between calculation and joy.

Still, just like his friends and neighbors, Ham Dillon grew up on a farm, which meant he was tempered by labor almost from the time he could walk. In the earliest days of spring he and his brothers were in the fields, setting fires to burn off the winter thatch. With the spattering rains of April, as the pink-and-white blossoms of the peach orchard dipped and tossed in the breeze, they were out working the soil alongside the hired men.

To put the corn in, one of the boys drove a horse-drawn wagon dragging a plank behind by one end—up one way, down the other, then crosshatching from the other direction, till the field was a checkerboard. Then seeds were punched into the ground at the intersection points with a handheld corn stabber: *One for the blackbird, one for the crow, one for the cutworm, and one to grow. . . .*

Planting the hay was more of a struggle. Later on Ham used to laugh about how he stumbled around with that wheelbarrow seeder. It was a box about twelve feet long, set up over a wheel and shoved along by hand. Using this contraption, he said, was like trying to roll two fat men in a big coffin over rough ground.

So it went through the spiral of the seasons. Ham would go

blackberry picking with his brothers and come home scratched with a bucket of half-squashed fruit; his mother put meat grease on his chigger bites and checked his hair for ticks. By July the hay was tall as a man, or taller. Good for playing games in. A boy could thrash into a hay field like a runaway slave, get shot, fall and roll in the cushiony crackle, and lie there briefly dead. This just before the long, hot work of the harvest: first scything, then pitchforking hay onto the big wagon. Sometimes they'd have to drive the corn harvester through gusting, late-summer thunderstorms to get the crop in, but that was all right; if he caught cold, Ham got doses of homemade blackberry cordial.

Late autumn was the time for repairing tools and equipment and for hauling in wagonloads of sawdust from the local mill. This was thick-scattered on the barn floor for the cows and other livestock—they spent twenty-two, twenty-three hours a day in there during winter, like maximum-security prisoners—to help soak up a monumental amount of manure. Sometimes Ham would be out before dawn in the crucifying cold, headed for the barn, where he would fill up the manure spreader, hitch it up, and go rolling out toward the frozen fields as the sun broke the horizon line.

Still, he was profoundly attached to this life. There was a clarity to it, a sense of knife-sharp divisions. The difference between night and day meant a whole lot less in the cities, where block after block of blue-gas torches threw a skittery light on nightcreepers and insomniacs. Not on the farm. On the farm, after sundown, it got dark. Nights with no moon it was dark as a pocket. Same thing with working and resting: farmers got a bone-deep experience of both. After a long day in the fields scything hay, a man knew when he was sitting down.

So Ham Dillon learned the lessons of the farm. He learned that simple tasks, faithfully repeated, have dignity to them. He learned tenacity in the face of nature's blows. He learned he was expected to get himself to school every day, no excuses. Mama Dillon didn't think any snow was too deep to walk through unless a boy stepped off the porch and disappeared.

Above all Ham was taught to respect the teachings of God.

IT WAS A SUNDAY MORNING in late spring, 1894. Ham was sixteen.

He was sitting in church, the same church he'd been coming to ever since he was a baby: Mud Pike United Brethren, a frame building with a modest bell tower located northeast of town. Now that the two oldest were back from college for the summer, the brothers were sitting as usual in their birth order; this put Ham in the center, a position he was coming to feel was just and natural.

He craned his neck toward the front, at the little altar dusted with wildflowers. No sign of the preacher yet. Ham Dillon liked church. He liked watching Reverend Aspinall, rough-hewn and thick-necked, giving the folks Hail Columbia from the pulpit, and the way the parishioners lobbed *hallelujahs* back at him, mostly the amen corner on the men's side. He liked the fat book the preacher waved at them sometimes, *Fox's Book of Martyrs*— especially the story about the man who was tied to a stake, had his abdomen split open and filled with corn, and then was flung to the hogs. He liked the little rugs of sunlight thrown by the church's windows onto the rough wood floor.

The place had its quirks. Miss Halsop, for one—the elderly lady who doggedly accompanied the hymn singing on piano, searching for tunes in the cracks of the keys. But even as a boy Ham always felt the power of the place. His neighbors too: for most of them, church was an experience that went right to their vitals. It was more than just strength of belief, a faith in God as their rock and their refuge. A lot of the Bible stories seemed like pages out of their own lives. These were tales filled with plowing and sowing, with fatted calves and storehouses of grain, with ruinous hailstorms and plagues.

At last Reverend Aspinall appeared from the vestry, Miss Halsop sounded a chord, and together the congregation rose for the singing of "Count Your Blessings." After it was over, and they had thunderously reseated themselves, Aspinall set down his hymnbook and glowered at them.

"In the name of the Father, the Son, and the Holy Ghost," the reverend moaned, *"who liveth and reigneth . . ."*

Ham loved the words: this tidal, symphonic language that went back three hundred years. Sometimes he felt as if the sound alone healed and sustained him. First Reverend Aspinall would fling out some tale of divine wrath, about the rain of frogs in Egypt or Jesus and the money changers; and after it would come the falling-off, the adagio, as the worshippers slumped to their knees and chanted:

O Lord, most merciful Father, we have erred and strayed from Thy ways like lost sheep. We have followed too much the devices and desires of our own hearts. We have offended against Thy holy laws. . . .

Drilled and drilled, from the time he was a small boy. The books of the Bible in order: *Genesis, Exodus, Leviticus . . .*

Ham looked to his right—past Ed Watkins, spit-shined, on the aisle—to the ladies' side of the church. He saw a small field of women, row on row, as organized as corn. Girls about his age dotted here and there. He picked out Millie Carnahan, who was sitting forward a couple of rows wearing a new dress, lavender gingham puffed at the shoulders, and a pert little straw hat with a trailing black ribbon. He studied the curve of her neck, her arched chin. Very proper she was. In church anyway.

He was staring at her now, hunched like a predator in the weeds; then some instinct turned her head and she caught his eye. Immediately she swung back again, and as he watched the color of her neck change, he smiled and smiled. Ham got a kick out of flirting in church. Most courtships began in church, after all. Nothing wrong with it. You had to meet girls someplace. He peered past Millie, looking for Lydia Phipps.

Then he came to as he heard the preacher quote one of the old, magic phrases:

"Joseph and the coat of many colors . . ."

Naturally Ham had never told Walter, William, and the others just how much he relished this story—and as he got older, he had to laugh at it himself. But it nourished him nevertheless, touched a chord of ambition that only seemed to grow stronger with the years. Ham had even acquired a phrase for this: "audacious self-esteem." He had come across these words in a book—one of those tattered palm-sized volumes of advice that were common as colds, but there it was, his credo in a nutshell.

"Help me, heal me, for I have sinned!"

Startled, Ham looked toward the altar. Reverend Aspinall's homily on Joseph, whatever it was, had long since ended, and Marcus Ragsdale, the town pharmacist, was up front now confessing to something. Long-faced, long-limbed, he stood before the congregation flapping his hands as if his fingers were ablaze. Every Sunday a few of the parishioners, in the grips of the Holy Spirit, would hoot and holler this way.

"I have coveted my neighbor's goods! I've spoken harshly and in anger!"

A couple of lackadaisical amens rose and died in the back. Ragsdale was well known as one of three or four habitual and incorrigible confessors; all members of the Mud Pike, men and women, were encouraged to speak if they felt the need, but Ragsdale was up there practically every Sunday, blowing the back dust out of his closet.

"On Wednesday I lay abed late!"

Why didn't they make phony confessing a sin?

There had been occasions in the past—a few—when Ham

knew he'd seen the real thing. Real remorse. Choking and weeping. And they served a purpose: the penitent got a big stone off his chest. Still, Ham Dillon had never made such a public display in his life, and he didn't plan to. Things were going just fine, and any sins of his, he figured, were strictly between him and God.

In this way he was starting to accumulate secrets.

2

NOT QUITE THREE YEARS LATER, in the spring of 1897, Maggie Thompson—genteelly gripping the hand of the conductor—descended from the day coach of the Evansville & Indianapolis Railroad and onto a brand-new concrete platform. Everything was new—the track itself, the A-framed station waiting room, even the name of the town, painted in bold red capitals over the doorway:

ELNORA

For Owltown was no more. It had just been renamed in honor of the wife of a local merchant who had given a barrel of money to expand the commercial district. Now it took up a full nine blocks.

As the train went clacketing off in a swirl of dust, Maggie paced slowly toward the end of the platform, the points of her shoes peeking from beneath the long pleats of her skirt. Two loungers, taking the sun on a bench, watched her as she passed.

Like everything else here, they were new too, though they didn't look it. Since the day the station opened, they had filled the job of noticing who got on and off the train.

Maggie ignored them. She always ignored strange men. A girl of twenty, she was porcelain pretty in a determined sort of way, with high-piled, dark blond hair; she wore a traveling costume of pale and dark yellow, right to the yolk-colored feathers of her hat. In style she was a notch or two above most farm girls, even farm girls on a big trip. The loungers slid a look at each other and went back to watching her some more.

"Maggie? Honey, where are you going?"

The girl turned and looked down the platform toward her mother, who stood in the middle of a broken blockade of suitcases and steamer trunks. Expensively dressed herself, in scarlet and brown, Mrs. Thompson had a more brightly lacquered look than her daughter and, from the flutter of her hands, seemed to vibrate at a higher pitch.

"I'm just seeing if Daddy's here," Maggie Thompson said. Cupping one hand at the side of her face, she peered through a window of the deserted waiting room. Then she went around the side of the building and saw the hard-packed lot, the double-length hitching post. No one in sight. She shook her head at her mother.

Meanwhile Mrs. Thompson was sizing up what she could see of the edge of town. For all her fine clothes, she had known some rough living in her time, and nothing about the place scared her. Still, she hoped it wasn't too backward. A salesman with a snootful had obtruded himself on them during the train ride, and when he found out they were going to Elnora, he had gone on and on about the owls. Especially how they eat their prey whole and then vomit up the hair and bones. "Take a walk in the woods!" he cried. "You'll see! Piles and piles of owl barf! They're like these little mouse-sized skulls and crossbones with hair stuck to them!"

People.

Moments later came the creak and bang of a wagon driven in haste, and Mr. Thompson pulled up in the station lot. He was big, red-whiskered, apologetic. "Tried a new shortcut," he panted. He had a farmhand with him to help tote the luggage.

It was sitting at the front of that laden wagon, steadying herself with a flat palm, that Maggie got her first good look at the town. With her parents billing and cooing beside her—they were a little revolting that way—and headed for a new home she had never seen, the girl studied her surroundings with wary, immigrant eyes. A. R. Stalcup's General Store and Livery, the blacksmith, the post office, Shufflebarger's Bank: all these lined the rutted main street, along with a couple of new cafes with chintz curtains in the windows. There was a library, the hired hand told her proudly, inside the pharmacy. This consisted (she discovered later) of a small bookcase of cast-off volumes standing against the back wall—just a few feet, in fact, from where doleful Marcus Ragsdale toiled away with his mortar and pestle, his sins darting through his mind like minnows.

THE NEXT SUNDAY the Thompsons attended local services for the first time. Mrs. Thompson was well-bred enough to recoil slightly at the name Mud Pike Church, but she didn't refuse to go. Her husband thought it was a good meat-and-potatoes operation. Maggie didn't care one way or the other. Before long the three of them became a fixture there.

Here Ham and Maggie met in the early summer of 1897.

Now nineteen, Ham had just finished his second year at Wheaton College. He was two-thirds of the way toward his degree and had come back home for the season's labors on the farm. His older brothers, Walter and William, had moved away and become big-city lawyers.

Scanning the women's section at church that Sunday, in his

automatic way, he spotted a slim, unfamiliar girl. She was dressed in summery white taffeta, her face half shadowed by the meringue of her hat. Ham slumped, trying to get a better look at her face. No luck.

Finally Reverend Aspinall pronounced the benediction. Miss Halsop slaughtered the recessional, and the congregation spilled outside into the sunshine. It was always a lively scene on the lawn; for these farm folk, mostly tied to their own patches of ground, this was the one time in the week they could count on visiting with their neighbors. In moments laughter and eager gossip had drowned the buzz of mayflies and the snorts of horses tethered under the trees.

Reverend Aspinall stood with an angular female parishioner, one of her hands pressed firmly between his own, listening with an air of compassionate depression. Meanwhile Ham was using his mother to wangle an introduction to the Thompsons.

"You're Ham!" Mrs. Thompson cried, first thing, as if she were giving him wonderful news. "Your mother goes on and on about you."

"I'm sure she does," he replied. His gaze stole toward Maggie. Ham was used to causing a flutter in pretty girls, but this one met his eyes dead-on.

"Well, well, well," Mr. Thompson said. "Well, well, well."

"Your mama tells us you're a college man," said Mrs. Thompson.

"That's right."

"And what exactly are you doing there?"

"Oh," Ham said, "filling my head with a lot of nonsense."

He could see now that Maggie's eyes were a dark gold flecked with brown. Honeybee eyes.

His mother began explaining all about the Thompsons—how they had moved up to Elnora from Kentucky, and were consolidating two large adjoining farms here.

But Ham barely heard what she said. She had to repeat it all for him later on.

A S T H E N E W E S T A D D I T I O N to the rural gentry of Elmore Township, which included Elnora, the Thompsons naturally came to the Dillons' place for Sunday dinner soon after. And a couple of weeks later the Dillons, en masse, went to pay a call on the Thompsons. They arrived just ahead of a summer storm: the first spears of rain were popping the dust in the front yard, and gusts of wind were tossing the trees, as they mounted the steps onto the Thompsons' front porch.

The home itself, from the moment he entered the front hall and faced himself in a little mirror fretted with gargoyles, gave Ham the lightly dislocated feeling he'd had on first meeting Maggie. From the road it looked like any other big farmhouse—he'd been riding by it for years—but inside there was something unfamiliar, subtle suggestions of tastes that were rich and strange.

Save for a couple of details—the clump of dried onions hanging in the hall, the butter churn he glimpsed through a side window—this might not have been a farmhouse at all. The musty parlor, where they found the hired girl lighting candles against the storm, had a stiffly cultured atmosphere, a whiff of the museum. On the mantel there was a sizable bronze bust of somebody—Benjamin Franklin, it turned out; on a side table, an arrangement of South Sea shells (individually labeled) under a glass dome, and next to that, a bowl of assorted wax fruit: beautifully tinted, amazingly lifelike, but what farmer would ever have it around? In the corner stood a melodeon with a Turkish shawl tossed across it, whereon lay lugubrious sheet music at least a generation old, fanned out like a poker hand: "On a Lone Barren Isle," "She Wore a Wreath of Roses . . ." Over the fireplace hung a reproduction of a Raphael Madonna cradling the infant Christ, a little too beneficent by candlelight.

The feeling was much the same in the dining room, where the families soon gathered. On the table was good, solid Sunday food: fried chicken and greens, with a frosted pitcher of crab-apple cider, and in the center a four-tiered jelly cake on display under glass, with a couple of flies patrolling the perimeter. But there was nothing farmlike about the presentation. The tablecloth was glossy white linen (instead of checked oilcloth), the matching napkins stood like bishops' miters on the plates, and the flatware was heavy silver.

While Mr. Thompson worked his way through grace, Ham glanced with slightly dampened spirits at Maggie's bowed head.

Mama Dillon was impressed anyway. The blessing was barely over, and Mr. Thompson had just given that sigh which is often the prelude to eating a great deal, when she started pointing at the decorations and bric-a-brac and asking questions. Arthur Thompson hunched his shoulders and busied himself with his soup; but his wife replied at length. Meantime there was nothing heard from the young folks but the clink and slurp of polite feeding.

It turned out that Emma Louise Thompson was anything but farm-born; she was a refugee from the upper ranks of Philadelphia society, an actual runaway. In fact, she and Arthur Thompson had . . .

. . . and here Emma paused and looked humorously dramatic . . .

Well, they had eloped.

"Eloped!" Evangeline Dillon cried. "Gracious!" Immediately she was rapt.

Ham eyed his mother, bemused; how fascinated the old girl seemed to be by this rather ordinary bit of news. It must be, he thought, that all women had a high-romantic chord in them somewhere, and no amount of hard living could completely pound it out.

The gist of the story was that Arthur Thompson and Emma Pfeiffer had met in Granville, Ohio, at a peace party after the Civil War. Emma had come west to visit some cousins; Arthur had just returned home after serving as a private in the Union army and losing a finger at Lookout Mountain. (When his wife paused and told him to show everyone, Mr. Thompson raised his hand but not his head.) "I just took one look at him and that was that," said Mrs. Thompson, her eyes youthfully wide. "So he traveled all the way to Philadelphia to ask for my hand in marriage, and Daddy practically threw him down the steps. Didn't he, sweetheart?"

"I don't remember," said Mr. Thompson, his voice muffled by biscuit.

The upshot, Mrs. Thompson explained, was that on a summer's night in '66 she had fled her father's home. It was like something out of a storybook, she said: creeping onto a ladder after tossing down her luggage, while Arthur and her lady's maid waited below. Oh yes, Emma added, she had also stolen the family silver. It was kept in a large walnut case inside a velvet sack, which she had lowered down in her basket.

"Surprised the heck out of me," Mr. Thompson muttered.

"Well, it was supposed to be mine one day," Emma said, "and I certainly wouldn't have gotten it otherwise. We're using it now," she added.

Ham felt the weight of his knife and fork. Odd: he was eating with stolen property.

Once married, the Thompsons rode in a covered wagon to Illinois and homesteaded there. Emma went from a city mansion, and a world of top hats and high teas and rides in the park, to a two-room log cabin with a dirt floor—where, as she put it, "I didn't know a pig from a mule." Her father disowned her.

Rain was rattling the windows now, blowing against the house. Cool, damp air crept through the cracks into the dining room. Starting with nothing, Emma continued, Arthur Thompson had worked his farm fiercely and soon achieved a modest fortune. From Illinois the Thompsons moved to Somerset, Kentucky, where Maggie was born in 1876. . . .

As quickly as it started, the rainstorm had vanished, leaving behind dripping eaves and the reviving peeps of birds. Sunlight, in fresh geometrics, appeared on the table and the faded dining-room carpet.

"Maggie's your only child?" Evangeline Dillon asked, a little sympathetically.

Oh no, replied Emma. They had another daughter, Elizabeth Alice, five and a half years older. "But Allie fell in love back in Somerset," said Emma with a sentimental sigh, "and she got married there, so when Arthur heard about the farmland in southern Indiana, and the coal mines and what all, well, we had to leave her behind. It's the way of the world. Still," she said, "I wish you could see my two girls together." She gave Maggie a melting look. "Two blossoms from one stem."

Maggie looked at Ham and, to his delight, rolled her eyes.

Evangeline said, "It's too bad that your father hasn't had the joy of them."

"Oh, well, he's trying like mad to make it up now," said Emma. "He's been sending us things. That melodeon."

"Oh, that's good," Mrs. Dillon said. "And you've written him back?"

Emma looked at her with eyes like little stones.

"Will you?"

"We'll see," said Emma. Lifting the tiny bell beside her plate, she rang for the hired girl as if summoning a fairy.

.   .   .

HAM CAME AWAY from the Thompsons that day with a fresh liking for both Maggie's parents. For all her la-de-da ways, Emma Thompson had turned out to be dramatically independent, and her husband was obviously capable of much more than just mumbling into his soup. These were formidable people.

He tried to tell Maggie as much the next Sunday afternoon, when he took her out for a buggy ride. The way her folks got together, he said, that was quite a story. But to his surprise, Maggie did not want to talk about it.

They rode without speaking, the horse's hooves dragging the road. As they clopped along, Ham's appraising eyes grazed the side of Maggie's skirt, slowly, all the way down to her shoe tips. It's true, he thought: you never know what their legs look like till after you've married them.

Usually talking to girls was like falling off a log, but this one made him feel like Sisyphus.

"So how's your sister doing?" he said.

Maggie gave a faraway smile. "I was just thinking this morning," she said, "about something Allie told me once. That the two of us weren't really farm children. That our being on a farm at all was a big mistake. The stork brought us there by accident."

"Is that what you think?"

"Well, we get it from Mama." Maggie turned her little heart-shaped face toward him, her forehead shaded by a blue-checked sunbonnet. "You've seen her. You tell me. Is it any wonder we're a little spoiled?" She gave him an arch glance and looked away.

He watched her proud profile. There was something extraordinary about this girl, something regal and down-to-earth at the same time; and something else too, a vault of privacy in her he was starting to take as a challenge. The day would come, he thought, when her pretty clothes would be scattered on the floor, and she would yield herself up to him in ways she hadn't imagined. She would give up the key to that vault.

"I haven't seen her since Christmas."

"Mm?" Toasting several fantasies together over a low flame, Ham barely heard her. "Who?"

"Allie. It's been six months. The longest stretch since I was born."

"So what's she like?"

"Allie? Well, she's more outgoing than I am. Or so people say."

"You two get along?"

Maggie cocked an eye at Ham.

"Sure," she said. "Allie's a peach." She gave him an uninformative smile and returned to the view.

While Ham's whip slashed idly at the summer weeds by the roadside, she slipped into a daze. It was easier than talking about Allie. In her bruised and unforgiving way, Maggie did love her elder sister. But it was family-style love, the kind that starts off flowing like a river and then builds up a lot of sediment.

Allie was five and a half years older: this was the great, irreducible fact that had colored everything between them. From the first Allie had blotted out the sun, taken up the oxygen. But what style she had! Once when the girls were maybe twelve and seven, they'd been out in the back yard watching their mother dithering over killing a chicken. It was writhing and squawking and spewing feathers while Emma—who was still a little too refined to kill anything—held it with both hands and emitted little *eeks*. Finally Allie marched over and took the bird, placed it on the ground, put her heel on its neck, and yanked its head off.

Great flapping about, by both mother and bird. Blood everywhere. Allie turning grandly, face spattered, holding up the chicken as if to imaginary crowds. What registered with Maggie then, squatting wide-eyed by the well, was Allie's terrible zest for life.

She remembered her big sister flashing past her on roller skates, arms flat out of sight inside her dress. Climbing to the top of a birch tree one day just ahead of a thunderstorm and swaying there in the wind and rain. The self-dramatizing streak in all this Maggie didn't see for years; what she felt was a mixture of awe and envy, with a dollop of fear thrown in—it daunted her, the toss of that red-gold hair. And it produced in the younger girl a wild garden of self-doubt. How in the world could she ever compete?

Yet there was a bond between them too. If Allie was a show-off, she also served Maggie well as advance scout, slashing her way through the thickets of girlhood and returning with regular reports. It was Allie who waded out into a new swimming hole, poking with a stick for the step-off while Maggie waited on the bank. It was Allie, not their mother, who taught the little girl how to sew for her dolls, how to piece a quilt by the age of five. Maggie still remembered sitting beside her sister, mesmerized, while Allie carefully cut out the bright blocks of fabric, then pinned two blocks together, a red and a blue, and marked with a pencil where Maggie should put the stitches. She still had that quilt.

And it was Allie who made such a party of it the night Maggie got her first cramps. Allie appeared at the bedroom door that night, a finger to her lips, holding a long-necked bottle of the Thompson home remedy for female troubles—whiskey with some dried snakeroot marinating in it. But instead of the usual tablespoon she had with her a couple of shot glasses filched from the sideboard downstairs. Setting them out on Maggie's dressing table, she sloshed out a couple of slugs and then, when they were both settled, toasted her. "Welcome to womanhood, sister," she said, with a depraved gleam in her eye. They clinked glasses and tossed off the whiskey, choked and laughed and shushed each other.

Oh, and the lies too. What wonderful lies she came up with. Allie used to tell adults who didn't know her very well the most outlandish things. How she and Maggie had a little brother, for example, who was once stolen by the Gypsies, and then recovered, but not before he'd learned how to play the accordion. She would offer up these fake confidences with eyes full of ravaged innocence and bag her victim a good four times out of five. Maggie would sit kicking her little legs and pursing her lips to keep the giggles down. Once she blew the joke by laughing and Allie didn't speak to her for three days.

They both had a temper. For both had grown up believing that the world should bend to them: as their mother often reminded them, they were hybrid flowers, the only farm-girl aristocrats in Kentucky. When she was thwarted, Allie might toss her head and stamp her foot; Maggie more likely withdraw. Either way, through all their years growing up together, the two sisters never apologized to each other, no matter what. Any apology would have been a patch of ground irretrievably lost.

She became aware of Ham's voice. Then it stopped.

"Excuse me. What?"

"You know what I've been doing the last five minutes?" he said. "I've been reciting Webster's Reply to Hay. Learned it in the fifth grade. No, no, it's all right," he said, laughing, as she stammered something. "Boy," he added with a wink, "there's not a fella alive could get a swelled head around you."

She sat, too embarrassed to think of a reply, as the horse clip-clopped through the heat and haze.

"So how do you like Indiana?"

She felt she owed him a thoughtful answer.

"Well . . ."

"Gee! Gee!" Suddenly Ham was tugging hard at the reins as the horse, out of habit, automatically tried to turn down the lane to church.

"Sorry. What?"

"The people are nice," she said. "The land seems . . ."

"Hot? Flat?"

"It is flat," she said.

"It sure is," he agreed happily. "There's something about it, I don't know, it's like when you read about how sailors love the sea. Same thing here, there's a—"

"A what? A romance of the flat?" Maggie gave an unladylike little snort, and quickly covered her nose with her hand.

"You just can't help it, can you?"

"What do you mean?"

"This thing in you. This ornery streak."

"I do not have—"

"I'll tell you exactly what it is about this part of the country," he broke in. "A man can think out here. Make plans. Nothing gets in the way, they just shoot straight out to the horizon. Look around. See? No limits at all."

"To the future."

"Yep."

Maggie eyed him in silence, with the first inklings of real respect. Up to this moment she had shared her sister's prejudice against farmers, that even the best of them were hicks. But now she sensed the depth of his ambition.

She still had her doubts about Indiana. Sometimes all this relentless open space gave her the heebie-jeebies. As if some malign force lodged in the sky might suddenly descend on them all like an anvil.

Instinctively she hitched herself an inch or two closer to Ham. He noticed and smiled at her.

Oh dear, she thought. Oh well.

In the years before the Thompson family came to Elnora, it was Allie who mostly gobbled up the men. Allie was radiant, spirited, a living John Singer Sargent. Maggie was a pistol. And as she grew up, Maggie became a student of the difference.

She had watched while men, the weaker ones, drooped and dropped things around Allie, flattened under the wheels of her charm. Even the suave ones could lose their color. Amid all the traffic—Mrs. Thompson, still playing the society matron, loved giving little dinners—there were a few, of course, who gave Allie the go-by. Some fellows even cast a speculative eye on the kid sister, or just turned to her for a little company.

But Maggie barely gave them the time of day. She figured they must be using her to get to Allie. And sometimes she was right. Their teacher back in Kentucky, Mr. Hardin Lincoln Hale, he was one of those. Always acting extra interested in the younger sister's progress.

To Maggie—who, like many children, had a knack for seeing grown-ups as unflattering caricatures of themselves—Mr. Hale was a walking inanity: a slight, bony man with slicked-back hair and a forehead the size of the capitol dome. So imagine her surprise when Allie came to his defense.

Of course, it was like that sometimes having a sister. If you said black, she'd say white.

Still, she'd never expected Allie to take it so far.

With a jolt Maggie went toppling onto her right elbow. Ham Dillon's buggy had struck a rut in the road that rocked her sideways. Instantly he reached over and righted her, asking again and again if she was all right.

Maggie thanked him as she blinked away her sunstruck reverie. He does have nice manners, she thought.

A little quick with the hands.

3

THAT WEEK a vigilante group called the Black Avengers took to the roads again, waving shotguns and beating up individuals, mostly non-Protestant, whom they thought had drifted from the ways of the Lord. One night they spread-eagled a Catholic on his own front porch and extinguished a cigar in his open palm. A Methodist preacher who protested from the pulpit was rousted at 3 A.M. by the same gang and dumped in the middle of nowhere without his shoes.

Ham was enraged, and the only person he could unburden himself to was Maggie; so after church, as they sat side by side beneath a mulberry tree, he talked politics to her for the first time. He told her the Avengers were a moral blight. From there he slipped into an escalating rant about what was wrong with the whole country.

She'd never seen him completely serious for more than five

minutes before. He went on lambasting Swift, Vanderbilt, Gould, all the big capitalists. Did she have any idea what the railroads were charging now to ship crops? He seemed so gung-ho and can-do, seemed to think that he personally could gallop to the public's rescue. As she listened to him, she began to realize how his self-regard and his social conscience were bound up together, as hopelessly entwined as jungle vines.

"Lot of things need fixing," he said, "and I'm gonna . . ." He trailed off.

"I had this girlfriend in Kentucky once," Maggie said. "Her fella was the town banker. Kept telling her he'd be the next J. P. Morgan."

"Well?"

"Well, it's been ten years now, and the only thing he's got in common with J. P. Morgan is a big red nose."

He grinned. What a girl. The way she kept her personality furled like a flag, then once in a while let it snap in the wind. Around her he felt goaded to do great deeds.

He ducked forward to snatch a kiss. Didn't get much. Maggie was a head-ducker, a side-of-the-mouther. Once before she'd stiff-armed him so hard she left a little bruise on his chest.

Her resistance, of course, only roused him more. He was positive there were wonderful fires within her, a lusty little boiler room.

For the time being, however, whatever fires she had were obviously staying banked. So Ham, in his moral froth, had to take himself off to a whorehouse in Vincennes.

Located on the Wabash River about thirty miles southwest of Elnora, Vincennes boasted all the attractions of a little two-fisted river town, including brothels of every stripe. One of these occupied the top two floors of the municipal firehouse—the fire department having discovered that it had more beds than it knew what to do with. Here girls and their customers could be found sliding down the big brass pole at odd hours and wearing scraps of fire-fighting gear in bed. The building also shared a common wall with the town jail; if any gentleman got out of hand, the sheriff was only steps away.

It wasn't Ham's first trip. He had himself a time with a female whose name he didn't catch, and afterward the two of them climbed some spiral steps up to the watchtower of the firehouse, looking out over Vincennes. It was late afternoon. Below them, all was commerce and confusion. In the distance lay the winking brown waters of the Wabash River.

"See Gabriel's foot?" the girl asked. Though young, she had a gambler's squint and a lot of very used hair.

"What?"

"Way off there, on the bank of the river. That hollow in the rock. They say that's the footprint of the archangel Gabriel."

"Who says? The chamber of commerce?"

"Well, come on. It's a lot better than 'Look, there's a rock.' Don't you have any spirit of romance?"

Ham laughed out loud.

"I come up here a lot," she said. "I like to watch the river."

"You're not from around here, hunh?"

She gazed at him flat-eyed and turned away.

Probably pouting, he thought. Disappointed that he wouldn't go the whole hog. But he wasn't about to, not with any whore. Especially now, with his ties to Maggie growing tighter, Ham meant to be careful with sex. Death, insanity, chunks of your face falling off. . . . Some risks just weren't worth it.

Ham turned around and leaned back with his palms on the parapet's cool pocked stone. Yes, it was a mighty pleasant world up here. His gaze drifted across the other side of town to the red yolk of the sun frying over the Wabash. Closer in he could see more streets. Craning down, he watched the people far below scurrying along in search of sex or salvation.

· · ·

B Y NOW Ham and Maggie were trying to see each other more often, not just Sundays. But it wasn't easy. This time of year the farmwork was dawn to dusk, and beyond; besides, it had been a rainy summer, so the hay was hard to harvest, and apples and peaches were hailing to the ground. So they stole time whenever they could.

They did the same few things other courting couples did, the mundane and enchanted things. At the soda parlor in Elnora they split a tin roof—vanilla ice cream and chocolate syrup, with peanuts sprinkled on top—brought to their table by Marcus Ragsdale, who set down their spoons and took a step back, hovering a moment like some gloomy presiding angel. They walked in a birch grove outside town that was like a museum, where lovers since pioneer days had etched their initials in the bark. When Ham offered to do the same, Maggie gave him one of her sardonic looks, so he shrugged and moved on. But then she caught his arm.

Pulling out his penknife, he went to work, manfully cutting a heart in the meat of the tree.

Soon he'd be leaving again for college, but there was one big summer party left, scheduled for the end of August—a box social to benefit the Mud Pike Church. (Its roof had lost a few shingles, and the furnace was a standing joke.) For Ham it would be his last good chance to pop the question, and he decided to take it.

The picnic began in the buttery light of a late afternoon, on a stretch of lawn adjoining the church itself, not far from a grove of elms. Late arrivals clambering down from their buggies and wagons found several dozen people there already, with their checked tablecloths and cotton blankets all spread out, Mason jars open, bottles uncorked, plates beginning to rattle. At the edge of the trees was a large table piled with shoeboxes, and beside them a fretful Reverend A. W. Aspinall.

Amid all the laughter and bright talk, Reverend Aspinall was a trifle preoccupied—the reason being this same happy heap of boxes, each tied with a gay ribbon or pasted with a bright flower. Inside each box was a complete meal for two, prepared by a young and marriageable farm girl—chicken probably, this time of year, or maybe cold ham, along with corn, tomatoes, peaches, a dessert that showed off her skill, and the good tableware and napkins, all wrapped up in fancy paper. Plus one thing more: the name of the young lady who had made it tucked inside. In a moment Reverend Aspinall would start auctioning these boxes off. Young men would vie for them, one by one. Each winning bidder would learn his companion for the evening only when he opened the box and found her name.

And thus young people would socialize pristinely and at random.

Supposedly, that is. But it almost never worked out that way because most of the young folks wouldn't play by the rules. Nobody kept quiet. Girls told boys ahead of time what their boxes would look like. Sweethearts always did. So the results were fixed.

Over the years Reverend Aspinall had made a kind of dejected peace with this arrangement, since he couldn't do anything about it. He told himself you had to expect a few shenanigans at these little affairs, and anyway, it didn't rank with the betrayal of Christ; still, it nagged.

Reverend Aspinall stepped forward and smacked the table a couple of times with the flat of his hand.

Ham looked up. Stretched out among the other picnickers, with Maggie sitting primly beside him, he could see the minister just a few yards away—the blighted face with its dark gray old-growth eyebrows, its weary scowl. The young man still respected the reverend though temperamentally they were poles apart; if Ham was full of natural song, Aspinall was the blanket over the birdcage.

Just then somebody struck his shoulder, and Ham discovered his youngest brother, Dennis, going by, trailing girls. The two swapped grins at their woebegone minister, and then Ham watched as his brother went on picking his way through the crowd. Denny was sixteen, lean and dark like all the Dillon boys. In fact, he and Ham looked much alike, both lady-killers.

Denny was always horsing around. He might have been Ham's mocking shadow. And yet they were close, would have done anything for each other. Denny had the complicated sadness of a goof-off in a family of achievers, something Ham alone guessed at.

Aspinall whaled on the table again and hollered, and expectantly Ham settled a little closer to Maggie. She was wearing a dress of sky-blue gingham and a little straw hat with rose-colored ribbons. The engagement ring he'd picked out, an amethyst set in scrolled silver, was tucked away in a jeweler's box in his trouser pocket. He traced the outline of it with his fingers.

"Hello, everyone! Glad to see you." Reverend Aspinall had dredged up some good cheer and was shouting at the crowd. "The old Mud Pike's grateful too. She certainly thanks you all for being here." He said a couple of other things about Christian charity and then trailed off. Even on a good day he wasn't much for biblical banter. "Well!" he cried finally. "Anybody hungry?"

Herculean cheers from the young men.

The auction began. First Reverend Aspinall held up a red-striped shoebox with a wild iris at the corner, trying to ignore the squeal from a girl in the crowd, the furious signaling with her hands. He received a first bid of twenty-five cents. Then thirty-five. Sold it finally for a flat half-dollar to a young man in a tan suit. The girl was clapping her hands.

So it went. Each time various folks would bid just a little, for the hell of it, to sort of goose up the price—it being for a good cause, after all—but there wasn't much drama in it. Meanwhile Maggie sat still and thoughtful, twirling the stem of a wildflower in her fingers. She knew Ham Dillon would propose to her; if not tonight, then sometime soon.

If it be now, 'tis not to come; if it be not to come, it will be now; if it be not now, yet it will come—the readiness is all.

Yes, that caught her mood. She was gravely happy. Lately Ham had crept into her prayers.

He moved suddenly on the blanket, pulling himself to his knees, and Maggie came alert. Reverend Aspinall was holding up the next box for bid. It was hers.

"Quite a heft to this one!" the reverend was hollering. "A good square meal for some lucky young feller!" But Ham didn't even let him finish.

"One dollar!" he cried, throwing his arm in the air.

"One dollar! How about one and a half?" boomed the reverend, trying hard to throw himself into the proceedings. "Who'll say one-fifty? . . . One twenty-five?"

"One twenty-five!" cried a voice.

"One-fifty!" called Ham.

"Anybody else? Smells mighty good," the reverend crooned. He pushed the box against his nose and sort of hummed with pleasure.

"Make it one seventy-five!" said somebody else.

"Two!" shouted Ham.

Ordinarily that should have been that. A couple of phony bids, then the young beau would claim his box. That's what the reverend expected.

"Well, if that's as far as we're going . . ." he said.

"Two-fifty!" yelled a young man off to Ham's left. Heads turned, Ham's included.

It was his brother Denny, kneeling on a patch of blanket a good ten yards away. He had a grin like a slice of watermelon.

"Three dollars," said Ham uncertainly.

"Three dollars? That's weak as water, boy. Four dollars!" Denny cried.

Ham was getting it now. He was in for a public ragging. All right then, he thought, with cold glee. Let's go.

"Four-fifty!" he shouted.

"Five!" said Denny.

"Five-fifty!" yelled a new voice, female. Ham wheeled around the other way. It was his own mother, sitting off with some friends. She looked at him and shrugged.

"Six dollars!" This from Denny again.

"Seven!"

Ham didn't think he'd ever seen that fellow.

By now laughter was sweeping across the crowd. Ham was getting shouts of encouragement—"Don't you give up, son!"—amid all the ruckus, as bids came in from everybody, men and women both. Ham got himself some extra laughs with his scarecrow mime of bafflement and distress. Maggie sat looking down with a handkerchief pressed to her lips.

"Twelve!"

"Thirteen!"

Hell, he'd just bought a rolltop desk for that.

Finally Ham strode forward and made a great show of emptying his wallet onto the table right in front of Reverend Aspinall, and then sprinkling his pocket change on top of the bills. After that he turned to the crowd and shouted, "I also volunteer to fix the church furnace!" to a roar of applause. He held Maggie's shoebox aloft, like a warrior with the head of his enemy, and at last returned in triumph to his sweetheart.

Maggie didn't know where to look.

Later, with the auction over and everybody deep in dessert, a local quartet gathered near the shoebox table and sang. The repertoire was full of the tried-and-true, viscous old melodies like "Break the News to Mother" and "Could You Be True to Eyes of Blue If You Looked into Eyes of Brown?" But the song they kept coming back to that night, again and again, was a brand-new selection, the hit of the nation that summer, and one these picnickers were extra partial to because it happened to celebrate their own home state. Fresh from its debut at the Alhambra

Theater in Chicago, "On the Banks of the Wabash" seemed to capture like nothing else the plangent beauty of the heartland, even for city dwellers who'd never seen the heartland in their lives and didn't ever want to.

No wonder that Indiana natives were getting drunk on it. Or that later that evening, when the quartet had packed up and gone home, and the feast was breaking up, a young man sat propped against a tree with his legs straight in front of him, slowly picking out the same tune on a mandolin.

Here and there people still lingered, Ham and Maggie among them. He had decided he'd propose to her on the slow ride home, and he knew they ought to get going anyway, it was late; but the spell here was hard to break. A light wind corrugated the surface of the pond, where Reverend Aspinall's children liked to play at baptism. There were great streaks of soot in the western sky, and the sunset lay low in the grate. When the young mandolin player began to sing, in a voice that quavered but held the tune, Ham rolled over onto his back and gazed into the sky.

For the first time in weeks, he thought of the prostitute in the watchtower.

"Oh, the moonlight's fair tonight along the Wabash
From the fields there comes a breath of new-mown hay.
Thro' the sycamores the candle lights are gleaming
On the banks of the Wabash, far away."

4

A LLIE HALE got word of the engagement of her sister, Maggie, to Hamlet Dillon, by mail the following week. Maggie tucked the big news pretty far down, after a couple of paragraphs about corn weevils. She always had to work up to the personal.

"And I suppose I should tell you," she wrote, "that I'm to be married next year to a farmer here in Elnora. Imagine that! You'll have to forgive me, dear. I know we always promised each other we'd never ever marry farmers, etc., etc. But this one's different. He's going places—or anyway, he seems to think so. A college boy too! Daddy says I couldn't do better if I looked all over God's green earth. . . ."

She'd forgotten to tell his name until the P.S. "There is one difficulty," she added then, "which is our getting engaged on such short acquaintance. This has caused a little talk. Daddy says ignore it, but some of the girls here just go on and on. They're convinced it's a great romance, and are a little put out with me that I don't need the fainting couch every time they mention his name. Oh well, we were never that sort, were we, you and I? . . ."

Allie read the letter twice, then refolded it with a knife-edge crease and slipped it into the pocket of her apron. She felt the paper crumple as she leaned forward on her stool and plucked up a rag from the shed floor. Then, bracing herself with her free hand against the flank of the cow, she started wiping dried mud off its udder.

That fall of 1897 Allie was living with her husband, Lincoln Hale, and their three children in a frame house on the outskirts of Somerset, Kentucky. She and Link had moved into it when they first got married, on October 25, 1888; nearly nine years ago now.

Most people, Link included, thought they were happy enough. Unaware that milking the cow had become Allie's favorite thing in life. More and more she liked getting off by herself where she could think, or not, as she chose. She liked to watch Bea munching away at the hayrack in her bovine trance.

"You and me, sweetie," Allie told her once. "Sisters under the skin."

The cow's bag was filthy this evening—Bea had been cooling off in a hog wallow—but finally Allie tossed the rag aside, dragged the bucket over and got it set. Then gently she began working the teats. A moment later came the sound of milk drilling on metal.

So this boy had proposed to Maggie after a box social; that's what she'd written. Like the ones Allie went to in Somerset when she was a girl, back when the boys were pursuing her like the Furies. Even Archie, that poor mope. One summer—she must have been sixteen—she'd made a fine big Bundt cake to be auctioned off, and of course the boys were all bidding on it like crazy, but Archie won at last. And he was so happy right up to the moment he took his first bite. She'd frosted that cake with whitewash—as a joke, and really aimed at somebody else, but the way he'd looked at her, with that uncomprehending hurt . . . After that she tried to be nice to him, and even took him shopping with her once. But he simply stood outside like a sheep in the rain, waiting while she went inside the stores.

The rattle of milking time had brought the cat curling around the doorway into the shed. He was a butterscotch-colored tom who lurked wild in the neighborhood but always showed up here for snacks. Now he trotted up and parked himself beside the bucket. Allie angled one of the teats like a gunner and aimed it. The cat caught the first squirt on his forehead and the second in his mouth.

She didn't often think about that, about the fun she'd had flummoxing the boys. The memories were all in shards anyway, a smashed mirror of slicked-down hair and mooning faces. She didn't even miss them, all those lovestruck clerks and farmers. She could never have married one of them.

Only one thing she mourned: her youth. She had had a kind of genius for being young. She had given herself to it without reserve. And youth had abandoned her anyway.

Her bucket nearly full, Allie caught it by the handle and carried it over to a tall can that stood nearby. With a heave she lifted and tipped, let the warm milk come foaming out. She dribbled the last of it down to the cat—who spun in circles trying to catch the drops—then took the bucket back and resumed her seat on the stool.

Mortal, immortal. Mortal, immortal. Like a chant, like a bell, she could still hear those words. She'd learned them studying the Greek myths in school. "The Rape of Persephone," that was her favorite: the beautiful young girl kidnapped and forced to become a queen. What a notion that was—*what a thrill*—to be a slave and a queen at the same time! But nobody talked about that, of course.

Her husband, Link, had taught her the story of Persephone—

the squeaky-clean version, out of a book. Of course, he wasn't her husband back then; he was just the young teacher who'd taken over at the local one-room schoolhouse. At first he was a puzzle to her. Lincoln Hale had grown up doing farmwork, or so he said, but you'd never have known it. He had that bony, brainy look that stamped him as an intellectual, or at least intellectuals the way Allie imagined them then: quiet men who thought a lot about Europe. He had an air about him too, as if he had suffered heartbreak, or some other literary disease, and hadn't fully recovered yet. Allie liked all that about him.

Not all her classmates did. The boys didn't respect him because Mr. Hale never beat anybody. But Allie had never taken to males of any age who went around puffed up like roosters and acting tough.

Mr. Hale was nothing like that. She admired the tremors of his personality. The ripples of a fine intelligence, that's what they seemed. Why, his post here at the school was only a way station. He was studying nights to be a physician, he said, and one day soon he'd be leaving for Chicago. . . .

Later on, after she graduated, and he kept turning up at the Thompsons' house, he still never forced his attentions on her. Never presumed or insisted. He seemed content with her as the quicksilver beauty, the butterfly no one could trap.

And so she married him.

Astonishing everyone! That was part of the fun. Eighteen, impetuous, Allie had no idea then how often girls married their teachers. Or how often they came to regret it. But in a wink, it seemed, Link's grave, intricate way of answering her questions about the world, the lovely Delphic quality of their courtship, all that had vanished—leaving nothing behind but this marriage with its minor acts of tenderness and its coward tranquillity.

Her milking done, Allie emptied her second bucketful into the can and then searched about for its metal top. She couldn't find it. After rummaging among rusty tools and chicken droppings she finally picked up a piece of board and used that as a cover instead. It would do for now to keep the mice out. She'd have one of the boys take the can to the cellar later.

Toting her pail, Allie opened the shed door and stepped out into the plum-colored evening. An oak, the biggest tree in the yard, loomed off to the left; along the hedge borders grew daisies and starbloom, like little crimson trumpets, the scents of flowers and foliage mixing with the flatulent odor of cooking as it drifted into the yard from next door. She followed the path that ran like a brown worm through the thick grass, leading toward the back door of her house.

Allie knew she bore a lot of the blame for this marriage; she'd been willful and childish to go through with it. Still, they might have been happy, she thought—might have, that is, if Link had kept his promise to her and become a surgeon, if he'd moved up and out into the wide world. But he hadn't. He bought all those thick medical books, he attended some classes, and what did it come to? Nothing. Link had the brains, it turned out, but not the drive. He was run by some littler engine.

Instead he got work managing a general store in Somerset, bringing his paycheck home every week and dropping it like a stick at her feet. He also picked up a little extra cash as a part-time deputy sheriff for Pulaski County. All in all, he had cobbled together a decent living for his family. He was good to the children, a patient husband—as long as she didn't mention his medical career.

So being appalled was just part of her life now, like the wallpaper. How could she, in the glitter of her youth, have married a plodder, a provider, a man so surpassingly ordinary? He wasn't even a failure. She had heroically looked beyond his physical appearance to the man within, and been utterly deceived. He had lied, either to himself or to her. It came to the same thing.

She paused a moment at the back door, listening to the ragged pulse of the crickets. Then, setting her bucket down, she impulsively caught up her skirts with one hand and trod slowly, with high-lifting steps, along the side of the house through the un-mown grass. When she came to the edge of the parlor window, she stopped and looked in.

There he was at the desk, his frail form bent forward, leaning into the green mandarin glow of the kerosene lamp. He was copying something into a ledger. As she watched, he laid down his pen, flexed his fingers, shook the hand out, then picked up the pen and resumed. He did work long hours and almost never complained. He was faithful to her. Some limp part of her even loved him. She shook her head.

Maybe Maggie would do better. Allie certainly hoped so. At least—and here, returning toward the back door, she paused in mid-step, caught by a little rush of apprehension—she wished Maggie happiness. But if Maggie married *too* well, what would Allie be left to feel but even worse about her own life than she did already?

A sister was always a threat that way.

The truth was, Allie wanted good things for her sister, but not—well, as their father would say, not enough to choke a horse. A shaming thought, but there it was.

Allie plucked up her milk pail again and stood, biting her lip. She should make Maggie an outfit to wear on her honeymoon. A traveling dress. Yes. Something in brown serge, with a tight little jacket and satin collar and cuffs . . .

For Maggie was dear to her—in a rather faded way perhaps after these last rough years, but dear to her nonetheless. Allie genuinely wished her well.

5

AS IT TURNED OUT, Allie did make a honeymoon dress for Maggie, but it wasn't brown serge. It was an airy rose-colored crepe, and the hat (store-bought) was a wide-brimmed straw, trimmed with wooden cherries and one of those beekeeper veils. A summer outfit, in short, for Ham and Maggie weren't married right away, but nearly a full year later.

The two families had decided Ham should finish his last year of college before the wedding. And the following summer of '98, as he turned twenty-one, he lingered on the Dillon farm a while to help with the planting and cultivating—savoring the days, his valedictory labor in these fields. The wedding was set for August 10.

But the engagement period beforehand wasn't the happy idyll Ham and Maggie had hoped for. First, a couple of Maggie's girl-friends went into odd snits and sulks, while insisting that jealousy had nothing to do with it. Then Maggie's mother declared herself in charge of everything, the whole shebang. Full of that iron politesse born of her days as an Eastern belle, she began organizing the wedding with the air of one determined to accomplish her mission coolly and with minimal loss of life.

The lovers snatched what little time they could together, which wasn't much, with Ham either away at college or busy on the farm. That last summer he gave her a locket to wear around her neck; inside was a tiny oval picture of him. Maggie spent more time studying that photograph than she did with the man himself.

Came the wedding day, at long last—scheduled for late afternoon at the Thompson home, Reverend Aspinall to officiate. Ham's mother commandeered the kitchen from early morning on, working half a dozen women like serfs. Soon provocative domed platters and napkin-draped bowls began to dot the dining-room table. When no one was looking, silver candelabra appeared on the mantelpiece, with candles grand as organ pipes, and the great horseshoe-shaped archway leading to the parlor sprouted peach-colored roses. In a bedroom upstairs stood Maggie, the eye of the hurricane, while Allie fluttered about helping her dress, along with their mother and a couple of friends, one of whom kept reaching over the heads of the others to do something vital with the bride's curls.

Around four Ham arrived like Coriolanus, trailing friends and relations. Mr. Thompson stood at the doorway pumping the hands of the guests. In the parlor Miss Halsop, dressed in orange, sat down at Dr. Pfeiffer's melodeon and fed the noise.

Finally, at a signal from Reverend Aspinall, she struck up the wedding march. The time was a couple of minutes past 5 P.M.

Two eight-year-olds crammed against the wall sang sotto voce ("Here comes the bride, big, fat, and wide . . .") as Maggie, squeezing the stems of her bouquet as if she had the devil by the throat, slowly descended the stairs. A sentimental sigh arose from the women as they closely scrutinized the bride. She was wearing pale yellow, pearl-throated, daisy-crowned. Maggie paused on the stair, a vein jumping near her eye.

Ham stood at his place under the rose-bowered archway looking up at her, as rapt as a man can be who knows he's yielding focus.

Then Reverend Aspinall began the incantation. "Dearly beloved, we are gathered here . . ." Its soft spell wove through the parlor and the hall, among the host of the assembled, and touched every warm, suspended face.

"Albert Hamlet Dillon, do you take this woman . . ."

In his conscientious way, Reverend Aspinall always added a unique touch to every marriage service he performed, some little watermark to set each one apart from all others. This time he had picked out special words for Maggie and her future:

"Proverbs thirty-one, verse twenty-eight," he rumbled. " 'Her children stand and bless her; so does her husband. He praises her with these words, "There are many fine women in the world, but you are the best of all." ' "

Slowly Maggie blushed. Her sister, Allie, matron of honor, put a hand to her throat.

Then the rings, the kiss. The bride blinked tears.

The first wave of guests, like heroes, stormed the food.

MAGGIE WAS TRULY ENJOYING HERSELF for the first time in ages. Married! Turning her head about in this state of dazed elevation, she spied her mother, fiercely festive, holding court nearby. Mr. Thompson beside her with a smile as stiff as a board. Poor Daddy.

Ever since they were small he had always called the pair of them, Allie and Maggie, the Princess and the Pea.

Well, the Princess had had her day. Now it was the Pea's turn.

She returned to the gabble of voices around her. Several

middle-aged neighbor ladies were welcoming her to the matrons' club.

"Now you take sleeping right up next to a man," said Mrs. Wampler. "You might not think so, but that can be the trickiest part of married life." She had a hunch and a squint, and her dress was a cheerful Armageddon of summer colors. "Take Horace and me. I can sleep through pert near anything, whereas Horace, he's different. He wakes up if a mouse sneezes. And I'm a flopper too. Now this is the type of thing that can lead to some bad feeling between a husband and a wife if you don't keep an eye out, and if it happens to you—I'm not saying it will but it might and if it does—the two of you got to sit down and have a good talk—"

"Talking, that's the key to a good marriage," Mrs. Dupree put in.

"Well, I don't know about that," said Mrs. Wampler, frowning. "A lot of people talk who don't have a thing worthwhile to say. Some husbands I know in particular."

"What's your point, then?" said Mrs. Dupree.

"My point is they might have to go to two beds."

"Oh, for heaven's sake."

"I think the most important thing in any home is a good Christian foundation," said the third woman, Mrs. Pike. She was thin, blue-eyed, and wan as a wax candle. "There's a lot of things I don't know, Maggie, but I do know this, that whatever storm or tragedy may come into your lives, you and Ham can ride it out together if you keep your faith in God."

Mrs. Wampler looked at Mrs. Pike, trumped.

"Just give him lots of love," Mrs. Dupree said. She made her face all scrunched up and confidential.

"Well now, you got to be careful about that too," said Mrs. Wampler. "Don't you ever lose your self-respect, dear. Some of these women cling to their men like cat hair."

Meanwhile over near the archway, Maggie could see her new

husband talking eagerly to some friends. Farmers like himself, all scrubbed and duded up for the occasion. He loved them, he was like them, but how different too. Farmers being, as a rule, laconic, even-keeled men, who worked like Trojans; Ham swung an ax as hard as anyone, but with a passion he never disguised.

He finished his story, whatever it was, to a burst of laughter, and one of the men slapped him on the back. It came to her for the first time, with a surge of pride: I'm a politician's wife.

O VER B Y the front window, Allie Hale took her glass of lemonade and sat down alone on the divan. Her dress was a dark caramel color, which set off her reddish hair. All afternoon she'd been registering, a little wearily, the double takes of men.

Where was Link? Not by the liquor table. Of course not: years ago he'd decided that booze threatened him, so he had cut it out completely. Allie admired that in her husband. To the extent that one can admire a negative.

Behind her she heard some women discussing wedding dresses of the past, in almost molecular detail.

"My wedding skirt was at least three yards around," said one, "and it had this crocheted insertion about two inches wide, made out of number fifty thread . . ."

"Well, mine was georgette crepe . . ."

There was Ham. He was talking with that sour-looking preacher who'd performed the ceremony. She watched her new brother-in-law press a five-dollar gold piece into the minister's hand.

Then Ham turned his head and caught Allie's gaze. He smiled and nodded to her. She smiled back. When he detached himself from the reverend and headed toward her, she began to sit up slightly.

"Excuse me?"

The voice said it again: "Excuse me." The sound was like a fly buzzing against a screen. Allie looked around. She found a wild-haired little woman holding a plate of food. The person leaned forward, timidly insistent.

"Excuse me. May I sit here?"

"Oh, of course," said Allie automatically. "Please." She waved a hand at the spot beside her.

"Thank you!" said the little woman. She seated herself with alacrity, placed the plate on her lap and unscrolled some silver-ware from her napkin.

Allie looked back at Ham, who had stopped a few yards away. He gave her a soft smile, held up his hand, and faded off.

"You're the sister of the bride, aren't you?" said the woman slyly, as if she was on to something nobody was supposed to know.

"That's right."

"I don't think the two of you look much alike," the woman said.

"Oh?" said Allie. "Some people say we do."

"But of course," said the woman, "not all sisters resemble each other. My goodness, my sister and I grew up looking so different, my father used to say Mama got up to something with a Bible salesman. It was just Daddy's little joke, but the way it used to get Mama going, oh my stars . . ."

And with that the frizzy-haired woman was off on a full-blown monologue. If it had a theme (and perhaps it did, to a subtle and deep-reaching mind) it was her memories of childhood which, based on the evidence, had been stuffed with minutiae, the only relief from which, as far as the listener was concerned, came from her digressions, like little day trips, into the suburbs of her thinking on various topics of the day, each of which, from the monumental on down to the minuscule, she gave equal weight and full attention, and thereby demonstrated an admirable sense of democracy and fairness.

There is a kind of boredom that's charged with anguish, as

Allie soon remembered. She looked around for Ham but didn't see him. No rescue.

Then again . . . Maybe it was just as well, she thought. Allie and Ham had met once before, last Christmas, when the Hales had come up for the holidays, and the moment she saw his avid eye and quick charm she had stopped herself like a diver at the edge of a cliff and just disappeared, emotionally vanished. They weren't friends.

Allie set down her lemonade and smoothed her hands on the long sheen of her lap.

"That's a lovely dress," said the talkative woman.

"Th—"

"WHERE YOU HEADING?" cried Denny, leaping in front of Ham as the groom crossed the parlor. "Don't you want your wedding present?" Ham could see it, that well-known look in his brother's eye—that look of the joker when he has a hot one on the stove. Denny was always dangerous that way.

"Listen, Den," he said, stopping. "Don't do anything too—"

"No, no," said Den. "Don't thank me yet!" He disappeared.

Ham continued across the room on his way to see his mother, who sat enthroned in a Morris chair near the sideboard. A guest was just squeezing her hand and going, and for a moment he saw her quite alone amid the swirl of the party. Aside from the dress she was wearing, which gave her an air of glum gaiety, she looked just like always: dull-eyed with determination, her face like a cracked field.

Ham came up and stood beside her.

"Having a good time?" he asked.

She looked up at him and nodded. "Of course."

"I love you, Mother," he said then, looking into her eyes.

At once her face got flushed and complicated, and a silence ensued.

Finally she said, "I feel the same way about you."

Ham smiled, brushed her cheek with his hand, and moved off in search of Maggie. He didn't see her anywhere. Maybe she was outside.

ED WATKINS, the Dillons' hired man, stood on the porch. Alone, yet serenely self-contained. Near his feet a little boy was playing with a cigar-box train. Not far away a heavy-haired young woman seemed to be looking for someone. Her fingers drifted to her lips as she peered here and there.

"Want to know how to get rid of those warts?" Ed asked affably.

"What?" The woman colored and snatched away her hand. "I don't know what you're talking about. What do you mean? What warts?"

"Those there," said Ed.

"No, I certainly . . ." The young woman paused, then furtively scanned the porch. "All right," she said finally, in a tense half-whisper, "how do you get rid of them?"

Ed reached out and took her hand. She flinched but let him. He held the hand before him, raised his other one above it, and after a moment of silence intoned:

"Erum, orum, urum, og . . ."

The woman yanked her hand away and stalked off. Unperturbed, Ed returned his attention to the little boy playing with the train.

"Whatcha up to there, partner?"

"Ed! Psst!"

He looked around. It was Den Dillon, signaling to him down in the yard. "Come here!"

"Howdy there, Den. What's—"

"Come on, gimme some help. I've got his wedding present." He slipped out of sight.

Ed was descending the outside steps as Ham appeared in the doorway.

"Hey, Ed. Seen my wife?" Ham said.

"Nope."

"Say, Ed—" But Ed was gone.

Ham turned back inside. He was hungrier than ever for a good armful of bride.

Then he spotted her, coming down the hallway with the photographer, who was lugging a safari's worth of equipment. Ham started toward her, but just then a hand came down on his shoulder from behind, hard as a pump handle.

"Mind if I shanghai you for a second, young fella?"

Ham turned to find a thick-spectacled gent of about forty, wearing a loud but expensive-looking auburn-checked suit that exactly matched the color of his hair and mustache. He offered a gap-toothed grin.

"Know who I am, young fella?"

"No, sir."

"I'm your Uncle Alva."

"Sir?"

"Arthur's brother. Arthur, your daddy-in-law."

"Oh. Well. Hi there!"

"Welcome to the family, son." Uncle Alva stuck out a meaty hand, and Ham shook it. "Well, now. You're quite a piece of horseflesh."

"Where did you travel from, sir?"

"Granville!"

"Ohio?"

"Yessir. O-hi-o. The state of grace."

Granville, Ohio. Just like Maggie's parents, Ham thought, who were about to pull up stakes and move back there themselves. Arthur Thompson had bestowed a 240-acre farm on Ham and Maggie as a wedding present, but otherwise he was selling off the rest. Less than two years, he'd been here.

Her daddy had a restless foot, that's what Maggie said. The pioneer curse. He'd set up somewhere, get successful, knock it all down, and move on. Still, people around here wouldn't be all that sad to see the Thompsons pull out. Emma and Arthur, who had arrived with such pomp and promise, had never mixed much. Kept to themselves, like an aging Romeo and Juliet. Somehow, though the heat of their passion must have cooled long ago, they had never shaken off the selfishness of rapture.

"Well!" cried Uncle Alva. "Bet you've been getting a lot of advice on how to handle married life, am I right?" He was waving a lit cheroot.

"I've gotten some," Ham said. His eyes kept shifting over to Maggie. Why didn't she come to him?

"Yeah, lemme tell you something, just about everything you hear 'bout marriage is a lot of swamp gas," Uncle Alva declared. "I'll say this, though. I've known that little girl over there"—he gestured toward Maggie—"all her life, and there's one thing I know for sure."

"What's that?"

"Don't break her heart, son. Go ridin' off. She'll yank you right back out of the saddle." Uncle Alva stuck the cheroot in his teeth and gave him a full-rictus grin.

Ham looked at him in dumb surprise.

The scrape of a fiddle brought him around. The musicians were coming through the front door to get a little punch and wedding cake before the hot work of dancing started. Through the back window he could see the hired girl on a ladder stringing Japanese lanterns in the oak trees. A farmhand appeared from the side doing jagged little backsteps, dragging a sack of cornmeal. Heading for the old silo site, a huge rectangle of exposed concrete that would be serving as the dance floor.

When he reached the edge, the farmhand muscled the bag upright and opened it with a flourish, then let the bag fall like a dead man on its side, spilling seed. From his haunches he began scattering handfuls of grain across the cement, slickering up the surface.

With a deft pantomime Ham got away from Uncle Alva and in two strides had his arm scooped around Maggie's waist. He planted a kiss, full and hard, against her tight little mouth.

"Can you two-step in those things?" he asked, nodding toward her shoes.

"Hey, everybody! Everybody!" It was Denny at the front door. He was calling to the whole parlorful of people. "Come on out on the porch, would you? We got a present out here for the happy couple, and I don't think you want it indoors!"

With a wash of trepidation Ham let himself be borne out the doorway amid the stream of wedding guests, Maggie still at his side. In moments the porch was crowded with peering faces.

"What are we looking at?" barked Uncle Alva.

Across the yard, through a gilding of dust and failing sunshine, Ham could see Ed standing near an elm tree. Beside him was an enormous crate.

With everyone assembled, Denny sprinted from the porch steps over to it, turned, and faced them all.

"It was daggone hard to find the right present!" he yelled. "But I finally got it! Tell me if this don't make you think of my brother!"

He reached over and popped the front on the crate. There was a rustling and banging and then something—a huge bird— spurted out.

It raced here and there in high dudgeon, making horrible noises, while Denny and Ed sprang around trying to keep it in bounds. Up on the porch the quick ones were telling the slow ones what it was. Finally the peacock stopped, flared its tail to the maximum, and screamed.

"I call him Albert!" Denny cried.

PART TWO

"Of course you'll expect something
    original,
But I'll tell you before I begin,
That there's nothing original in me,
Excepting Original Sin."

—ALLIE THOMPSON,
written in her mother Emma's "memory book,"
October 24, 1888, the day before Allie's marriage
to Hardin Lincoln Hale.

6

EVERYBODY SAID the same, if you didn't count those two old birds down at the post office. They were probably the oldest men in Elnora, and they spent their days playing dominoes at a little side table beside the stamp window, squabbling about this and that, getting whipped up like shaving soap over nothing at all. So naturally when somebody stuck in the mail line asked them, just making conversation, if they'd ever seen a bigger hailstorm in their lives, the pair of them sat back, eyeing each other with a sort of sly senility, till finally one of them said sure, there'd been hail this-big-around back in the thirties, and the other said no, bigger, and they fell to arguing about the average size of a hailstone seventy years ago, their only point of agreement being that it was bigger than a human head.

But those two aside, nobody claimed to remember anything heavier than the Great Hailstorm of 1905. It descended on Elmore Township like one of the plagues of Egypt, on a freak afternoon in late April, battering the farms that lay between Odon and Elnora. All the early plantings of corn and tomatoes were slaughtered, buildings pitted, livestock left gashed and bleeding. One farmer died making a dash from his smokehouse to the kitchen door, his skull cracked like a coconut. Afterward people stood numb amid the ruins, like civilians after an army has swept through.

Ham Dillon's place got pounded as bad as anyone's. Aside from damage to the porch and some pieces of the roof, the house stood up all right, but his barn was a piece of standing debris, a few cows were dead and his threshing machine smashed beyond repair. It took weeks to get things back in shape, and on this mild blue day in June he was still at it. Crouched on the roof of his house, the knees of his overalls damp from a morning shower, he was driving a nail through a soggy wood shingle. The blows of his hammer echoed like gunshots over the countryside.

Like his neighbors, Ham was brisk and steady at his work, farmers being a disaster-toughened lot accustomed to laboring hard just to get back to zero. But Ham brought something else to plain tasks like mending the roof: a rare spirit, a knifelike vigor. It wasn't just that times were good, that farm prices were finally shooting up after a lot of bad years; every fat capitalist, every headline writer in the country was ballyhooing this new century as the Age of Optimism, the Cocksure Era. Ham Dillon's confidence went beyond that.

Twenty-seven years old, and what a farm he had already. In the six, nearly seven years now since he'd married Maggie, it had grown to four hundred acres, and he hoped to expand even more—if they ever sorted out who owned the adjoining property. (The Addisons had been chewing each other up with lawsuits over it ever since the old man died.) Sitting back on his heels now, on the mild slope of the roof, Ham looked out over the vast spread of sun-dusted land, stretching all the way to the creek line where the Addisons' began. He could see one of his hired men in the middle distance with a mule and a plow in the muck, still playing catch-up in the wake of the big storm. Just beyond lay the melon field thick with vines, a crucified scarecrow in the middle of it, wearing an old hat and shirt of Ham's. And way off yonder, past all that, a round barn with a cap like a factory whistle. All his.

Ham Dillon was a popular man in Daviess County, with the votes to prove it. The year before, 1904, he'd been elected to the post of trustee of Elmore Township, which made him political boss over a good-sized chunk of territory, thirty-six square miles and maybe twenty-five hundred people. He was the tax assessor, the job dispenser, the Solomon, the fixer. He supervised and controlled all ten district schools. Saturdays he always spent in his office in Elnora, visiting with constituents who came streaming up the stairs to see him, worked up about some pothole or some pig down the well. It was rare day somebody left Ham Dillon's office not feeling better about whatever it was, because they knew if Ham couldn't get results on the telephone, then by golly he'd go out there and take care of it himself. Though he sometimes moved with a shamble now, a little touch of Lincoln, just enough to put folks at ease.

Of everything he had to do as trustee, running the schools was dearest to his heart. He was his own first choice for substitute teacher, respected even by the older boys, and he acted as master of ceremonies for the cipher contests and spelling bees when two or three schools at a time went head to head.

On the roof Ham was rummaging for his next nail when a woman wearing a gray-checked calico dress came out the kitchen door and stepped into the yard, smearing her palms dry on her apron. Seeing no one there, she turned and paced slowly backward, looking up, squinting against the late-morning sun.

It was Maggie's sister, Allie Hale. She was up from Kentucky visiting.

Shading her eyes with one hand, she regarded Ham in his sprinter's crouch, framed against the sky.

"The kids are about to explode," she called to him. "You've got to come on."

Ham steadied himself against the pitch of the roof and peered down at her. Wisps of her reddish hair twisted in the breeze. Her shadowing hand kept him from seeing her face.

"Tell Harold if he kicks up I'm not buying him any weenies," Ham said. "He'll behave."

"What makes you so sure?"

"He knows I mean it."

"Why don't you just come ahead?"

"All right, all right," Ham said. "Be there in two shakes. You know, I could get this done a lot faster if you'd come up and help me," he called, but she was disappearing back into the house.

A minute or so later, standing on the back porch, Ham slung out the last of a dipper of drinking water, saw it land like a rope in the dust, then drag-kicked a chicken to one side and pushed through the screen door into the kitchen. His children were in there, Harold, six, and Ruth, four, the boy blowing bubbles out of a toy pipe with all his might, too fast, while his sister ran around after the floaters, her little hands outstretched, smacking them dead. The moment they caught sight of their father, the pipe clattered to the table and they flew to him, baying.

It was hot as blazes in the kitchen. That dragon of a stove was on, and a stagnant undersmell of bread or biscuits hung in the air, overpowered by the sharp stench of lye. Maggie was working at a counter by the sink, her face bright with heat. She was making soap.

"Lord God," said Ham, his eyes starting to water. "How come you're doing this in here?" But Maggie kept her back to him, whacking away at her pan of lye and pork grease with a wooden spoon. Maybe she hadn't heard him.

"Honey?" Ham slipped up behind her and kissed her slick neck. "Why don't you shift all this out to the summer kitchen?"

She paused long enough to tell him it was too late now, then reattacked the soap. She went at all her chores this way. Ham had joked with her about it, how his overalls took more of a beating on the washboard than they ever did out in the field. Here she was now, four, maybe five months pregnant, and still no letup.

While the children whimpered and tried to climb up his arms, Ham looked around for Allie. She wasn't there.

"All right," he told the kids. "Get ready. We're going." As they fled, he turned back to his wife. "You sure you don't want to come?"

"I'm certain. The last thing I want to see is a two-headed baby." She gave him an acid little smile, then turned and started working the sink pump to wash her hands.

Ham left the kitchen then, went through the hall and on up the stairs, his footsteps in alternating rhythm with the thumping of the little pump. *Clunk, thump. Clunk, thump.* "Here comes the bride." That rhythm. Or no, not anymore. Now it was more like the interlocking machinery of marriage.

Maggie had done her share, no doubt about it. She believed in his future in politics, that someday they would all be lifted triumphantly off the farm; she was counting on a life of silk and calling cards in Indianapolis or Washington, D.C. (her ambition being even stronger than her instinct for privacy). But in the meantime she wasn't lying in bed dreaming about the future. She was up scrubbing and sweeping and making carpets out of rags and kitchen curtains out of feed sacks. He was proud of her.

Still, working as hard as she did had a way of closing her off from other people. Even Ham sometimes. Maggie sang in the choir, tried to be a good political wife, but that shuttered part of her personality—which he'd been so tantalized by in their courting days—had actually grown, not shrunk, during the years of their marriage; now she often wore a look of thin-lipped determination. He could usually jolly her into a smile, a loving touch, if he tried hard enough. Not lately, though. She was having a rough pregnancy. He knew she was sick a lot, but she wouldn't give him the details.

In their bedroom Ham stripped off his shirt. Then he poured some tepid water from a pitcher into an enamel basin, soaked a rag, and slopped it over his face, neck, and armpits, at the same time stooping at the window to peer up at the sky, as automatically as a city man checking his watch. No rain clouds; good. The new corn, already a foot and a half late, couldn't take another soaking. Going to be a hot afternoon, he thought. Good news for the lemonade man. Whistling, Ham rummaged in a drawer for a clean shirt and pulled out a fancy one with red stripes. So he'd be easy to spot in the crowd. Then he sat on the bed to pull on his shoes—the marital bed with its swamp mist of memories.

The whistling ceased.

It wounded his vanity as much as anything that he had misjudged Maggie, the way she would behave in bed. When they were courting, he used to imagine how he'd go about it, picking the lock of her passion, like a thief, with meticulous fingers. The feel of her body beneath him, bucking and vaulting. But he'd been mistaken. Maggie had a scrappy style of lovemaking, but its very energy came from her passionate refusal to surrender. Those times he did tease her over the brink left something sour and embarrassed in the air.

And yet her love for him, her devotion even, was real enough. Maggie just felt more comfortable admiring him across the dinner table, or watching him striding in from a field brushing grain dust off his clothes, than when he put out his hand to touch her. Well, now he knew. The cold can be devoted, like anybody else.

Ham buttoned his shirt, combed his hair, and studied his face in the beveled mirror. Just for five seconds or so. Never longer.

· · ·

WHILE HAM DRESSED, Allie was in the guest room getting ready to go. Unlike Ham, she had never been much for mirrors. In her younger days she'd had that high confidence of a girl who knows that getting a little mussed is just another way to look devastating.

But that was a long time ago. Now she sat at her dressing table languidly contemplating herself in the looking glass, an earring motionless in her fingers. This had become a form of meditation, surveying the signs of decay.

Allie was nearing thirty-five, still beautiful. More so than she knew. Age had done her a subtle favor, softened her. If anything she now attracted even more men—those legions who are frightened off by startling beauty but come slouching back at the first signs of age. There was the warmth of experience in her gray eyes, a promise of comfort in her body. But either she didn't realize that or she didn't value it. Otherwise she wouldn't have put her money—thirty-seven cents—on a gaily beribboned mustard pot with silver label reading: Orange Flower Skin Food, Now Regarded as Very Essential to Beauty. Allie Thompson, who never gave a fig for all that stuff. Weeks ago she'd bought it, and still it sat in her suitcase unopened. Maybe she should try it out today.

She was startled by a tap at the door, and the earring clattered on the glass-topped table. There was no time for skin food. She joined Ham in the hallway and together they went downstairs to the kitchen.

Ruth was there, head cocked, humming to herself. A great bow now clung to the side of her head like a huge, tenacious butterfly. Down on one knee, Maggie was giving the little girl's dress a last flick clean with a dishtowel.

"So what are your plans?" Ham asked his wife.

"Later on I'll stop by Mrs. Lascoulie's. See if she's doing any better." Maggie stood up, her back to him. "After that there's an Eastern Star meeting."

The Eastern Star was the semisecret women's arm of the Masons, the equally semisecret brotherhood Ham belonged to. All the prominent men in the area did. Ham called the Eastern Star a coven and pretended to be afraid of it.

"You'll be back when?"

"A little past dark."

"You're doing too much."

"I'll rest tomorrow," she said.

Allie watched as he walked over and encircled Maggie's waist from behind. She slapped at him backward with the dishtowel.

"That's my sweet girl." He nuzzled her neck, knowing it would annoy her, and kissed her on the cheek.

"All right, troops," he said.

It took more than half an hour to reach the fairground by buggy. Harold rode with his father on the springboard up front, while Ruth nestled in the back seat with her aunt. As they wheeled onto the main road, Allie was singing "Four and Twenty Blackbirds" to Ruth, and nipping off her nose with two knuckles over and over while the little girl squealed with glee; this led, naturally enough, to the story of how the elephant got his trunk, which Allie related, and Ruth absorbed, as a nonstop astonishment; but by the end of that they still had not reached the fair, and Ruth was tired of stories. Now they were caught in a slow-moving clog of other buggies and wagons. Up front, Allie noticed, Harold was sulking about the delay.

Harold was a large, charmless child, to Allie's mind; though he did seem to be a student of charm in others; in fact, Harold's most attractive quality was his obvious fascination with his father. When Ham entered a room, the youngster was likely to drop whatever he was doing and follow his dad's movements with the eyes of a hunter seeing his first stag. But otherwise he was a stolid sort of boy who managed to convey a surprising amount of menace for a six-year-old. One day (Allie was there) Maggie had to take Ruth on her knee and tell her she didn't have to play Prince and Slave all the time just because Harold wanted to.

"You like boxing, right?" Ham said to his son, breaking in on the boy's bellyaching. "Well, did I ever tell you about the feather-weight championship of the world, the one fought right here in Indiana, back when I was your age? Never been anything else like it. Ike Weir, the Belfast Spider, versus the challenger, Frank Murphy. Otherwise known as the Man Who Can't Be Damaged. Believe you me, that was a monster fight. Eighty-four rounds, they went at it."

Harold scowled. Hooked in spite of himself. "Who won?" he asked.

"Well," Ham said, "they come out for the first round . . ."

Allie rolled her eyes and leaned her head back. She was smiling, though. As a father Ham knew his onions.

With a lurch the buggy picked up speed; the traffic jam had unsnarled and they were trotting along again. Allie felt good being outdoors. Some kind of constriction or gloom had settled on her just over the past few days—why, she didn't know—but lifting her face now, she felt all her vague troubles blowing off with the breeze. She'd been here visiting now for three weeks, and it was still great to be away from home.

Home being the place she was always pregnant. Allie was the mother of five now—a good mother, she knew that. Still, there were times she felt as if she'd been carrying passengers most of her life. People always touted having little ones as a woman's greatest joy, but soldiers in battle had a better chance of coming back alive.

Not that Allie was scared of it herself, not anymore. She had reached a point beyond fatalism. No delivery would ever kill her. She was going to live and live and live, whether she liked it or not. As a result, she never worried about her health.

Her husband, on the other hand, might have failed as a doctor, but he was going great guns as a patient. Over the years Link Hale had developed a whole list of symptoms. That tremulous quality, that poet's sensitivity she had once so responded to, seemed to have turned malignant. For the past four years he had been getting regular blasts of electricity for what his doctor called "scrivener's palsy"—writer's cramp, in English. At least once a month Link went to an office to have electrodes strapped to his hand. His physician, Dr. Carstairs, had grown very enthusiastic about electricity. With his encouragement, Link was also using something at home called an electric flesh brush, which ran on batteries. It was supposed to calm the flits and fidgets that occasionally attacked his body. Link claimed it worked. Sometimes, while she lay in the dark pretending to sleep, Allie would feel him creep out of bed like a thief, and a moment later she'd hear the hum of the flesh brush coming from the next room.

Jouncing along in the buggy, Allie suddenly wondered just how much of all this Ham knew about. She had talked to Maggie about it, never to him. Still, tell a wife, tell a husband. For some reason this distressed her.

Just then a horse and buggy shot past on the right, with a flailing, red-faced driver aboard and a woman holding down her hat with both hands. Delighted, Ham half rose and hooted something at the back of the vehicle, which was already dissolving in a cloud of dust and small stones. "That horse there's an ex-trotter," he shouted to Allie back over his shoulder. "Hubert bought him right off the racetrack. Thought he got a good deal."

Allie laughed gaily at that. So Ruth did too.

Now Ham was circling around to the hitching area on the edge of the fairground. The children sat up at the sound of the music, a mishmash of styles coming from different directions—a piccolo, an oompah band—just as if they had struck up especially for Harold's and Ruth's arrival and were competing furiously for their attention. Ham pulled up in the shade of an oak and the kids clambered out.

Allie was about to follow them when Ham swung around in his seat. "How the elephant got his trunk?" he said.

"I didn't think it up," she answered.

"Well, you've got a way with a story anyhow. Speaking as one old tale spinner to another."

"Oh . . ."

"You ought to hear Ruth talk about you when you're not around." He reached a hand toward Allie's face, and she flinched. "Whoa," he said. Lightly, almost clinically, Ham ran his fingertip from just beneath her ear all the way down along her jawline, to the tip of her chin. Then with a strong thumb he stroked her cheek, brushing the edge of her lips. "Just wanted to say thanks," he said, and finally withdrew the hand. He gave her an easy smile, turned, and jumped out of the buggy.

Hauled along by the children, she and Ham were soon working their way through the whoop and clamor of the fairground. Set on a big open field, it was laid out roughly in sections: the first they came upon was a long double row of white tents, flag-festooned, with their flaps up, showing off all the latest labor-saving wonders from cream separators to hand-cranked washing machines to battery-operated outboard motors to sheep sheared in half the time, right before your eyes—each of these miracles staked out by a jungle-eyed sales agent. In the wide, littered lanes between the tents people strolled, or jostled, or dashed and dodged. Drums beat, bells rang, and the air was full of money and science and self-congratulation. For it wasn't just the manufacturers of the products, but the people here too—every farmer and farmer's wife and clerk and hired hand—who knew they had helped to make this day. They were all part of the song of American progress.

"Lemo! Ice-cold lemo!" cried the red-lemonade man. "Five cents, a nickel, half a dime! Ice-cold lemo!"

Harold was trying to tug his father straight to a destination of his own, but Ham was already running into people he knew in the crowd, and he kept stopping to swap a few words.

"Horace, you old chicken thief! Mrs. Burns, how you been keeping?"

"She had seven teeth out just the other day," cried Horace proudly. "Seven teeth and not a yelp out of her. She sure has nerve that way."

"Well now, isn't that fine?"

Mrs. Burns ducked her head, shyly delighted.

Harold muttered and fumed. Ruth meanwhile was gawking at all the delights of her first fair, catching thrilling glimpses of peanut vendors and a balloon man. She discovered a stick of licorice in her hand, apparently put there by God, and began sucking on it while their little group worked its way forward, past the last of the tents now, onto a dusty little byway lined with booths and platforms. Every few feet along here some man seemed to be yelling.

"I'll tell you what I'm holding up here, folks, and spare you the lather of suspense. A solid gold ring, my friends! Gold! The priceless mother of metals, toiled for on the steaming slopes of Madagascar! And look, my friends, I take this ring, glorious, golden, eighteen carats, and I place it in the package with the elegant notepaper and the pens and the India-rubber eraser you can bounce like a ball. Who takes it, ladies and gents, for a quarter of a dollar?"

". . . No, we do not guarantee that Princess Hair Tonic will grow hair on the back fence. What we DO claim . . ."

". . . Every price hammered down to the lowest notch . . ."

". . . You, sir! Don't skitter off! Look at your lady friend beside you just a-languishing and a-drooping for the unspeakable beauty of the item I hold in my hands . . ."

Toward the end of this mad gauntlet they came upon one of those freelance evangelists—a bulging-eyed little man underneath a mail-order toupee, hollering at the passing stream of fairgoers about the horrors of "eternal regret." Allie just glimpsed him as they went by, but the word *regret* lodged in her mind, and she found herself wondering as she trailed along after Ham and his boy whether this cocky brother-in-law of hers had any regrets.

Just then Harold, running ahead, almost collided with a unicyclist, who spun adroitly out of the way, then with a man wearing a sandwich board advertising King the Diving Horse. "We're almost there!" Harold shouted, knowing they were getting near the Geeks and Freaks Tent, officially known as the Hall of Wonders. He pointed. There it was. Allie, holding Ruth by one sweet-stained little hand, spied a man in a boater and bow tie in the middle distance; standing on an elevated rostrum, he was waving his arms and hollering with the fervor of a man freshly baptized. You could almost believe that he'd just stuck his head inside the tent and seen the five-legged cow for the first time in his life.

Ham stopped short, leaving Harold, who had hold of his hand, straining forward like a mule in the mud. His father had caught sight of another booth off to the right, a counter with an overhang made of two-by-fours. Framed there was a pretty young woman, not quite in profile. She was dark-haired and willowy, no more than twenty, and in her perfect stillness she had the gauzy look of a maiden musing at a windowsill on a rainy day. Overhead was a sign:

KISS ME

FOR PITY'S SAKE

25c

"Come with me a second," Ham said, and headed for the booth. Allie and the children trailed along.

"Why, Mr. Dillon," said the girl, coming out of her reverie.

"You can't tell me business is bad," Ham said. "I don't believe it."

"Business has been excellent, Mr. Dillon," she replied archly. "I'm all tuckered out."

She didn't seem like a maiden anymore. For a farm girl she had an odd sort of insolent languor. Maybe that's why she had been asked to work this kissing booth for charity—a campaign, as Allie could see now, underway to repair the Widows and Orphans Asylum. There were leaflets on the counter, along with an open cigar box half full of coins, and a photograph tacked up of a building with a ruined roof.

"Does your father know you're here?" Ham asked, roguish.

"Why, Mr. Dillon," the girl said. "You wouldn't tell on me, would you? He'd just blister my behind."

She was bold as brass, this girl. And there was Ham, shoveling it right back. Not introducing his family. Then something else touched Allie, not a thought but a flash through her vitals.

She was jealous.

It wasn't just dislike she felt for this girl and her lazy Mediterranean way. Allie felt like pitching her into oblivion. And maybe Ham with her.

Now it came to Allie in a rush of clarity, the cause of that nameless gray weight that had been sitting on her spirits lately. Living right there in the same house with Ham and her sister, she had managed to keep up an icewall of denial about how she was starting to feel about her brother-in-law; until this silly exchange with a farm girl whose name she didn't even know, catching her with her guard down . . .

Instinctively she knew that this was the start of the irreversible thaw, the first tricklings of desire, the flooding of her defenses. In a heartbeat, it seemed, they were down, all down.

Dazed, Allie realized that Harold, who was standing next to her, was muttering something under his breath.

". . . twenty-six, twenty-seven . . ."

"What are you doing, Harold?" she said.

"I'm seeing how long it takes to get to the Hall of Wonders," the boy replied, not looking up. "Twenty-eight, twenty-nine . . ."

The young woman meantime was working her wiles on Ham to try to get him to buy a kiss. Allie knew it couldn't be more unimportant, yet she was riveted anyway.

"Mr. Dillon, you have to kiss me," the girl said, wheedling. "It's the Christian thing to do."

"I don't know," said Ham. "You're talking to a man in the public eye, Lorraine."

He seemed cooler now, Allie thought. A little remote. Good.

"Why, I know you're a public man," Lorraine said. "You're a politician, Mr. Dillon."

"That's right."

"Which is exactly why I trust you," she cried. "You have to protect your good name. Really," she added, leaning forward, her eyes taunting him, "you wouldn't believe what some men expect for twenty-five cents."

Ham thought a moment; then he fished a dollar bill out of his pocket and laid it carefully on the plywood counter.

That topped her. She blushed.

"I believe I'll just make a straight contribution this time," he said. "Maybe one of these days . . . You be good now." Leaving the dollar on the counter, he led Allie and the children away toward the Hall of Wonders. "Nice girl," he said as they walked along, "but she's getting herself a reputation."

"Fifty-nine, sixty, sixty-one," said Harold.

Allie was still too addled by her own thoughts to care much where they were going. Why hadn't Ham kissed that girl? Moments ago it had been the last thing Allie wanted to see, but now that he hadn't done it, it seemed like a bad sign. First he'd been so free and easy with her; then suddenly he'd balked like a horse at a jump.

Oh dear.

No, no, she thought. I respect him for that.

Thus consumed, Allie was barely aware that she was moving forward with Ham and the children into the Hall of Wonders. When her surroundings finally swam into focus, she found herself staring at a tap-dancing chicken.

There was a strange blue glow in the tent, whose source she couldn't trace. But the inky light only made the effortful stylings of the chicken, which was dancing inside a wire-mesh cage, even more peculiar. That, and the faint, rancid odor of something burning. It turned out to be coming from the hot plate, or stage, on which the chicken was performing.

With a wince Allie turned and moved away from Ham and his children, trying to gather her thoughts. It wasn't easy, surrounded on all sides by a deformed netherworld of Wild Men from Boola Boola, with body hair like the manes of horses, waving their spears; the two-headed baby, afloat in a jar of sparkling brine; and the Woman with the Body of a Spider, whose opiated and cynical face, and filthy costume, made her practically as hideous as if she'd been the real McCoy. Shaken, Allie fumbled her way to a stool off to the side, next to the shell game, and sat for a while getting her breath. Once she lifted her head and caught the maleficent gaze of one of the banshees from Boola Boola, who had paused in his hopping and was watching her. Her eyes flashed back to the sawdust.

Her niece came running up. "Aunt Allie! Look what I have!" Ruth cried, pointing proudly to her upper arm. A real sailor's tattoo!

"I know the first thing your mother's going to use that soap on," Allie told her.

"No!" The little girl clutched the place on her arm.

Ham and his son joined them then. Bribed with a weenie, Harold had finally agreed to leave the Hall of Wonders and try the rest of the fair. As he stood next to Allie though, he glanced over and discovered the shell game. Now he was wild to play.

"Not on your life," said Ham. "We're going."

"But, Papa—"

"Forget it." He started to move, but when Harold balked, Ham turned back and with an exasperated sigh squatted down eye level with his son.

"It's not a game, boy," Ham said. "It's a cheat. That ball there? He doesn't really put it down. He fakes it. The way you do that, see, is you pick the ball up with your index finger and the back part of your thumb—see, like this—and then you *pretend* to put the shell on it. Okay? It's for suckers. Let's go."

Harold allowed himself to be dragged away this time, but all the way out of the tent he was looking back at the shell man with a new respect.

"How do you know that about the shell game?" Allie asked Ham as they strode along. He answered with a wink.

For the next couple of hours the family enjoyed all the pinwheel pleasures of the fair. The children became sticky and popcorn-specked. Ham kept it up with friends and constituents, passing out encouragement and advice—a lot of advice. (Some grumbled that Ham Dillon kept his advice in a magic pouch—no matter how much he gave away, it was always full.)

"So, Frank, that old dog of yours had her pups yet?"

"Yessir, she did. Dropped 'em just last night."

"So they're Republican pups," Ham said, giving him a little elbow. "Ain't got their eyes open yet. Now when they do, you make sure . . ."

Allie was calming down. Now that she was out of the freak tent and surrounded by happier sights and smells, her craving for Ham was passing, her universe returning to normal. To her relief, the figures in her own constellation—her children, her sister, her husband—reappeared in their usual places, as steady as the stars. When she looked at Ham now, all she felt was a little bewildered.

They were deep into the afternoon, and the children were starting to stagger, but there was still one thing to be done. Ham insisted that before they left, they had to see the fat men's race.

"This is just about my favorite thing in life," said Ham. "Big shots lookin' silly." So they made their way to a field on the edge of the fairground where preparations for the race were in progress. As they found themselves a spot near the finish line, Ham was telling Allie about Mr. Yeager, the squat little owner of the hardware store in Elnora, who had wanted to run the past couple of years but had always been denied a spot on the grounds that he was too thin. Lately though, to achieve his goal, Mr. Yeager had been single-mindedly porking up and was finally going to run this time, having been declared fat by acclamation.

The race was minutes away. Ham and Allie were actually out of sight of the starting line, which was located near the base of a steep grassy slope some yards to their left. Adding the hill had been a new idea this year, probably to provide more fodder for mockery, which was already rife among the spectators.

Gradually, like cattle before a thunderstorm, the crowd fell uneasily silent, and a thin gas of suspense began to spread under the broad blue sky. Then, not quite when anyone expected, came the pop of a pistol and everyone was yelling and cheering instantly, before a single runner had come in sight. Ham and Allie cheered. The kids cheered too.

It was unearthly, Allie thought, even as she hollered her heart out with the rest, how they seemed to be rooting for no one at all. They might have been cheering a stream of ghosts. She could almost see them as they fled by, heads high, full of promise.

She was roused by a fresh burst of noise, and looking down the line, Allie saw the first fat man come heaving over the hill.

"It's Mr. Akers!"

"Charlie Charlie Charlie!"

Seconds later an even more immense individual appeared, close on Charlie's heels, and the crowd went into a rattling frenzy now, yelling for Mr. Akers, the respected banker, or urging on Mr. Brisbane, the distinguished hotel owner, as the two warriors jostled for the lead, faces puffed, bellies sloshing.

"Catch that wagon!"

"It's SUPPERTIME!"

Mr. Akers' suspenders had come loose and were bouncing on his backside. Mr. Brisbane had lost a shoe. And then a third man appeared—the mayor! Mr. Niles, the mayor of Washington. A roar for the mayor. He was followed by Mr. Yeager, who came high-stepping along like a Tennessee trotter holding up a home-made sign reading YEAGER'S HARDWARE, smiling maniacally and waving with his free hand to the spectators on both sides. And after him came Judge Hilary Houghton, a slab-sized jurist who ran the district court. Except today. Today he was running fifth.

"Hey, Judge!" Ham yelled. "You gonna get beat by somebody carrying a *sign*?"

People were straining for a look at the finish when there came another shout from downwind and a sixth contestant came teetering up over the brow of the hill, to the fresh delight of the crowd. Mr. Sweeney it was, the postmaster, trailing so badly he seemed to be in some event all his own. He was running a disciplined race though, locked in a sort of alarmed waddle with his eyes fixed on the horizon.

"Exit, pursued by bear," Ham cracked.

But his words were lost in a great cry, and a clanging of pot lids, that erupted down at the finish line. Mr. Brisbane had nipped Mr. Akers with a red-faced surge at the end, and was now having his back pounded, and his hand pumped, by a throng of hearty partisans.

Shepherding Allie and the children, Ham set out to find Judge Houghton.

"He's on the circuit court here," Ham said as they walked along. "Tough old bird. There's something I've got to ask him about."

They found their man swilling lemonade and gasping next to a barrel near the finish line.

"Fine race, Judge," Ham said.

"Fine race, my ass," muttered the judge. He was past fifty, with a heavy, pouched face like a bag of old meat, and lank gray hair matted with sweat. His glowering eyes made Allie think he was furious, till she realized he was just exhausted.

"Guess you got a bad start," Ham suggested, fighting down a smile.

The judge eyed him darkly, still breathing hard.

"That grass still slick from the rain last night? Tough to get your footing, I guess—" And then Ham broke wide open with laughter and smacked Judge Houghton on the back. "Sorry, Judge, it's just . . . The things a man has to do in politics. Makes you wonder if it's worth it, right?"

Judge Houghton showed no signs of wondering at all.

"You want to talk to me about the Addison land?" he said after a pause, filled by the sound of his raking lungs.

"Well—"

"I can't discuss anything about the case. You should know that, son."

"Sir," said Ham, still more amused than anything, "I just—"

The judge turned his attention to Allie.

"You must be Maggie," he said.

Allie blinked.

"No, sir," said Ham, rallying her with a touch, "this is Allie Hale. Maggie's sister. Up here on a visit."

"Oh. Beg your pardon. Up from where?"

"Kentucky," Allie said.

Not far away the Brisbane loyalists were struggling, with only partial success, to hoist their hero onto their shoulders. But Allie barely noticed, and whatever the judge said next she missed completely. Being mistaken for Maggie had been like a rush of tide against a sand castle. Her newly restored peace of mind shifted and crumbled, and she glanced toward Ham, stricken, uneasy.

・ ・ ・

THEY DIDN'T STICK AROUND for the pie-eating contest.
For Ruth and Harold it had been a long day, and now,
stunned with cake and weenies, they had to be lifted limp into
the buggy. On the way home they slumped together in back. Allie
sat by Ham.

The rough way Judge Houghton had treated him didn't seem
to bother Ham any, as he filled Allie in about the Addison heirs
and all their squabbling over this land he liked.

"So you wanted the judge to let you know which way the
wind was blowing?"

"If he'd been willing to tell me, sure," Ham said. "Don't want
to waste time being nice to the wrong people. Oh well, who
cares?" He laughed again, flicked the reins and the horse moved
into a quicker trot.

It was still full daylight when they reached home, close on six
o'clock. The house was empty; Maggie wouldn't be back from her
Eastern Star meeting till maybe eight. Upstairs, Allie took off her
niece's dress and hair bow, and the little girl fell into bed like a
sack of flour. Then Allie came back down. Ham and his son were
where she'd left them, out on the front porch. Ham was sitting in
a rocker, still in a fine flow of spirits, with Harold in his lap; the
boy, though ornery and overtired, had been insisting he wouldn't
go to bed till he'd heard the end of the Ike Weir–Frank Murphy
fight. Ham didn't mind.

Allie took a chair nearby, next to the smoldering smudge pot
set out to keep the mosquitoes away, and looked at the children's
swing hanging motionless from the big catalpa tree across the
yard. She heard the *thap* of a cabbage moth against a window. In
another couple of hours the trees would be filled with sparrows
heralding the sunset like a thousand squeak toys.

And after that Maggie would come home.

Allie sat listening to the rise and fall of Ham's voice, the timbre and the texture of it, hearing the words without taking them in.

When she finally glanced over, she saw that Harold lay with his head on his father's chest, his mouth sagging open, drooling a little. In the innocent stupor of childhood, even Harold looked cute. Ham was still going on, half audibly, with his lullaby about the boxing match. When she raised her eyes, she found he was looking at her.

Ham smiled. It was the look of a tender father who sees himself observed. But as their eyes, Allie's and Ham's, held each other's, she saw this paternal tinge fade, saw it replaced by something else. A more penetrating look, magically balanced between the pleading and the predatory.

She knew he would then, if she would let him. Probably he'd already divined the desire in her, sniffed it out like an animal.

With the next breath she felt, not joy at the discovery. Or even fear. What rose in her was an almost lyrical regret. Allie remembered that silly man preaching at the fair, his coyote moans of eternal sorrow. Well, this would be hers. It was sad she and Ham had met too late, but the way things were . . . They had spouses, children . . . *He was married to her sister* . . . What could be crueler or more final?

"He's out," Allie told him, to break the spell.

Ham looked down at the top of his son's tousled head. "Is that true, boy?"

She would gain something, however, by refusing this affair. She would earn the consolation of all tragic heroines: depth of soul.

"Harold?" Allie cooed, leaning toward the boy. Harold struggled to open his eyes. "He's too pooped to peep," she said. "Put him to bed, for goodness' sake."

"I know it's supposed to work this way," Ham said, "but as a politician, it always makes me nervous when the kid falls asleep while I'm talking." Lifting his son under the armpits, he stood with a grunt and then, cradling him in one arm, one-handed the door open and disappeared inside. Allie heard him mounting the stairs.

A couple of minutes later Allie went upstairs too. When she reached her bedroom door, she hesitated.

Then Ham came out of Harold's room and spotted her down the hall. He came and stood beside her.

"You going to lie down too?" he asked.

"Thought I might."

Smiling, he brushed her jaw with his finger again, but quickly, sort of chucking her under the chin.

"Don't do that," she said, and slapped his hand away.

"What? What? What's this? Are you hitting me?" Ham cried, and they tussled with each other, hands grappling, till they ended in a clutch against the bedroom door.

"Sh sh sh . . ." he went, like a kettle. "Don't wake the kids."

His face had never been so close to hers. All of him seemed concentrated in an eye, a cheekbone.

"They won't wake up," Allie whispered back. She'd crossed a line into some new zone, but with no consequences yet. Some part of her longed to stay paralyzed right here, in this state of sinless exaltation.

She watched the humor in Ham's eyes go out. He pressed his open palm softly against her cheek and left it there. Then pressed the side of her neck. Her hair. When he kissed her first, lightly, he might have been taking crumbs from her lips. The second time she was in undiscovered country.

Only once, after he had drawn her inside the room and they had settled, she backward, onto the bed—the corn shucks in the mattress making a soft, slow rustle, like the hiss of a wave on the shore, one sound—only when he had unbuttoned her dress at the throat and slipped his fingers under the strap of her shift, did she put up a hand to stop him. But he took the hand, kissed it gently, and she gave herself up to the aphrodisiac of guilt.

7

ALLIE REMAINED at the Dillon farm for another two and a half weeks, until the first of July. And her affair with Ham, once ignited, spread like a fire in a coal mine. They seized what few chances they had, making love in the woods and once against the barn wall with the cows looking on. Or they talked, eagerly, trading their most treasured yarns, their best stories about themselves. Every past foolishness or defeat exalted them in the other's eyes.

As the morning approached for Allie to leave for Kentucky, neither one had to ask if the affair would continue. The only question was how.

By the time she left, they had the sketch of a plan.

She arrived in the Nicholasville train station next day, following an overnight stop. Link and a couple of the older children met her at the station. Allie was surprised to find, riding home in the family buggy, that she was mildly glad to see Link. Taking a blurry sort of interest in her husband was actually a pleasant change from the pounding fever of the past two weeks.

It was a beautiful afternoon. Link held the reins lightly, keeping an easy pace. They were clopping down a shadowy lane overhung with elms, with ivy trails of sunlight on the road.

"By the way," she said, "Ham told me he'll be coming down this way next month. He wants to look at some horses."

"What horses are those?" Link asked.

"I don't really know. You children remember Uncle Ham?" she said, turning her head toward the back seat.

As it turned out, Ham couldn't get down to Nicholasville until September, more than two months later. Allie, as the date neared, was in a state of high-vibration anxiety, shot through with something feral and hungry: it was a lot to try to disguise. Would he never get there? What if he canceled the trip? What if he came only to tell her they couldn't go on, and she was left with nothing but those few delirious days in June? The specter of this—interspersed with moments of crawling guilt—left Allie snapping at her children over nothing and in and out of tears. So that, eager as she was, her first sight of Ham at the front door gave her a jolt not entirely pleasant.

Ham showed up blithe and randy. So keen himself that he hadn't fully considered just what it would be like to be constantly surrounded by her family, till that first night at supper when he found himself looking at a whole table of obstacles, laughing, talking, snatching the salt. But Allie had a plan ready, and the next morning, while Link was off somewhere sniffing out tax cheats for the government, all five children magically disappeared, the littler ones to school, Louise on some cockamamie mission cooked up by her mother. Even the hired girl was on the other side of town, flirting wistfully with the grocer while he ground her fifty pounds of flour. Meantime Ham and Allie were in the master bedroom, making love like enemies condemned to each other's arms. That sex could be so intimate, yet so impolite, was an ongoing revelation to them both.

That night Ham lay in the Hales' little guest room unable to sleep, gazing at the pinecone wallpaper by candlelight and thinking, or trying not to, of what might be going on in that master bedroom two doors down. There was an odor in his room, too, which he knew he would never forget—the scent of cured tobacco sifting down from the attic. Like a lot of other folks around here, Link used it as an insecticide, and the smell had become a permanent part of the house now, even in winter. For months afterward the toxic allure of that aroma, in that room late at night, would come back to Ham every time he lit a cigar.

Days passed. Here and there, in the hallway, in the milking shed, he and Allie managed a fugitive caress. That was all. Otherwise Ham passed his time strolling around Nicholasville, or traveling the few miles north to Lexington, viewing the horses and hemp. It was his first trip here, to the bluegrass region of north-central Kentucky, and the sight of the beauty and muscle of all this horseflesh in the rolling fields—Thoroughbreds, Appaloosas, harness racers—was a tonic to his blood. It took the edge off his impatience while he waited for the other thing he'd come for: the right moment to talk to Link.

Finally it arrived one quiet evening while he, Link, and Allie were sitting at the kitchen table playing gin rummy after the kids had gone to bed. After a fresh deal the three were grouping their cards, musing. Out of the silence Ham told Link there was something he'd had rattling around in the back of his mind. A sort of proposition, he said. How would Link feel about maybe pulling up stakes and moving his family to Elnora?

Link looked up from his cards, and for the first time Ham did too. Allie stared at her queens, before she remembered she should look up too.

"We could be neighbors," Ham said, and he gave Link a smile, easy, medium-strength. "I could get you a teaching job in my district right off the bat. Your wife here tells me you used to be a real good teacher, and as an old student of yours I guess she should know. Didn't mean to say old," he added, turning to her with a wink, and Allie smiled faintly. "Anyhow," Ham said, returning to Link, "I got ten schools to look after, so I can pretty near guarantee you a spot. Maybe you could buy yourself a little farm too. Expand over time. Lot of good opportunities there . . ."

Link squinted at him.

"I appreciate the offer, Ham," he said at last. "I surely do, but . . . Well, we're settled here."

"I'll tell you the truth," Ham said, relaxing back in his chair, scratching his neck. "It was Allie's visit this summer put the thought in my mind."

"How so?"

"Well, she and Maggie got their first chance to really spend some time together in a hell of a while. Sort of got a chance to be sisters again. And to Maggie, I'll tell you, that meant a lot. So then I got to thinking about the kids, yours and mine, this whole slew of cousins who barely know each other, how great it would be if they could all grow up side by side. Everybody"—he jabbed the fingers of his hands together—"you know, closer like . . ."

Ham trailed off, winded by the enormity of the lie. Sleeping with Allie, that almost seemed like the prelude to sin right now, not the sin itself. He'd just broken through some further moral barrier like so many rotten boards.

Link turned to his wife.

"Has he talked to you about this?"

"He mentioned it. I told him to ask you."

"How do you feel about it?"

"The truth?" Link nodded. "I'd like to go," she said.

Link laid down his cards and shook his head in perplexity.

"My God, what is this?" he said. "Honey, it's thirteen or fourteen years since I taught school. I'm out of practice. The books would be different."

"Not that different," Ham said. "What do we teach? Reading, writing, figuring. The eternal verities. Come on, I can get you a license."

The two men studied each other across the table. Ham observed the glum light in Link's eyes—it seemed perpetual, that look—the pale planes of his face, the bureaucrat's hair slicked back like dark-blond wood, the thin, negative mouth. Weak, Ham thought, but not a fool.

Link meanwhile was starting to reconsider. He had to admit he was flattered by the offer. Not by the job so much, but by Ham's plain desire for a closer relationship with him and his family. Link had always liked Ham. The way he came into a room like a fiddle player, always bringing the party with him, that could be a little intimidating, but all in all Link thought of him as a friend.

So finally, with a sigh of wonder, Link said he would sleep on it.

Next morning, however, he was against it again. He told Ham he definitely wasn't interested. A man whose emotions were easily roused, Link had been stirred by Ham's lace-edged descriptions of sisters side by side and the children all playing together. But this was pretty thin stuff by the light of day, and once all the sentimental sea foam had blown off, Link was back to his stubbornly practical frame of mind. He cleared a space on the breakfast table and showed Ham on paper. As a clerk he was making $1,500 a year. Teaching in Elnora would get him—according to Ham himself—no more than half that. Any farm income, that was just pie in the sky. On top of which, Link said, he'd just taken a civil service exam to get a better federal job here in Kentucky, and if that came through the way he thought it would, he'd be sitting pretty.

Ham countered with a paean to American agriculture. After those rough times in the nineties, he said, this was the golden age for farmers. Crop prices were shooting up. He could get Link an insider's price on some fantastic land investments.

Link shook his head. Besides, he said, he already had his eye on a bigger house right here in town.

"Well, if you buy it, I'm not moving in," Allie blurted.

Link looked at his wife in amazement. She flushed. Ham burst out laughing.

"I don't like the house," she said.

The topic hung fire over the next few days, till it was time for Ham to leave. Link was baffled, and a tad irritated, by the way Ham and Allie kept pecking at him about the move—how healthy it was for boys to grow up on a farm, that kind of thing. At the train station Ham practically stumbled backward with his suitcase in his hand.

"I feel like a vacuum cleaner salesman," he said with a slightly desperate grin. "Hate to leave without knowing I've clinched the deal."

Sighing, his brother-in-law said he wouldn't close the door on it entirely, that was the best he could say. And when the train finally pulled out of Nicholasville, Ham sat by a window, rubbing his hand on the prickly plush of his seat, worn out from lying. He'd have to leave it to Allie now.

It took another week for Link to capitulate. The way Allie kept rhapsodizing about her sister and all her new friends in Indiana, he finally couldn't withstand her. What settled things was the moment she slipped up behind him as he worked at his desk and murmured into his ear, "If you only knew how badly I want to go, you'd say yes." Whereupon she gave his cheek a maiden's kiss and faded out of the room.

That night Link wrote to Ham and told him all right, look out for a school.

Ham pulled the open envelope out of his pocket after dinner

and showed it to Maggie. "They're doing it," he said in a tone of mild surprise. "They're coming."

"I'm still not sure I understand why," Maggie said. "I wouldn't have thought that Allie . . ." Would ever give me the chance to lord it over her this way, is what she left unsaid. Her husband could buy and sell Link Hale ten times over. Did she really want her sister moving to the same town? In her mind she began to tick off the pros and cons.

Next day Ham wrote back to say that a teaching post had fallen open. Sudden departure. Death in the family. Could Link start at once? He could bring the whole tribe, and while they looked for a suitable home they could all stay with the Dillons. Why not? There was plenty of room.

That settled it. All seven Hales came spilling off the train in Elnora on October 6, 1905.

8

FOUR ADULTS and eight children under one roof. Not to mention the hired help. If Ham and Allie had had trouble stealing time together in Nicholasville, here at the Dillons' it was impossible. In fact, with Maggie still recovering from a hard birth and nursing a brand-new baby, Allie found herself the de facto woman of the house: riding herd on the children, keeping the place clean, cooking most of the enormous meals. Maggie, her domain invaded, watched warily while her sister, constantly harried, her hair coming down in damp spirals, received her baptism of fire as a farm wife. Nights Allie sat ruefully massaging the muscles of her own neck.

Link started his teaching job at the Bowman School, just outside of Odon. Always a man who liked to keep himself neat, he dressed each morning now with a grim, particular care.

It was a Friday, his first on the job—a clear fall morning,

gusty, with fallen leaves whispering and tumbling around the schoolhouse. Link was at his desk making calculations on a piece of paper about the type of farmhouse he needed to find for his family: rooms so big by so big, allowing for this and that. . . . The children were outside at recess. He could hear their shouts, the rush of running feet, the clatter of a can along the ground. Melancholy sounds. Somehow the exuberance of children always depressed him.

The building was like a lot of one-room schools: a long gray rectangle with a pointed roof, a door at one end, and three windows along each side which rattled like gunfire when the west wind blew. Virtually everything looked familiar to him from his teaching days in Kentucky. There were the same rows of double-seat desks, heavily gouged and initialed, with inkwells for pigtail dipping; the same big cabinet by the door, kicked to hell and back, where the children kept their lunch pails; the rusty potbellied stove; the American flag (shy a couple of stars) that had never known a breeze; the half-clean water bucket with the tin cup hanging on the wall. About the only things Link hadn't seen before were the stuffed owl in the corner wearing a doll's bonnet, and the fat dictionary which lay open on its own oak stand and was chained to the wall. In one of his first acts as trustee Ham Dillon had put dictionaries in all his schools. Adults who'd never seen one still turned up sometimes to take a look.

Meanwhile Link's right-hand drawer was filling up already with items he had confiscated. This morning he had seized a bean blower, and when its owner called him a knock-kneed puke, Link had smacked him sharply across the back of the head, a show of violence that surprised them both.

There was a loud thump. Link looked up. The bean-blowing boy evidently, protesting his punishment; he was spending recess in the woodbox with the lid down. The only other child in the room sat toward the back, gazing out the window. Ethel Lee Wylie was a remarkably pretty nine-year-old with dark hair and wondering eyes, the lustrous braid down her back tied with a blue satin ribbon. She never went out for recess. Two years ago Ethel Lee's father, while splitting some kindling, had reared back with his ax and caught his little girl on the head with the blunt end. Since then, there were times Ethel Lee looked directly at whoever was talking to her, other times when she seemed to be looking a little off to the side. Or up. In Link's opinion, up was worse.

Nellie Popp.

That's who Ethel Lee reminded him of. It had been hovering at the edge of his mind all week. Nellie Popp was his daughter Marguerite's favorite doll. Marguerite, who was seven, liked to read selections from the daily paper out loud to Nellie Popp. Only the sensational bits: "Eskimo in College," "Lumberjack Dislocates Jaw Yawning" . . . His daughter read each item as if reporting a public emergency, sometimes switching to her police voice or her baffled-medical-establishment voice, while Nellie Popp—who had a rosy-cheeked china head and eyes that closed when you tipped her over—sat at her elbow listening to this litany of amazements with a look of poleaxed wonder.

" 'Maniac Conducts Prayer Meeting . . .' "

Link sighed. What were they all doing here in Indiana? He wasn't even sure Allie knew herself, hard as she'd pushed to come. She could be a little rattlebrained, especially lately.

He rose, went to the nearest window, and pushed it open. Just outside, two boys were taking turns throwing stones straight down into a puddle. Another went by them, frog-marching across the schoolyard in a world of his own, his arms going all raggedy man. Children were so peculiar. Over by the big oak he noticed three girls playing jump rope. Their chanting rang in the air:

Matthew, Mark and Luke and John
Went to bed with their stockings on
Luke and Mark

Scared Matthew in the dark
And John woke up with his stockings gone.

A sharp sound brought his head back around. Ethel Lee had just spotted something, some bug or spider, on her bench and smacked it dead. She held her palm up for him to see, looking at Link with eyes of triumph.

At least he hoped she was looking at him. From this distance he couldn't quite tell.

L INK WAS EDGY, but he didn't rebel. Not because Allie made things easier for him; she had all she could handle just running the household. But Ham was keeping a weather eye out, and as soon as he saw Link's darkening face, he stepped right in. Ham took his brother-in-law under his wing, introduced him to people, worked overtime trying to bind him to the community.

With some success too. For one thing, Link was pleasantly surprised by the great respect teachers enjoyed here. This was part of a general reverence for learning in America's farm communities; rural Americans were more literate than city folk, in fact, because farmers had a hard-bitten work ethic, along with a lurking inferiority complex, that drove them to fashion the best schools they possibly could. For the first time in his life, Link found himself esteemed by complete strangers.

All the while, Ham stood by his side with a benedictory smile and a detachment that was hardening like plaster. He was as gregarious as ever, and slapped Link on the back enough to raise a bruise, but when Link wasn't around Ham barely gave him a thought. Ham had decided to strangle his own guilt in its cradle. In for a penny, in for a pound.

Besides, he thought, any man who took on a woman like Allie and didn't cut the mustard—well, he was asking for it.

One windy afternoon Ham took Link down to show him Washington, the bustling county seat. They visited the B&O railroad yards on the west end of town, where workmen scrambled over engines in the roundhouse like bugs on lunch, where fat, frowning gents with their derbies and cigars strode in and out of small brick offices, and a few Weary Willies, part of the army of bums who were always catching rides on the freights, kept in the boozy shadows near the fence. It was the coming of these railroad yards ten or fifteen years before that had given the town such a shot of energy, turned it from a hay-sucking backwater into an oily, grimy, noisy, busy mini-metropolis, with new stores, new houses, new churches, and a whole slew of new saloons. Catching Link by the arm, Ham steered him east from the train yards up along Main Street—which was brick-paved now and striped with trolley tracks—talking up the attractions.

There was the great Cabel and Kaufman, sellers of farm supplies, with big sacks of feed stacked outside like a flood levee. Here, Neal & Eskridge, where Ham stopped in for cheroots: a grandly crespuscular general store as full of fragrances as a harem; it had half an acre of merchandise and a ceiling of embossed tin. Farther up they passed by the livery stables, the billiard hall, the Meredith House—a salesman's hotel Ham had a couple of blue stories about—and then Slank's Eats, where they peered through the window at the waiter as he maneuvered between rows of feeding men with saucered cups of coffee running all the way up his arms. "See what I mean?" Ham said. "We never had that till we got the railroad yard." A few steps on, Ham stopped in front of the Teatro to read the poster. As he muttered eagerly over the copy, he told Link all about how much he loved theatricals—Shakespeare, fancy whistling, you name it, he liked them all.

"How about you? You ever go to the show?"

"Once in a while," said Link. "Not too much."

"I'll keep an eye out for something good."

The brothers-in-law moved on up the wooden sidewalk. It was getting colder. Ham came to a stop again, so Link did too. He was starting to feel like a dog that way.

"See that?" Ham said, pointing across the street.

It was a wide beige-brick building with a recessed front door. Charity Lodge Number 30 of the Free and Accepted Masons.

Link didn't know much about the Masons, beyond what everybody knew: that they had chapters everywhere and that George Washington or somebody had once belonged. Not to mention thousands upon thousands of America's political and business elite since. Like any club, it satisfied two contradictory but equally powerful drives: the impulse to band together and the impulse to exclude. But Masonry had flourished not just as the ultimate old-boys' network but also because it struck other grand chords—the patriotic, the religious, the charitable. And the magical. Part of the lure of the Masons was their aura of many-veiled concealment. Their handshake was one of the world's most famous secrets, and one of the best kept.

Here in the Washington chapter there was a meeting or two every month, but most of the deal making and wheel greasing went on day to day in the game room on the second floor, where members played pool, poker, and pinochle in a manly fog of cigar smoke. That's where Ham was pointing, to one of the upper windows, where a man in vest and shirtsleeves stood looking out, holding his pool cue like a sentry on duty.

"Feel like meeting a couple of fellas?" said Ham.

A bare five weeks later, thanks to his brother-in-law's nimble lobbying, Link was elected to the Masons. Being a brother in the lodge wasn't something Link had ever aspired to, but as he studied the booklets in the run-up to initiation night, he grew more and more intrigued. Its doctrines seemed to be a fine reinforcement of Christian principles. Controlling your passions: he believed in that. He liked the symbols of the square and compass, reminders to be ever forthright and moderate.

On a polar night shortly after Thanksgiving, Link was initiated into Masonic Lodge Number 30 in the big third-floor hall. When he first appeared in the archway, flanked like a death-house prisoner, he discovered a grand chandelier, suspended by a central cable and alive with candles. Their jumping light gave an undersea shimmer to the whole room, and to the scores of Masons seated in orderly silence along the side and back walls, two or three rows deep. Each man was gazing at Link. Each wore a business suit, white cotton gloves and a short white apron. Link had been told in advance what to expect here; still, it was a daunting sight, his first eyeful of two hundred men dressed in symbolic emulation of Christ the carpenter. A white-gloved hand nudged him forward.

He was brought to the eastern end of the room, where he stood before the Worshipful Master and two other high officials of the lodge. The Worshipful Master—a moonfaced man wearing a top hat—asked Link a series of ritual questions. Then he was led around the room and examined by others. Did he believe in God? Was he committed to the service of his fellow man? For the first time Link noticed that the windows facing the street were all shuttered. The smoke and the scent of hot candle wax, growing denser, spoke to him of martyrdom and transcendence. He saw Ham Dillon sitting in the crowd.

Finally Link was brought to the very center of the room, where a small altar stood. On it were the temple Bible, and a square and compass. He knelt before the altar and bowed his head.

A brother Mason with a long snuffer was dousing the candles of the chandelier. As the shadows in the room stretched and deepened, Link greeted them with a feeling of gloomy exaltation. But just before pitch-darkness fell, three other candles were lit on a tall stand to his right, and he became the central figure in a Caravaggio.

He was inducted into the Masons—into God's army, it felt

like—on his knees, with his hand on the Holy Bible. Out of the dark the Worshipful Master conjured an apron made of white kidskin and placed it in Link's upraised hands as if it were made of glass. "May the record of your life and conduct be as fair and spotless as this," he said.

Link gazed at the apron, morbidly transfixed. After tonight, he would be allowed to wear it only once more: the day that he was buried. Allie had already made him a nice cloth one for meetings.

Moments later the women, down in the game room on the second floor, heard the convivial roar and thunder of their husbands descending the stairs. Mounds and platters of steaming farm food were already laid out for them—or for Link really, since it was all in his honor, as Allie reminded him, hugging his elbow hard. Ham made a comic demonstration of eating standing up, claiming to show the approved method of leaning forward to keep one's apron clean.

Men and women poured up to Link to congratulate him, while he laughed and babbled his thanks, half the time on the edge of tears.

For on top of everything else, he had just learned the handshake of a first-degree Mason, and he felt—he couldn't help it— overjoyed to be in on the secret.

9

IT WAS QUITE A WEEK. Just a few days after Link's induction into the Masons the Hales finally found a home of their own. The religious cultists who'd been encamped there more or less vanished in the night, one step ahead of the bank, leaving behind a good-sized, gray-gabled house located at the crest of a horseshoe drive on about thirty acres of land. What's more—and Ham ballyhooed this feature—it was barely a half mile from the Dillons'. In the leaden chill of a late November afternoon, he took Link and the older Hale boys, Denton and Arthur, on a tour of the place, upstairs and down, enthusing over things while the Hales moved from room to room as gravely as generals surveying a field hospital. Especially Denton, the eldest son, a weedy fourteen-year-old who stared at everything with the same desolated face. When the four of them finally stood outside again, on the wraparound front porch, Ham was still trying to win him over.

"Hear this?" he said to Denton, striking the porch with the heel of his boot. "Travel near or travel far, that's the sound of home." Ham gave him a wink and was rewarded by the boy's reluctant smile.

Link said the house would suit him. That was the main thing.

Next day Allie walked over to explore it alone. She checked the kitchen first and liked it: the oiled maple floor and soapstone sink, with the hand pump perched over it like an iron bird; the embossed blue-steel cookstove; the woodbox big enough to take a nap on. With gingerly steps she descended a procession of pitched planks into the dank cellar. There she found a few unmarked canned goods still on the shelves, caught the sharp smell of unsunned stone and earthworms. She prowled the rest of the house, mentally deploying furniture, assigning curtains, imagining flowers.

In the empty parlor she gave a skip and a twirl.

Finally she stepped out on the porch and, hugging a shawl around her to cut the chill of the wind, looked up the road and across the fields. In the distance she could see Ham driving a two-horse team, harrowing a field for winter wheat. His two oldest were with him: Harold, with a man's hat sunk down around his ears, astride one of the horses, and little Ruth—that had to be her—riding the back of the harrow for ballast. Watching the three of them, Allie smiled in a tender, faintly proprietary way.

The purchase of the house was handled through Ham's bank in Washington. Link and Allie sent for their goods, which arrived the second week of December. After the punishing stress of living at the Dillons', it was a grand thing indeed for Allie to see her own belongings being lifted off the wagon.

And though Link was secretly disappointed to wind up so near the Dillons'—it was like living in the shade of a great tree—he was very glad to be master of his own establishment again. At the supper table that first night he improvised a long grace, which made the children fidget, and insisted they finish all the bread on their plates. It was, he reminded them, the staff of life.

"YOU CAN'T keep your things on worth a damn."
He snatched at a button, a ribbon. She squealed and jumped back.

"All I have to do is look at you, and your clothes fall off." He gave a sharp pull. "You should be ashamed of yourself."

"You'll tear it," she protested, laughing, till her laugh died in a sharp intake of breath. "Stop," she whispered.

There was a silence.

"What is it? Do you hear something?"

Allie didn't answer. She had just noticed that panic and lust sound a lot alike.

"Relax, honey," Ham said. "I'm busy here." He began prying and tugging at her underclothes again. One yank more and she was naked to the waist. Roughly he flung away the shift, as if flinging off every other thought, every memory. It caught the air and ballooned, sighing, onto the rug. She fell back on the bed and let him strip off the last of her clothes.

"Happy now?" she said, lying there.

He forgot to say yes. The sight of her, after so many weeks of waiting, left him wavering, as if unsure what to do next. He fumbled off his own clothes without a word.

He was raring to take her. But something strange happened, something he didn't expect. He knew by now that in bed, her guilt was gunpowder to them both; that he was ready for; but after that first spasm of nerves she slipped into some other state he hadn't seen before, not in any woman—ravenous but cool, a cat with her kill. She was taking him this time, methodically, and taking him by right. When it was over he lay on his back uneasily.

No other woman had ever stripped him of his sense of humor.

"Penny for your thoughts," she said.

"Just picking out the birds," he said. "By their calls. Ever do that?"

They lay side by side in her bedroom, talking of this and that, while Allie toyed with his hand in the warm cave of the sheets. She was savoring the way she felt today: calm and corrupted. And tenderly protective too, toward Ham. Wasn't he younger by six years? For once it didn't bother her. It was strange, this peace.

1 0

THE TWO FAMILIES spent Christmas Eve together at the Dillon house. Shortly after dark the Hales came streaming inside, package-laden, puffing and stamping off the cold in that cheerfully exaggerated style that has always belonged to the holidays. Dillons shepherded Hales into the parlor. There were cries of pleasure at the snapping fire in the hearth; at the tapestry of scents that filled the room, pine and cedar and blackberry cake; at the blue-needled evergreen decked with popcorn strings and homemade angels. Every red candle, every nut dish added its touch to this cozy conspiracy—including the wind snooping in the chimney and the frost chiseled on the windowpanes.

The Hales weren't the only guests. Mama Dillon, Ham's mother, was already enthroned in the armchair nearest the fire, with a crocheted shawl across her lap. Ed Watkins was at the sideboard fetching her a cup of punch. Ed didn't have much to do around Mama Dillon's place anymore; the boys were long gone and the old lady had sold off a fair-sized chunk of her property. But he had stuck around even so, gravely filling the role of hired hand emeritus and taking care of the aging Mrs. D.

Allie had not been looking forward to coming tonight. But now, chafing her hands before the fire, she realized that in this snug and magical atmosphere it wouldn't take much— just a slight trick of the mind—to pretend that all was well between the two families. She would pretend, even in her heart, tonight. She would give herself Christmas. At once she felt much better.

Turning from the hearth, she almost stepped on the bright brown shoes of her nephew Harold, who was blocking her way like a toll taker. She couldn't tell at first what was wrong with him—something, obviously. But it was hard to know what with his sunken little personality. Then she looked in his eyes. They were dull and crowded with desire. It was a look that went beyond the innocent greed of six.

"Hello, Harold," she said.

" 'Lo, Aunt Allie," the youngster answered, breathing through his mouth.

"So," she said finally, "what do you want for Christmas this year?"

"Everything," the boy replied. "And a gun."

Nodding, Allie patted Harold on the head and eased past him, on her way to the refreshments. But just then Maggie caught her elbow and yanked her into an embrace.

"Oh, thank you, thank you," Maggie whispered tightly in her ear.

Allie caught her breath and stepped back. "What for, for heaven's sake?"

"The ginger cake. That was so nice."

Allie gaped at her. Who ever went anywhere without bringing food?

"Well, I'd better put it in the warmer," Maggie said finally, her eyes dusting the floor. And she was gone.

Allie gazed after her, nonplussed.

It all made sense enough to Maggie—even though being so demonstrative was costing her, and she pushed into the kitchen toting the ginger cake actually blushing. She was attempting, in her clumsy way, to get close to her sister again. More like when they were girls, way back, before Maggie had grown so full of envy.

As briskly as a nurse with a bandage, Maggie unrolled the cloth from the gingerbread, tested it with a thumb, made a half-satisfied face. Then she slipped it into the warmer, up near where a string of dried apples hung. The bang of the little door disturbed a litter of new piglets nestled behind the stove, and they emitted a few sleepy squeaks.

The turning point, for Maggie, had come this past week when she showed up at the Hales' house with "Christmas clothes" for the children. Allie had blanched when she laid eyes on the basket, and that's when Maggie realized—well, she'd known it in the back of her mind all along—that this was just like the charity visits people made to the coal-mining families this time of year. Suddenly, with the clothes at her feet, she was embarrassed at trying to humble her sister, and from that moment on Maggie swore to herself she'd do better. She would be a real friend. It was no wonder Allie had been acting a little odd around her these past weeks, the way Maggie had been behaving.

Why did Allie always bring out the worst in her?

Licking her sticky fingers, Maggie left the kitchen and returned to the party.

Quite a little do it was getting to be, full of boisterous family jokes and good-fellowship. There was one threat to the reigning merriment when Ruth lost a struggle with Harold over the last walnut cookie and started to wail, but just then Mama Dillon leaned in and told her sharply, "I cried because I had no shoes until I met a man who had no feet." What that meant exactly nobody knew, any more than Ham had known when Mama D used to tell him the same thing twenty years before, but it was enough to make Ruth shut off like a siren, and wander away in a daze. Before long the children were allowed one present each, as a Christmas Eve treat, leaving the younger ones sprawled out on the floor, painted by the firelight, with toys of an improving nature—miniature carpet sweepers and Noah's Arks.

Meanwhile Ed, coaxed with another glass of punch, read aloud a letter from his brother. That Ed had any family at all had come as a revelation to the Dillons. He had always said there was no one. But finally age—or maybe some sneaking suspicion that he was not, after all, a walking embarrassment to the name of Watkins—had moved him to rekindle old ties, and produce this sudden brother.

"Well, Santa Claus can't get down here in Arkansas," Ed was reading, his spectacles well down his nose, "as it is too muddy, so I won't get nothing much but that's okay. Well, brother, my pup can fight and pull hair like a baby. The pup is twenty-two inches long and weighs ten pounds and is growing like a billy goat. . . ."

The news was all about the mud and the dog, separately and together, and Ed read it through to the end with great satisfaction. Then he heaved a sigh, carefully refolded the letter, and tucked it into his shirt pocket.

"You know, talking of the mail, they're fixing to start this home delivery scheme here," Ham remarked as he got to his feet.

"My stars," Maggie said.

"I pity the poor fella has to carry it all," Link said.

"Who'll be doing that anyway?" Maggie said. "Sweeney?" Sweeney was the postmaster.

"No," said Ham. "They're going to have like a little contest."

Passing behind the women, he gave Allie's shoulders a quick squeeze, and she felt the sudden voltage of his fingers.

"Any fella who's interested will have to take this civil service exam," Ham went on.

"Just to hand people things?" Maggie scoffed.

Ed, who had acquired a new devotion to the whole idea of mail, had been listening closely. "That's about the best job I ever heard of," he said.

"You should try for it, Ed," Maggie said. "You'd make a great whatchamacallit."

"You should," Ham said. As he poked the fire, he laughed. "Give those young bucks a run for their money."

"What about that exam, though?" said Allie.

"Those fellas ain't never tangled with an autodidact," said Ed.

"Course, somebody might object to your taking the test," said Ham, sliding a broad look at his mother.

"He can suit himself," the old lady said shortly. "That's all I know," she added sharply to Harold, who was tugging at her elbow about something. "My hat blew off."

"That means Mama D doesn't want to talk anymore," said Maggie, leaning forward to shoo the boy away. Mama D, fighting off help, grasped her walking stick like a gondolier and heaved herself out of her chair. "Too many children," she muttered, shuffling across the room.

"Where you going, Mama?" Ham said.

"Going to see what the owls are up to," she said, and disappeared.

Ham's eyes stayed on the doorway she had gone through.

"What?" said Allie.

"My old man used to say that when he wanted to get off by himself," Ham said. "I never heard it from her."

"Maybe she misses him tonight," Allie said. "What with the holidays."

"Sometimes I think the older people get, the more expressions they use," Maggie said. She was dangling a string of yarn, and a cat, up on its haunches, was batting it like a speed bag. "Gets to be like they're talking in code," she added.

"So how does Mama D fill up her time now?" Allie asked, touching her coppery hair with the heel of her hand.

"Spends a lot of time on the telephone," Maggie said.

"Talking to who?"

"Not talking to anybody. Just listening in. She likes that party line she's on better than the gramophone."

Allie lost her voice for a moment, and she fingered the lace at her throat. "You mean she listens to the gossip?"

"Never was the type before, but it's a good way to chase off the blues, somebody her age. Now she's got the straight skinny on everybody." Maggie gave a little bark of laughter. "Whenever the sound fades out she starts snapping at the hired girl to run outside quick and pour a cup of water on the line. Claims it helps her hear. Ruth!" she added sharply. "You keep twisting it, that little head's gonna come right off in your hands."

A pinecone popped and showered sparks in the grate.

"I don't believe I'm on that wire," Allie said absently. There seemed to be a roaring in her ears.

"No, that's right. They're on the other side of the road from us," Maggie said. "We've got our own little show. You ever listen to Mrs. Ives? Two longs and a short, that's her house, and when that phone rings, receivers go down all over the neighborhood."

Bored, Ham crossed the room and did a big flop on the couch, the kind he made when he wanted to attract children. In moments Harold, Marguerite, and Ruth were clustered around him like little courtiers. Allie turned her head away. She didn't feel like looking at Ham just then.

"Is Denton all right?" This from Maggie in a whisper, her head ducked close to her sister.

"Denton? What do you mean?" Allie looked around. She saw

him curled up in an armchair in a far corner of the room: the dark head, the introverted heap of knees and elbows.

"He's very quiet," Maggie said.

"Ever since we came to Indiana he's been like this." Allie gave a ragged sigh. "I keep waiting for him to snap out of it."

"Maybe we ought to find him a girl," Maggie said.

"A girl?" The thought of Denton with a mournful fistful of posies caught Allie off guard. She blurted out a laugh, and for a moment she and Maggie were merry together.

"Well now, I don't know," said Ham, in a big, stagy voice, stretching out his arms like a giant just waking up. He was responding to some remark of the children's. "I think maybe if the Wild Man was here, he'd have a thing or two to say about that."

"Do the Wild Man! Do the Wild Man!" the children screamed.

"Naw, I'm not gonna do the—"

"Do the Wild Man! Do the Wild Man!" the children cried.

"I said I'm not—"

"Do the Wild Man!"

"All right, one time."

Instantly the children backed away, leaving Ham sitting quietly alone on the couch. But slowly he began to sag, as if he were a pile of melting ice cream. A simian fog came into his eyes, and he made a few guttural noises. Ruth gave a little scream of anticipation.

With one swing Ham was on his feet, arms hanging. The children scattered. Grunting, he scanned the room. The only thing stopping him from eating children right away was his deep stupidity about what exactly a child was. Muttering, he slouched to the table, picked up a book, sniffed it.

"Unh," he said. "Not child."

More grunts. He picked up a lamp. Sniffed it. Pretended to burn his nose. This brought laughter from the children—and

Allie too, caught up in it now, clapping her hands, while Maggie (who had seen this bit before) looked on without expression.

Then suddenly the children fell silent. They realized they had made a tremendous error. Laughing had caused them to move, and the Wild Man was very sensitive to movement. Now he knew where they were.

Now they dodged and squealed in sweet fear of the Wild Man, and froze like statues trying to fool the Wild Man till finally, after barely missing the other children with great sweeps of his paws, Ham lassoed little Ruth. Bug-eyed, at the very pitch of pleasure and terror, she shrieked while her father turned her sideways and made a great show of eating her like corn on the cob.

Allie was gazing at her lover, the amusement in her eyes shading into something soft and rapt. Once she thought to glance at Denton, to see how he was enjoying his uncle's shenanigans, but he wasn't even watching.

"All right," Ham said finally, sinking back on the couch and wiping his mouth with his sleeve. "That's all for tonight."

At once Ruth and the others were jumping up and down in front of him.

"Do the Wild Man!" they hollered.

"That's it, I'm telling you. Wild Man can't eat any more children. Wild Man's full."

"Do the Wild Man! Do the Wild Man!"

"All right, one time . . ."

A COUPLE OF DAYS after Christmas, the twenty-seventh or twenty-eighth, Ham gave Allie a silver broach. ("If Link asks, tell him you've had it for years," he said. "Men never know.") It was Ham's first real gift to her, and she lost it almost immediately. She searched everywhere. Ham treated the whole thing as a joke, but Allie was miserable—guilty for taking it and guilty for losing it. The next time they made love she lay limp and splayed, in a posture of penance.

But even through the ugly shimmer of her self-recriminations, Allie stayed dedicated to the affair. Sleeping with Ham—the sex itself, and the wild rise of feeling that came with knowing she was the ruler of his heart—gave her, more and more strongly, a sense of her rightful destiny reclaimed. This she clung to far more tightly than the broach.

Then in the first week of the new year, 1906, Link received an official letter postmarked Kentucky. He came home from school one day to find it on the salver in the front hall, the envelope already torn. Clipped to it was a note from Ham, saying the post office had gotten it mixed up with his own mail, and he'd opened it by mistake.

It was the results of the civil service exam Link had taken the summer before, when he was applying for a government job. Good news, the examiners said: thanks to his excellent score, Mr. Hale was being offered a post as a gauger, or customs official, at a bourbon distillery outside of Nicholasville. The salary was three times more than Link had ever made in his life.

Link didn't know what to do. He and his family had been in their new house a mere six weeks, and to uproot them again . . . Still, this was an opportunity that whispered to him in the night. It would solve so much. For despite Ham's Trojan efforts on his behalf—which Link sincerely appreciated—he realized the moment his eyes fell upon the letter just how emasculated he felt living here in Indiana. He hated owing everything he did or had or would ever be to his brother-in-law.

In February he took the train to Kentucky to see the distillery for himself and shake a few hands. While he was gone, his son Arthur had the croup and Dr. Porter came to call. Upon his return, Link sat the family down and told them he had decided to take the job.

Desolate, Allie lay in the crook of Ham's arm staring at the ceiling of her bedroom. She didn't even know the ceiling yet, the cracks and grooves in the planks up there.

"I'll have to go with him," she said.

Ham said nothing. Just kept one slow knuckle moving in the groove of her spine, low down, again and again, feeling the fine hairs.

"I suppose I can visit sometime. I can try."

"Mm-hm." Ham turned his head and nudged her hair with his face, the way a horse will sometimes, and she turned to look at him, but she didn't get the chance because he kissed her then, and the next moment they were clasped together, reaching and gripping, but languorously, easy as athletes, since they'd made love today already. "Oh, I need this," she said.

"No," said Ham. "Not 'I need this.' . . . 'I need you.' Say it." Pushed up on his palms, he shifted a little, not quite out of her.

"I need you," she said, trying to engage his eyes. They were washed out, impersonal.

"Say it again."

"I need you." He drove, and this time she cried out. "I need you," she whispered, and he drove again, and a tear slipped from the side of her eye and down onto the pillow. "I need you. I love you. I want you."

Late that week Ham and Maggie and Allie and Link had a powwow at the Hales' house to sort out what was best to do. Allie sat erect but unusually quiet. To Maggie she looked a little frail, almost like an old woman. Allie was taking this pretty hard, she thought. Still, it was a big thing, being separated from your husband.

For that was the consensus they were all coming to: that just for the time being, Link should move to Kentucky alone. A lot of his money was tied up in Indiana now in this land, this house. And Ham was right—wasn't he the one who'd said it?—the children needed some stability. Before uprooting them all again, it was only prudent for Link to make sure this job was everything it seemed. Down the road, in a year or two, when he was set up, the rest of the Hales would join him.

In the meantime, he could return for visits.

Link was a little confused how they'd come to this decision—he hadn't suggested it first, he knew that—but now he was all for it. This job was his big chance to become prosperous at last, to make Allie proud of him in a way he knew she'd never been. This time things would be different, he was sure. He was almost sure. Best though, at the start, to devote himself to his new situation with no distractions, without his wife there looking over his shoulder.

Meanwhile Ham and Maggie would take good care of his family. For the first time, he was glad they lived just down the road.

So it was that in March 1906 Link Hale left his family behind to take a post at the Curley Distillery at Camp Nelson, eight miles outside of Nicholasville. He rented a small house and had his belongings sent. Once settled, he still didn't regret how he was going about things. Even so, it was odd sometimes sitting on the porch by himself at night while the hired woman clattered in the kitchen. Somehow he'd lost his family. It made sense when he reviewed it all step by step, but there were times he couldn't help feeling as though he'd been left out back with the blowing trash.

1 1

IT WAS THE FIRST beautiful Sunday morning in spring. All around Elnora the peach trees were flowering in shell pink and white, fresh-turned furrows ran along the fields like mole tunnels, and the air was full of damp and acrid promise. It was wine before breakfast, this weather, and Ham—along with some other truant spirits—wasn't happy to be stuck in church. He had a train to catch too, in less than an hour, so he sat shifting impatiently in his pew, distracting himself now and then with glances at the women's section, where the worshippers sat slightly spaced, like chess pieces, to make room for their new spring hats. Reverend Aspinall was giving an interminable sermon. Today he was banging away about original sin. Whenever the reverend ran short of inspiration, Ham reflected, his first thought was to throw Adam and Eve out of the garden again. Though of course on a day like this even the minister was entitled to a touch of spring fever.

Since Ham was barely listening, he was surprised later that morning to find fragments of the sermon still sounding in his brain. He was aboard the train now, musing with an elbow on the window ledge, waiting to pull out of Elnora, when he realized the old Bible phrases were tolling like bells somewhere back of his thoughts:

"Cursed is the ground for thy sake." . . .

"In the sweat of thy face shalt thou eat bread!" . . .

God condemning Adam and Eve to be farmers.

That was irritating. Ham had never much liked this part of the story, what it implied about his livelihood—that when God was casting around for a punishment, farming was the worst thing He could think of. Ham didn't buy that. He figured it brought out the best in a man. But if you believed the Bible, farmers were all prisoners doing hard time in a penal colony.

As if you might be out plowing one day and look up and there would be Christ at the edge of the field with a shotgun on His hip and a couple of dogs.

With a jolt the train began to move. *Bup-bup, bup-bup,* it ground along the tracks, leaving behind the station platform, rolling past the big weathered grain silo on the edge of town. A spotted dog raced along beside the train yapping till it was swallowed by dust. The rocking acceleration of the train interrupted Ham's sour line of thought and replaced it with something else: relief. After a moment he realized why. Two women making demands on his time. A fellow had to be quick as a cat to keep it all going. Unlike a lot of gregarious men, Ham valued his time alone, and lately he'd had precious little.

And there was that near-disaster last week. The day Louise, Allie's oldest girl, came home from school early. He and Allie had heard the noise of the door first, then nothing, nothing at all for what seemed like a long time. They began to think whoever it was must have gone out the back. But when they finally emerged from the bedroom onto the landing, they found the girl standing in the well of the downstairs hall, looking straight up at them as if she'd been waiting there. It gave him a turn. There was no fuss—Allie came up with some light lie, and the girl seemed to believe it—but Ham well remembered that first shot of wonder in her eyes.

Ah well, let it go. As the train picked up speed, Ham lapsed into a study of his own reflection in the window.

He was on his way to Indianapolis, summoned there for a meeting that could set the course of his whole political future. With the state legislator from his district retiring—a prominent Washington lawyer named Padgett—the Democratic Party's executive committee was looking around for his replacement, and a couple of important men already thought that Ham was the pick of the litter. So he was headed to the big city now for what amounted to his first audition. He was to have dinner tonight with Padgett himself.

Turning from the window, Ham settled back with his head against the soiled plush of the train seat, remembering Indianapolis. He had been there once before, mostly to see the statehouse. From the visitors' gallery he'd peered down upon the heads of a hundred lawmakers in their gladiatorial pit, many howling like banshees. Amazing that it was their job to make the rules for everybody else to live by.

The journey on the train took most of the day. Then toward late afternoon the outskirts of Indianapolis appeared. Swaths of primeval forest gave way to scatterings of tall, ramshackle dwellings with little wired-in yards, in which chickens and small children staggered about under cat's cradles of strung laundry, and then came the scarred brickfronts of factories with their rows of flashing windows. The train was slowing down. Buildings and signs loomed close to the tracks now, and Ham watched them as they clicked by:

Finally the train slid into the station and with a jolt, and a great exhausted hiss, began disgorging its passengers.

Ham yanked his cowhide suitcase down from the rack above, settled his city hat on his head, and eased down the aisle through the press of travelers. Moments later he was crossing the lobby of Union Station. He was glad to see it again, this vast, clamorous, light-shot space, cut with twisting smoke—picking his way through the treacherous, unspooling throngs, the hurriers, the stoppers, the impossibly baggage-laden, everyone an obstacle to everybody else, the air smelling of shoe polish and muddy with a thousand voices. Swinging his satchel, he found his way outside and hopped a trolley with the careless ease of someone who had lived here all his life.

With his arm around a pole, he became just one more buoyant spirit in a buoyant town; for in this Age of Optimism there was no place in America more optimistic than Indianapolis, no place more enthusiastically on the push. Indianapolis was certain, that spring of 1906, that it was about to burst into blossom as the nation's next great city, the next Chicago, the next New York. Factories were being thrown together as fast as tar-paper shanties—ironworks, cotton mills, beef- and pork-packing houses; there was a symphony now, and a big new art museum; but better than all this, Indianapolis had a lock on the future. It made automobiles.

Indianapolis was the beating heart of the new auto industry, the most exciting industry there was and the reigning symbol of this twentieth century. Shiny new Marmons, Nationals, Coles, Pathfinders, Chevrolets, Duesenbergs, and more, all spewing out of its plants, gave folks here the feeling they *were* America now.

Those few who fretted that not all the big automakers were headquartered here (conspicuously Ford), that the whole business might slip away somewhere else (Detroit was mentioned), these people were slapped down as nervous Nellies and nitwits. And the complaints of a few old mossbacks, those who didn't like all the coal smoke streaming into the skies now from so many new factories, office buildings, and hotels, these were hooted down too. If houses had to be painted darker colors now because of the drifting soot, so what? Businessmen and politicians had taken to calling it "good clean smoke." They announced that coughing exercised the lungs and strengthened the chest. "Boost!" they cried. "Don't knock!"

From his perch on the rocking trolley, Ham caught the industrial tang in the breeze and scanned the urban panorama as if he owned it. He had always been a man with a gift for happiness, and he was filled with it now—that kind of rambunctious arrogance that had always been the most perfect form of happiness to him.

Even today, Sunday, he could see stirrings of life down Illinois Street. He looked sharply too, as the trolley swept by, having spent an evening or two in that neighborhood before. The Levee, it was called, and it was the heart of the sporting district. He remembered the gamblers he'd seen, men in hard derbies and loud vests from as far away as St. Louis and Chicago, outside the casinos, sauntering like kings. He remembered the diamond rings one of them wore, on all four fingers, like brass knuckles. The German beer gardens exhaling liquor and song, the dandies and panhandlers, he remembered those too, but most of all he remembered Queen Mab's, the city's most elegant whorehouse—there, he thought, that might be it now, fronted by chalk-white porch columns that seemed to rotate in the distance as he passed. Young and short of money, Ham hadn't gone in there, but he'd stood outside and looked at it for a while. He'd heard that all the girls wore chiffon, drank champagne, and used flawless grammar. He liked good grammar.

Peering about, he tried to recall what other buildings around here were bawdy houses. Every night a forest of red lights appeared in this neighborhood; in fact, Indianapolis was said to have nearly as many brothels as New York. Another unofficial point of civic pride.

The Levee gave way to vistas of parkland and a lake, which was dotted with identical rowboats, the men at the oars, the girls with bright parasols cocked on their shoulders, very Parisian. Everything else was wheels, a great streaming of wheels: bicycles, wagons, trolleys, autos. Back home in Washington, Indiana, there were now four autos total, and when one passed another on the street it usually made the paper. Here they were everywhere he looked.

Slicing into the heart of downtown, the trolley finally dropped Ham in the city's central plaza, just steps from the Soldiers' and Sailors' Monument, a terraced obelisk that shot three hundred feet in the air and symbolized (depending on the day) war, peace, or Indiana. It was very late in the afternoon, and the slow spin of high society around the square in their cars and carriages, a Sunday ritual when the weather was good, was fast thinning out. But there was still a blur of cyclists riding themselves dizzy around the monument—and making pedestrians step lively—underneath a virtual circus tent of new telephone and electric wires running into the nearby government buildings and the first-class hotels that fronted the square.

Ham wasn't staying at one of these. He had the prudence of a farmer when it came to money, and knew he could get a much better rate at one of the stag hotels catering to salesmen, actors, minor lobbyists. He had booked a room at the Norris, just a couple of blocks from the antique-green dome of the statehouse.

After signing in at the front desk—the tiny lobby, with its

spittoons and defeated plants, contained odors going back five years—Ham found his own way to his room on the second floor. It was decently furnished, in a dog-chewed sort of way, and the back window offered a country-style view of a stableboy currying a horse. He noticed a sign on the wall: "Don't Blow Out the Gas." Too bad. It meant electricity hadn't gotten here yet. It reminded him too of all those vaudeville routines about rubes in the big city. Farmers blowing themselves up in hotel rooms. That was about the only kind of joke he didn't like, jokes about hicks.

He laid out his hairbrushes, his razor, and his shaving mug stamped with the Masonic crescent and star, on the little shelf under the mirror. Had a half-hour lie-down. Then he washed up, changed his clothes, and returned to the streets.

Threading his way through heavy foot traffic, past Italian chestnut vendors, millinery shops, Negro shoe shiners, a men-only restaurant ("Eat here," said the sign in the window, "and keep your wife for a pet"), he arrived at last at the Imperial Hotel, a swank watering hole for politicians and businessmen. He and Padgett had arranged to have dinner here. Ham eyed the hotel's enormous chocolate and buttercream facade and then trotted up the front steps. Inside he found a huge marble lobby with whispering fountains and standing palms. With a few minutes to kill yet, he decided to have a drink in the bar.

What surprised him, as he approached the grill's open doorway, was how quiet it was. Where was the roar of government shoptalk, the chiming of glassware? Then he remembered it was Sunday. The city had looked so crowded to him he'd lost track of that. That meant no liquor being served here tonight, no crowd of politicos. Disappointed, he stepped into the barroom, as still as a library.

It was a small but beautiful room, given depth and grandeur by a series of wall-filling rectangular mirrors in rococo gilt frames, and a large crystal-prismed chandelier depending from the ceiling. Otherwise, whatever wasn't made of brass was made of mahogany. But the place was dead. A bulb-shaped man in a dark suit was sitting alone at the bar drinking tea. There were tables too, ice floes of undisturbed linen and flatware, maybe three or four people eating. Ham crossed to the bar and edged in between a couple of stools, not far from the corpulent customer with the teacup.

He glanced over the sparkling glassware, hanging upside down like bats asleep, and the warm lights in the bottles of whiskey. With a restless sigh he ordered a mug of sarsaparilla and then, as the frosted handle chilled his fist, leaned with his back against the bar. He was a politician in a nearly empty room. He felt a little desperate. Cautiously he slid a look at the fat gentleman a couple of barstools away.

The man appeared well-to-do. In his fifties probably, he had heavy-lidded eyes, a double chin like a roll of dough, and a mass of greasy gray hair raked straight back and curling up at the neckline. He wore a glossy black coat, matching vest, wing collar, and black bow tie. In general, he had the look of a very large and expensively dressed bullfrog, asquat a leather lily pad a good deal too small for him.

Ham sipped from his mug.

"Evening," he said.

The stranger, who was moodily swirling the contents of his cup, glanced over at Ham. "Evening to you, sir," he replied. He had a rumbling bass voice, both seductive and belligerent.

"You staying here?" Ham asked.

"I am not."

There was a silence.

"What's your line?"

The man eyed Ham sideways again. Finally with two fingers he produced a card from his vest pocket and passed it over.

Ham read:

Ham regarded the man with surprise.

But Dr. Hungerford didn't notice. Cradling the teacup in his meaty hand, he drained the contents, then sighed, smacking his lips.

"Martin!" he commanded.

The bartender, redheaded and jug-eared, materialized before them. He took the teacup from Dr. Hungerford, angled it under the beer spigot, and gave a short pull. Then he set the cup back on its saucer.

Ham was surprised again. "Don't take this wrong," he said to Martin after a longish pause, still watching the winking foam in the teacup. "I'm just in from out of town. But I had this idea in my head you couldn't serve alcohol on the Sabbath."

"You can't," agreed the bartender.

Ham mulled this over. "Cup of tea?" he said at last.

"Yes, sir." Martin pulled him a beer and set a little flowered cup and saucer on the bar. Ham pushed away his sarsaparilla and settled himself on a stool.

"You are?" said Dr. Hungerford.

Ham introduced himself.

"Salesman?"

Ham laughed. "I'm in politics," he said.

"Politics!" Dr. Hungerford snorted, fixing him with such a malevolent eye that Ham recoiled slightly. "Well, well, so you're a politician, hunh? Well, well, well. You know, there's something I've been wanting to ask one of you fellas for a long time. You mind?"

"No."

"How is it you're able to walk like everybody else? I mean, with your head up your butt."

"What's that?"

"Is there some kind of trick to it?"

"Now wait a second—"

"A politician." Dr. Hungerford took a slug of beer. "That figures. Why do you suppose I'm sitting here right now?" he said to Ham, turning and wiping his mouth. "How come I'm not out somewhere making an honest living, instead of wasting myself in idleness and dissipation?"

Ham shrugged.

" 'Cause of this new damfool law that says I can't pursue my livelihood on Sundays, that's why!" Dr. Hungerford roared. "A damfool law passed by a pack of goddamn politicians! Sunday! Of all days! When thousands of people are sitting around twiddling their thumbs, looking out the window. Hoping maybe they'll see an accident. People who'd give their eyeteeth to behold a few plasmatic effusions or chat with the dear departed. But no sir. Can't do it. 'Cause those boys in the statehouse tell me I can't. No more spirit work on the Sabbath." The man smiled without mirth. "Man. If the Lord God had listened to the Indiana legislature, we'd all be Jews today."

He tossed off the dregs in his cup and thrust it toward Martin for another refill. The rings on his pudgy hand sparkled with pink and lime-green stones.

"You know what I think's crazy," cried Martin as he pulled the beer spigot. "These new regs on tobacco, they're really nuts," he said. "Did you know that manufacturing cigarettes is against the law in this state?"

"That passed?" said Dr. Hungerford.

"Last session."

"That's the church," growled the hypnotist. "The religious lobby. They're always sticking their nose where it don't belong. By the way," he added, "you got any cigarettes?"

"Yep," said Martin. He produced a leather case from his pants pocket and popped it open. It was full of smokes. After peering at them in a finicky way, Dr. Hungerford selected one. Martin showed the case to Ham, who shook his head.

"This goddamn mania people have for telling other people how to behave," said Dr. Hungerford, smoking. "That's what there ought to be a law against."

"You said it," Martin yelped.

"Where are these from anyhow?" said the doctor, waving his cigarette.

"Imported," Martin said. "From Kentucky." There was a snap of fingers from a far table. "Oops. 'Scuse me, gents." He set down the doctor's beer and melted away.

Ham checked his watch. He was due to meet Padgett in ten minutes. Maybe he should go out front and wait at the main door. More diners were trickling into the bar now, he saw. They couldn't all be staying at the hotel. This must be Indianapolis society: the men in ravenbacked evening clothes, the women, glamour-gowned, with their tiaras and feathered headgear. His eyes lingered on the ladies passing, their heavily insured throats and earlobes, the soft and stately stirring of ostrich plumes.

"You ever see Three-Finger Brown pitch?" Dr. Hungerford asked. He was leaning both elbows on the bar now, leaking smoke from his nose and mouth.

Sports, the universal language.

"Now there's one heck of a ballplayer," said Ham, sliding his arms onto the bar. "Man alive, I once saw him—" He heard the quack of a cork coming out of a bottle. Looking around, he spotted Martin at a distant table dribbling wine into teacups for a gentleman and his lady friend.

"I was just thinking about that bill to legalize Sunday base-ball," the doctor said. "Almost twenty years they been sitting on that thing. These holy rollers and their puckerbutt crusades. You know what I'd like to do with all them folks?"

As he crushed out his cigarette, Dr. Hungerford began to chuckle. It went on for a while, his laughter, like the bubbling up of a drain.

For the first time Ham wondered how long his companion had been belting back these cups of beer.

Martin returned, dragging a smelly gray rag along the bar. "I thought of another one!" he said. "They've got a bill knocking around the statehouse right now that would make having relations with another man's wife a felony. A felony! Did you hear about that? Five to ten years in jail, they say."

"Well now," said Ham. "Is that a fact."

"Put you in jail for adultery." Dr. Hungerford laughed explosively. Martin laughed too. It was a silent laugh, but his shoulders went up and down. Then the doctor belched with a sudden solemnity that made him seem more froglike than ever. "You know something?" he said. "Drinking beer out of these little doohickeys puts you half in the bag in a hurry."

"You all right, Doctor?" Martin asked.

"Sure, sure." Craning his neck, the doctor peered nearsightedly over Martin's shoulder. "What kind of whiskey you got there?"

Just then Ham heard a voice at his ear. "You Mr. Dillon by any chance?"

He spun on his stool. It took him a moment to recognize Arnold Padgett, since up to now he'd only seen the man from a distance, up on podiums giving speeches. There he seemed like a force of nature, but up close he looked about as remarkable as a scrub bucket. Mr. Padgett was slightly under average height, with a weak little sprout of brown hair, to all appearances buried in the bosom of middle age. He wore his pants high with an equatorial belt. But there was life in his eyes—a twinkle of a practical nature—and that well-known nose, which over the years had inspired a few editorials. Pounded to pudding in fistfights during Padgett's tempestuous youth, it had achieved the size and shape of a small pear. Legend had it he'd once had to be taken to the hospital to have his fist removed from somebody's mouth.

"Arnold Padgett," the man said. "I've seen that pan of yours in the hometown paper."

Ham never objected to a little lazy flattery. The men shook hands.

"Sorry to drag you up here on a Sunday," Padgett said as Ham fumbled out some coins and laid them on the bar. "My schedule's tight as a tick right now with all these bills we've got coming up for vote . . ." They were moving away when Ham was stopped cold by Dr. Hungerford's voice booming after him:

"Don't you worry about that adultery bill, boy! That thing'll never pass! If it did, three-quarters of you birds would have to arrest yourselves!" Ham walked on without looking back, leaving the doctor haw-hawing in the background.

He followed Mr. Padgett toward the rear of the restaurant, where a balletic headwaiter bowed them through an archway into another, far larger room Ham had not realized existed. Suddenly he understood the scale of the place, and why the cream of society liked to come here. It was like a slice of Versailles, row on row of snowy tables under a wedding-cake ceiling at least twenty feet high, with more crystal-drip chandeliers repeating into the distance. Pedestals of white marble were stationed here and there around the room, each topped by a large vase artfully bursting with roses. The gold-flecked walls were hung with paintings of cream-and-pink nudes and chubby cupids, and on a platform in the far corner a small string orchestra was unpacking their gear. Ham had never seen anything like it.

They were shown to a table, and Padgett ordered a bottle of wine and two cups. Then as the waiter was leaving:

"Hang on a second, son. You want a little something first?" Padgett said to Ham. "Something to wet your whistle?"

"No, thanks."

"You can start me off with a bottle of Coca-Cola," Padgett told the waiter. "Nice tall glass of ice." The waiter departed. "You ever try Coca-Cola? Real tasty. And it makes rats explode."

"Sorry?"

"I lay out little saucers of it in my horse stalls back home. Something about the carbonation, I don't know, rats just—*boom.*" Opening his menu, which was burgundy-colored and about the size of a two-by-four, Padgett gave an unbuttoned sigh. "The French-type dishes are all first-class here," he said, scanning the listings. "Just stay away from anything that says 'home-style.' It's an abomination in the face of the Lord."

Ham was still trying to get his bearings. He was used to providing the banter, but Padgett had him outgunned.

"Nice place," he said lamely.

"Yeah, it gets real high-toned here at night. Days it's more just a squat-and-gobble for the statehouse crowd, but after sundown the society folks move in. I imagine they fumigate the place first."

"What do you mean?"

"They hate having politicians in here. Look down their noses at us. Hell, they'd make us eat in our own restaurant if they could, like the coloreds."

"Come on."

"It's a fact. Most of them don't even vote, unless you count blackballing people out of their fancy clubs. How do you feel about starting off with oysters? That's what my grateful constituents generally want me to have."

They ordered and ate and shot the breeze, mostly about their little corner of Daviess County, and friends they had in common. Ham was beginning to like the senator's adrenalized down-home style.

"By the way," said Padgett, wiping a sheen of gravy from his lips, "Frank Deitz will be along to join us for coffee. How's that suit you?"

"Just fine."

"You know Frank Deitz?"

"Know of him."

Deitz was a political boss. He had no official job as far as Ham knew, just a half-sinister reputation as one of the top cornermen in the state Democratic machine. People said he was smart and tough as a boiled owl.

"Interesting fella, Frank Deitz," Padgett said. "A paragon of animals, in his way. He's the only man I know whose friends are more afraid of him than his enemies because his friends have seen him operate up close, and they know just what the hell he's capable of." Padgett was eating with a bulge in his cheek like a chipmunk. "You ever hear about the special election we had up here last fall?"

"No," said Ham.

"No reason you should. It was just an open city council seat— not even statehouse level—so a man of the stature of Frank Deitz, you wouldn't think he'd get into a foam about it. But no. It's an open seat and Frank Deitz wants a Democrat in it. Don't matter how teen-inesy the office is, he wants a Democrat in there. It's like a religion with him. Okay, so this election's coming up, and they got party men on both sides out in the Fifteenth Ward going through the usual monkeyshines, buying up votes one by one for five bucks or a box of cigars. And Frank Deitz is out here and there, squeezing folks where he knows he'll get their attention, all perfectly friendly as these things go. Till one day our boys come around the corner of this particular block they haven't visited yet—no reason for 'em to race on over, it's just a few raggedy-ass apartment houses—and what do they find but the Republicans have got there first and bought up every-body there in one swoop, and I mean everybody, right on down to the children, the unborn and the unthought of. Sewed up two hundred people. What the promise there was, I don't know for sure, but it must have been lip-smackin'. Running water maybe. Or lights. Everybody's crazy for lights now.

"Anyhow, when old Frank Deitz hears we've been torpedoed,

he knows he's got to do something about it. Somehow he's got to keep these people from voting because all by themselves they might be enough to flip the election. He's got three days. So he's in this big sweat now, and kicking a few butts around the office to help him think, when it comes to him. He realizes that what he needs is a Democrat with smallpox."

"What?"

"We still get these little bust-outs of it, you know. Not in the countryside much, out where you are, but here in the city it happens, you bet. When it does, people stick these little flags out their windows. Ever seen 'em?"

"No."

"You ain't never seen our smallpox flags? Damn, boy, you gotta pull your head out of the woods, get an eyeful of some of these A-number-one attractions we got here in Indianapolis, city of the future! Flags by day, lights by night. It's real festive. Colored lanterns, you know—blue, green, all kinds. Quarantine lights. 'Cause that smallpox, you know—"

"Yeah, I know."

"Anyway, the point is, Frank Deitz finds himself some poor sap with smallpox, not delirious yet, gives him a badge and sends him door to door in these apartment buildings telling everybody he's the sanitary inspector. Checking for cockroaches."

"Christ Almighty."

"Then about the time the guy's wrapping up his rounds, Frank Deitz puts in a telephone call to the Health Department. Anonymous tip. The result is one god-awful hoo-ha, naturally, and every one of those buildings gets sealed up just like that. Now nobody can get out to vote. The bug inspector gets arrested, of course, but he's not talking, or if he is, nobody can understand him 'cause his mouth is so stuffed full of money. Some of the cops on the case, well, they're on the party payroll too. So that's that. Election goes ahead. We win in a walk. And you know what Frank Deitz says to me afterward? Only time I ever saw him almost smile. 'Believe me,' he says, 'you ain't lived till you've walked down the street tipping your hat to a couple hundred quarantined Republicans.' "

Ham's jaw was still hanging. "These people in the apartment buildings. Did they get sick?"

"Not that I ever heard of," said Padgett. "Of course, I can't say I ever made strenuous inquiries. There are some things a man would just rather not know."

As he said this, Padgett's eyes lost their genial light, and they lingered on Ham in a disconcerting way, as if to measure the effect of his tale. Ham did his best to look blasé.

"So!" cried Padgett suddenly. "Let's talk about my retirement."

Ham sat up slightly. "Yes, sir."

"The party's nosing around for somebody to take my place next election, and your name keeps coming up."

Ham waited.

"Now I want to be entirely straightforward with you. The truth is that the party is also considering the cousin of the wife of some muck-a-muck. I don't know, I guess they owe him a couple of favors. On the other hand, there's something powerful on your side—namely, that this cousin's got the political visibility of a black cat in a dark closet and we need somebody who can win."

Padgett reached for the bottle and poured out a little more wine for Ham, and then for himself, murmuring as he did, "One more and that's the last."

"What's that?"

"Sorry," said Padgett. He looked grumpy. "Nothing, it's just . . . Shakespeare. Part of the price you pay for being a trial attorney, all those years making opening and closing arguments. Your head gets so stuffed up with Shakespeare, everything you do reminds you of some damn quote. It's like malaria, you can't get rid of it.

"As to this matter of my successor," he went on, setting the bottle down, "there's something else I want to be candid with you about. More candid than is good for me maybe, but . . ." He paused. "Have you asked yourself why I'm retiring?"

"Yes, I have," said Ham, lying.

"After all, I'm not but fifty-two, still got my back teeth, and there are things about this job that like me fine. Giving a real ripsnorter of a speech . . ."

Padgett was famous in Indiana for his oratory. The newspapers called him the Potbellied Stove.

"Believe it or not, I think you can even do some good in politics," he went on, "if you look sharp and stay on the balls of your feet."

"So why are you quitting?"

"Exactly! Why give up the colored fella brushing my coat in the cloakroom, and all those free rides on the trolley?" The light, which had reappeared in Padgett's eyes, faded again, as if it were supplied by a fitful dynamo. "The fact is, I've lost the stomach for it. You might not think I could say that, a man with a stomach this size. But it's so. You see, I didn't tell you that little tale about Frank Deitz to pass the time. I want you to have an idea of exactly what you're getting into. After all, you're a young man, full of ideals. I assume you're full of ideals . . ."

Ham tried to look full of ideals.

"I've seen a lot of young men get smashed on the rocks," Padgett said. "They come charging into town, want to take on all this corruption and double-dealing with a fire hose. Honesty in government! But you know what I've learned in my twelve sobering years here? Almost nobody cares about honesty in government. The rich don't care about it. Hellfire, they're dead against it. If government was honest, they'd go out of business, most of them. And all the poor want, when you boil it down to the bottom, is protection from the rapacities of the rich. In other words, the real constituency for honesty in government is so small you could just about wash it down with a glass of water."

Try as he might, Ham was having a hard time paying attention to this. He was starting to notice the women in the room. One young lady, crowned with iridescent feathers, sat with her head cockatooed sideways, nodding to someone. Another sat at a table of six eating like a bird—meaning she was looking all around her, up, down, and sideways, and then shoveling food in her mouth as fast as she could. Most acutely, Ham was aware of a tall beauty seated close by, with a corsage low at the cleft of her breasts. He could feel the candlepower in her eyes; they were turned in his direction. Society belle or not, he wouldn't have said, at that moment, that she was looking down on him.

"You familiar with the difference between honest graft and dishonest graft?" said Padgett.

"Honest graft?"

"Frank Deitz has a whole speech on it, but in a nutshell, blackmailing cathouses, embezzling from the state treasury. That's dishonest graft. Some of the brethren go in for that kind of thing, even though it stinks to high heaven and once in a long, long while it can even get a man arrested. But let's say you've got a spot on some transportation committee, and you get wind of where they're fixing to lay a new trolley line. You jump in, buy up the land, then turn around and sell it to the city. Make a handsome return. That's honest graft, Frank Deitz would say. Reaping the rewards of your foresight."

A wealthy matron passed by on her way to a table, moving with the dignity of one risen from the crypt.

"Honest graft," said Ham. "Whew." He had to smile. "You go in for that yourself?"

Padgett ran his tongue around in his mouth. "I've dabbled," he said at last. "Yeah, I suppose I'd have to say. . . . But I'm not proud of it." He fell silent. " 'Cause you know what? You know the problem with this whole awe-inspiring system? Out there in the world it's a hell of a thing trying to tell the good graft from the bad. You'd be amazed at the overlap. It's all one ball of string.

About the best a man can hope for is, do a great right, do a little wrong. . . . See what I mean?" said Padgett disgustedly. "Shakespeare again. Anyhow, it's time I packed up my ill-gotten gains and went back home to Daviess County. Figure I'll practice a little law again. A very little law. Do a lot of fishing. I've just lost my appetite for being up to my ass in moral ambiguity."

Padgett drained half a glass of ice water and sighed. "Still want the job?" he said.

All Ham wanted right now was for Padgett to shut up. The old gasbag was starting to get to him, running down politics this way—Ham's own profession—while at the same time, whether he meant to or not, throwing an uncomfortable searchlight on the young man himself. Ham had never felt such a vivid sense of his own flaws; they were as clear to him right now as veins in marble.

"Don't you want to know where I stand on a few issues?"

"You're a Democrat, aren't you?"

Ham nodded.

"Well, then. I don't guess you aim to reinvent the platform of the Democratic Party."

Ham toyed with his teacup.

"I appreciate the advice," he said at last. Just for something to say.

"I may have overdone it," said Padgett. "If so, my apologies."

"How are things going with the Sunday baseball bill?" Ham said.

"That thing? Getting that old piece of legislation through's been like trying to pass a kidney stone. Why do you ask?"

Just then some kind of ruckus broke out, a burst of voices. Ham looked toward the archway, and there spied a small man in a derby, his chin poked up into the face of the headwaiter. Backing away, the headwaiter pointed in the direction of Ham's table. The small man in the derby came hurrying over.

He barely glanced at Ham, but caught hold of Arnold Padgett's upper arm, bent down, and muttered fiercely into his ear. Padgett interrupted with a word or two. The other man leaned in and spoke as before. Finally Padgett excused himself from the table, and he and the newcomer walked into the aisle, where they could converse with more freedom.

At last Padgett returned to the table. "Sorry, I've got to go," he said. "A little brushfire we have to take care of. Like I said, we've got a lot of bills just now coming to a vote. Stay, stay," he added as Ham started to rise. "This wine here's too good to waste. Just let me see about the check. Be right back." And he was gone.

The other man was left for the moment fidgeting in the aisle, just a few feet from Ham. With that battered derby of his, mud-colored clothing, and scrawny neck—physically he was no more imposing than a plucked chicken—there was still something about him, an imperious roll of the eye, that left Ham little doubt he was looking at Frank Deitz. More out of nervous energy, it seemed, than anything else, the man abruptly veered in Ham's direction and came to stand over his chair.

"You're Dillon?" he demanded. In the soft dining-room light the stubble on his cheeks glistened like frost.

"That's right," Ham said. "I'm Dillon."

Deitz walked away again. Stood restlessly in the aisle. Then he came back.

"Don't know if I'll see you again," he said. "Maybe, maybe not. But you can take this home with you. I've got nothing against a man who won't let himself be bought, you understand? Maybe you're that kind, and if you are, that's okay. I've got nothing against a man who *can* be bought, either. A fella like that can be real useful. But a man who lets himself be bought and won't stay bought . . . he's the lowest thing that crawls."

He paced away into the aisle again as Padgett came hastening back clutching his topcoat, threw some coins on the table, and then stuck his hand out. Ham shook it, not standing up.

"It's a powerful argument for going fishing, isn't it?" Padgett said, not smiling. "We'll be talking. Okay, Frank, let's skedaddle." The senator departed with Deitz at his heels.

Ham sat in a brown study. Padgett was right about one thing. The wine was too good to waste. He doled it out for himself a little at a time, amid the sea roar of upper-class vocal cords, till he began to feel a buffer in his brain. Then he suddenly pushed the drink away from him. A little wine slopped over the lip of the cup.

Ham got up and headed out of the restaurant, sidestepping a frail old lady who seemed to be struggling to move under the weight of her own jewels. He glanced toward the bar, where he saw Dr. Hungerford sitting just as before, only leaning now with the full weight of his chest against the bar and breathing laboriously. With one outstretched arm he seemed to be trying to seize hold of Martin, who stood at the cash register with his back turned. "An eighty percent chance they told me!" Hungerford bellowed. "Eighty percent chance, and she was gone the next day. Just like that." He snapped his fingers tremendously. "Doctors."

Angrily Ham shoved the brass rail of the revolving door and spun outside into the night.

He walked a long way. The maidenly cool of the April night mingled nicely with the wine in his brain. He stopped at a street-corner tobacco stand, bought a cigar, and lit it at the lantern hanging there. Then, smoking, he strode on more slowly. Before long he had left the commercial district behind.

Eventually he found himself on North Meridian Street, one of the city's great residential areas. He stood looking at a double line of big brick houses trimmed in white stone, mighty verandas, long lawns.

All very peaceful, this mass disguise. Ham walked along studying the homes with a mixture of jaundice and envy. He passed cherub-encrusted fountains; a cast-iron deer. There wasn't much traffic on the boulevard tonight, just the occasional sputter of an auto going by or the *jing-jing* of a bicycle. Great skeletal fans of elm and black walnut trees spread above him, weakly in bud. It was getting chilly. He passed a young man in full mourning costume, right down to his black gloves and ebony walking stick, impeccably grieving. Ham ducked off Meridian and began to explore one of the more intimate side streets.

Money lived here too, obviously, but the houses were different, closer together, many Queen Anne style—scaly, with turrets, as if they had been assembled from parts of dragons. Here the porch swings looked like real invitations.

Then he heard the trickle of a piano coming from one of the houses and stopped a moment to listen. It sounded like Chopin. He thought of Louise, Allie's daughter. Pretty girl, Louise.

He remembered her again, standing in the well of the stairs, looking up at him and Allie.

Allie and Maggie. Again they began to revolve in his mind—one, then the other, on a slow carousel. This world here, the stone birdbaths and gardeners' quarters and smug money, this was what Maggie wanted. And now it was nearly in his grasp, maybe just an election away. (Padgett's warning that politicians were snubbed here didn't faze him, Ham always figuring that in his own way he was the Tamburlaine of charm.) Well, Maggie deserved success here, he thought. She'd been a good wife to him. Worked so damn hard. There were whole stretches she barely stuck her head up to take a look around.

At intervals the electric streetlamps threw down hard pools of light. He stopped a moment to watch two older ladies through an unshuttered window, lace up to their necks, looming godlike over some board game.

Still, he couldn't shake free of Allie. He didn't want to. She fired him with life: not just his loins but his imagination. And if big-league politics was really as depraved as Padgett claimed, well, that only made her more precious to him. To steer his way through such a corrupted world he would have to know Allie was tucked away somewhere. She would be the one pure place he could go.

For the first time he wondered if he and Allie should have a child.

His wandering way had taken him onto another block of handsome houses. Here the branches of trees from both sides of the street reached across and interlaced high overhead. Come summer, thick with leaves, they would make a cool tunnel against the sun. Ham was gazing up at them when he noticed a figure standing at a second-story bay window.

A young woman was facing the street, wearing a high-necked, cream-colored dress with a cameo at her throat. She was playing the violin. From this distance, and with the window shut, Ham couldn't hear a note. But what a picture it was. Captivated, he stood across the street watching the silent music.

She didn't see him, caught up in her own playing. Ham, who was still a little drunk, thought he had never seen anyone work a bow so well.

He was surprised to feel tears collecting in the bones of his face. He drove them down.

To master himself he concentrated on details of the woman's appearance. She was attractive, he could tell that much. The way her head tilted toward her instrument, the line of her delicately exposed neck, gave her an artfully vulnerable air. Like one of Dracula's victims. Ham began to peer at her frilled front, trying to judge the size of her breasts.

By now he knew he wanted a prostitute. He tried to flick it away, this idea, but once it had occurred to him he knew he couldn't conquer it. He had to do something with his lust and tears.

The violinist played on, but Ham wasn't watching anymore. He looked up and down the street. He was thoroughly lost. To reach Queen Mab's, the famous cathouse near the train station, he judged he should strike to the southeast. Find a taxi along the way. Maybe he'd come upon some other cathouse between here and there. After all, the town was full of them. All he had to do was look for the friendly red light over the door.

He started walking quickly, hoping he was going the right way. Soon the fine houses fell away, replaced by modest two-story clapboards and bungalows. Once or twice Ham thought he heard a swell of traffic noise and headed toward it, hoping to hit a thoroughfare, but he remained in a tangle of side streets, turning hopelessly this way and that.

At last, in a nest of cottages tucked in a cul-de-sac, he spied one of those fabled red lights. This'll be all right, he thought. He didn't need champagne, just a nice, simple girl. Somebody clean. He began to trot down the dark, deserted street.

It wasn't until he was within five or ten yards of the house that he saw another red glow, at one of the side windows, like the one in the front. Then he noticed the little triangular flags and the next instant the hand-lettered sign, QUARANTINE, pasted across the front door. A smallpox house.

Cursing, Ham backed away, then turned and sprinted the way he'd come. After running a couple of blocks, he slowed to a walk, recovering his breath. He was still lost. By now he'd given up any idea of finding a cathouse.

That is, until he bumped into a helmeted policeman, who pointed him in the right direction.

12

THAT SUMMER Maggie beat up a Gypsy. At least that's the way people talked about it, even in later years: some underoccupied old geezer would bust out with a horse laugh. *"Remember that time Ham Dillon's wife beat up the Gypsy?"* She never exactly landed a punch, but still and all, she wound up with quite a little reputation.

It happened one morning late in June. Maggie was sweeping out the dank little storeroom just off the kitchen—poking, *bap bap bap*, into a corner—when she heard an echoing tap coming from the front door. *Tap tap tap.* Three times. It came again, *tap tap tap.* Toting her broom like a rifle, Maggie came out into the hallway and crossed the parlor to the front door.

There on the other side of the fly screen was a shape with the sun behind it. Maggie opened the door with a cautious creak. She found a soiled and ragged man, large-featured, with a headful of black curls. His body was canted to one side, his dark eyes were dancing with mischief, and he held both hands behind his back, as if he might be hiding something. He looked as if he were trying to fascinate a six-year-old.

Maggie regarded him unentranced.

She'd heard the Gypsies were back. Every year they showed up about this time, twenty or thirty of them in their box wagons with bright-painted wheels, jangling pots and pans, and musical instruments, offensively picturesque. They camped out on church grounds mostly (preachers being a notorious soft touch for this type of criminal), and from there they'd begin their depredations of neighboring farms. A Gypsy might come to the front door, say, asking to buy eggs, while the rest of his family was out back stuffing chickens and vegetables into their shirts. Or they struck at night.

Maggie had already noticed that over the past couple of days somebody had been in her strawberry patch, and one of her chickens was missing. She opened the door wider.

"Ahhh," breathed the Gypsy. She had been about to give him what for and get rid of him fast; but to her surprise his face changed, and he took a slow step backward. He wore the look of a man struck by unexpected beauty.

"What is it?" she said tightly.

What was it? The Gypsy made a fuddled face. He seemed to have forgotten. Ah yes! Hunching his shoulders, he slowly, suspensefully, drew something from behind his back—something bright—and thrust it up for her to see.

It was a large bouquet of dyed chicken feathers. Green, red, purple, sky blue. A gorgeous curiosity. As Maggie gazed at it, the Gypsy's eyes peeked over the top, full of doleful hope. There was a silence. He proffered it votively, like a lover, but she didn't take it yet. Maggie had only one thought.

A gut instinct told her this bouquet had been made from the feathers of her own chicken.

"How much?" she said.

"One," her suitor replied. Meaning a dollar. He seemed sorry to have to ask for anything at all.

"Mmm," she said, reaching for it at last. She turned the bouquet over, examined it slowly. Her heart was hammering. This was the kind of stunt they were always pulling. First they steal from you, then they rub your nose in it. The Gypsy raised his eyebrows optimistically.

"Let me see it in the light," Maggie said, striding to the edge of the porch; Bert, the dog, slunk out the door and trailed after her. She held the bouquet just out of the roofshade where it could catch the sun. Across the yard, on the far side of the gate, she noticed his wagon, and the watchful faces of a woman and child.

"One?" crooned the lovelorn Gypsy, holding up one finger.

For reply, Maggie shifted the handle of the broom she was carrying, grasping it with both hands, and caught the Gypsy a sharp shot in the pit of the stomach. Shocked—just as if she'd been struck herself—she frantically changed her grip, and before he could straighten up, swung the broom like a baseball bat, hitting him a mighty blow with the straw end that sent him crashing against the square column at the edge of the porch steps. She kept swatting at him, like an enormous insect, but he wouldn't go down, so she went at him with her feet then, kicking, and when he cried out she shouldered him sideways, by main force, off the edge of the porch, where he lost his footing at last and pitched forward, raking his face on the steps just before he collided with the ground. Panting, she marched over to the bouquet, which had fallen unregarded onto the porch, picked it up, and heaved it after him. A few feathers exploded free.

Skittering down the steps, Bert sniffed the prostrate Gypsy all around, searching for signs of life. At long last the man lifted his head. Maggie watched him on tenterhooks. He scrambled smoothly to his feet and faced her, his eyes filled with awe.

To her horror she watched them narrow into slits. He started toward her.

"Get out of here!" she hollered, shaking the broom like trying to spook a horse. "Get off my property!" He kept coming. But the next moment he was checked by another yowl, this time from his wife, stretched halfway out of the window of the wagon. Obviously she was telling him, in their Gypsy language, to forget it, to get away from there, because the two of them exchanged volleys of abuse, which sent the Gypsy stomping about in an exasperated circle, till finally he stopped with a great sigh; then, throwing a venomous look at Maggie, he clutched his damaged bouquet to his chest and headed toward the gate. Just before he got there, he halted and pointed at the dog; made a knife-slitting motion across his throat; then scrambled aboard his wagon and with a crack of the reins, rumbled away.

Maggie told Ham what had happened, of course, and Ham crowed about it to everybody. She couldn't make him understand how frightened she'd been. He kept Bert indoors for a few days, just to be on the safe side, but all the time he was telling folks what a pistol he'd married.

The whole thing put Ham in such spirits he even talked about it in bed with Allie, breaking their unspoken rule about not discussing spouses. This irritated her. (Only a man, she thought, could be so monumentally unconscious; a woman, talking about another man, would know just what she was doing.) Then she thought, no matter, and nested deeper in the bed. Let him talk about Maggie.

After all, Allie was the one pregnant with his child.

Funny how a few weeks ago she had almost bolted. He'd come roaring back from Indianapolis, saying yes, all right, let's have a child; so eager, in fact, it had scared her, though she'd been trying before to convince him. She thought of those ancient maps of Europe: there was the known world, where the human race lived, and all around it the unknown world, represented by dragons with curling tongues. That night she wrote to Link in Kentucky, begging him to visit her. *"If you don't come,"* she wrote, underlining it, *"I don't know what I'll do."*

That was the tail end of April. The letter put Link in a state, of course—all the more so since he'd been in Indiana with her and the children not more than two weeks before, when everything seemed fine. He grabbed a train, but by the time he arrived Allie's spasm of conscience was over, and she spent the next week in a state of wild impatience waiting for him to go away. Why had she written? he kept asking her. What was the matter? Nothing. It was nothing. Nerves. She did seem nervous, that was for sure: she kept repeating she wanted to make love, but when he touched her, she could barely breathe. At long last Link did go back to Kentucky, leaving a puzzled kiss on her forehead. He would come back for his regular visit, he told her, in a few weeks, late June. Wonderful, she said, take good care, and she watched his train pull out feeling utterly spent.

The baby was conceived in early May. And now she lay six weeks later, with outlaw life inside her, in a cocoon of angry joy. Not only had she reclaimed lost territory—herself as a beautiful, headstrong girl, before married life got its mitts on her; she was taking new ground besides.

Strange, she thought, how betraying the marriage vow can develop so many good qualities. Courage, stamina, quick wits.

She became aware that Ham was stroking her hip in a way that conveyed both fondness and ownership. A silky, repetitive motion.

"What should we name the little bugger?" Ham said softly, his hand beginning to explore.

"Honey, I don't think that's going to be up to you," she said.

She shifted, then moved again, under the growing pressure of his fingers, wondering if she would ever feel guilt again. It could seize her like an epilepsy, she knew that now. But at the moment it was hard to think why.

ONE THING she was still worried about: making sure Link got back up for another visit. That would put him in Elnora twice in April and once in June—enough, she felt sure, to hide the paternity of the baby. Evidently this little detail hadn't crossed Ham's mind. (Men.) So in her next letter to Link she pressed him to remember his promise to come. She tried for a tone of lighthearted longing.

But she didn't hear back right away. Allie started to fret. Ordinarily Link was a letter machine: he wrote twice a week without fail—more than she did—and sent along fifty to seventy-five dollars every month (extras too, like the cream separator). By that reckoning, she should have heard from him three days ago. What was wrong? Had he guessed? Surely not. There was just some clog in the mail.

It was morning, about eleven o'clock. Cool for mid-June. Allie was on her knees, feeding hickory sticks into the kitchen stove. She added two tablespoons of kerosene; lit that; then she washed her hands in cold water at the sink pump and started mixing biscuit dough. If a letter didn't come today, she thought, she'd telephone Link in Kentucky. No, no, don't do that. People don't call on the long distance unless somebody's died. She couldn't afford to seem panicky again.

Smearing her hands on her apron, she went to the window facing the road and looked out. Nobody. Just last month they'd finally done it, introduced home delivery of the mail. A bell ringer of a day. It was still so novel, having letters brought to their own front gates, that some people couldn't help treating the man who did it with a touch of awe, like another Mercury, even though they knew it was silly. Who was it, after all? Just that old Ed Watkins in a uniform.

Back at the kitchen counter, Allie fetched a sigh and whaled into her biscuits. Whanging her spoon in the big red bowl, she mixed the dough, then rolled it out with strong strokes, like roadbed; after that, she began cutting the biscuits out, twist by twist, savagely. Once she heard a sound outside and went to the window again, but it was just Denton crossing the yard, dragging a shovel behind him with the lassitude of youth.

She was adding one last hickory stick to the stove—a little superstition she'd picked up from her mother, a prayer to the biscuit god—when she spied Ed's wagon through the trees.

Light as a girl she ran down the driveway to meet him.

"Ed!" she cried, waving as she ran. "Hi there, Ed!"

Ed froze. She had interrupted him as he was leaning from his seat to pop open the Hales' mailbox. This was a big moment. Ed opened the flap of every mailbox he came to carefully, with a great sense of occasion, as if there was no telling what he might find in there—which was exactly the case, in fact: for with the appearance of the mailbox had sprung up, almost at once, the happy custom of leaving little gifts inside it for the mail carrier. Mostly food. In the course of his slow daily round—twenty-four and a half miles of dirt road, with a few graveled stretches—Ed dragged into the daylight roasted ears of corn still steaming, fat slabs of pie, mounds of bright fruit. He had long since stopped bringing lunch. Sometimes he found other things too: notes from people asking him to pick them up something at the drugstore, or to be sure and tell so-and-so such and such. One man had left him eighty-nine dollars in cash with a rock on it, and a note: PLEASE DEPOSIT BANK. Everything he was asked to do Ed did. In his bright-buttoned uniform and smart cap, he radiated the grave contentment of a man who has both pride of place and no further ambitions—and who regards himself, on top of that, as the very avatar of the twentieth century.

"Howdy, Miz Hale," he said, sitting back on his wagon seat. The mailbox, for now, stayed shut. He looked down at her from his perch: yellow-haired, watery-voiced, affable as always. Allie had never seen a whisker's difference in the way he acted around people, from Mama Dillon to a perfect stranger. "Oop, steady there, steady!" he shouted now, yanking the reins, as the horse pulling the wagon did a two-step in her harness. "Look out there, Miz Hale, that's Sy Callahan's filly, she'll kick you into next week."

"How come you've got her pulling the mail?" Allie asked, catching up her skirts and stepping back. She could see Ed had a small packet of letters, tied with string, on the seat beside him. Probably hers. She wanted to snatch the mail and run, but that wouldn't do. You had to pass the time of day.

"Sy asked me to break her for him," Ed replied. "Tells me she's a spoiled outlaw kicking filly, but he's hoping maybe I can do something with her, you know, out driving all day long. Well, like I said to Sy, you can't hardly ever break a kicker from kicking, but hand her over if you want and we'll give 'er a whirl." Ed, who had been picking his teeth with a fingernail, turned his head and rifle-spat something into the weeds. "Yesterday she had a brainstorm about ten minutes out. Laid down in the road and kicked, and I sat on her head and let her do it . . ."

Ed went on about the horse, while Allie's attention wandered to the letters beside him. He did like to talk. Actually, she thought Ed and the job were a good fit: he was garrulous without being a gossip, which she considered a fine quality in a person who toured the community every day. Why, he was a tomb for gossip; she'd already heard a couple of ladies in town complaining about it.

"I always plant them thick and then thin them out after they get past the bug stage," Ed said.

"What?" said Allie, coming to. "Plant what?"

"My melons," Ed said. "Well, better be gettin' on." He started to hand her down her mail, then paused. "You gonna sign that road petition like you promised?"

"Sure, of course."

"That's fine." He handed her the packet. "I'll tell you, I could write a book about holes in this road. The road supervisor, I think he must have been hatched out of a monkey egg."

"Bye-bye, Ed," Allie said, turning away. She was tearing open a letter from Link.

Before heading up the road to the Dillons', Ed snuck a peek in the Hales' mailbox. He looked twice, but there was still nothing there.

Allie paced slowly up the drive toward her front door, reading.

FROM BEHIND a poplar tree nearby, Denton watched as the mail wagon rolled away in a smoke of dust. Then he turned away, moodily chopping at the ground with his shovel. Like his father, Denton had always had his spells of moping, but ever since the family had moved here from Kentucky, he had really gotten depressed. He was fourteen, that was part of it. But there was something else. In the rough-and-tumble world of farm boys he felt like an oddball: so mechanically gifted he had built his own bicycle part by part, but prone to a kind of mental paralysis around people, especially when they looked him full in the face. It didn't help that he hated farming. At least in Nicholasville, just outside Lexington, he had felt close to civilization and hope; here he felt lost and, what was worse, intimidated by the rubes.

The other boys knew he was different. They smelled it, as boys do. As long as his father was around teaching, they'd pretty much left him alone, but the day Link got on the train they threw his lunch on the schoolhouse roof. And that was just the beginning.

Of course it was summer now, and he wouldn't have to see his tormentors for a while. It wasn't any hardship for him to stay away from Ragsdale's soda fountain or the swimming hole. And yet: Denton was coming to the grisly realization that persecution is at least a form of companionship. More than ever in his life he felt cruelly alone.

Dropping the shovel, he wandered around the back of the house, along the edge of the peach orchard, and over toward the barn. He was supposed to be digging out the pigpen. He was supposed to be doing a lot of things.

Denton pushed the door—it slid sideways on a rolling track—and stepped into the cathedral of the barn. Automatically his eyes rose to the haylofts, to the dust spinning in the slatted light shooting through the rafters. This barn, its vastness and musty peace, was the one place on the whole property he liked. Just standing in this space somehow soothed his loneliness. Shuffling down the broad, straw-strewn center aisle, past cow flop and puddles of motor oil, he headed toward the far wall. He passed the vacant nests of barn swallows, some sleighbells and harness hanging from pegs, the swish and thunk of a stabled horse.

He was looking for the gun his father had placed in the barn for shooting varmints. Denton knew it was still there, had known for months, but it was only in the past few days that he'd begun making pilgrimages to it. There it was, stuck behind a can of turpentine on one of the back shelves, an old Iver Johnson hammerless. Amazing how fast it got dusty. Denton lifted the revolver out and carefully wiped it off.

Turning the weapon in his hands, he studied once more the loops and whorls in the nickel plating—beautiful, hand-engraved. Then he felt the heft of the thing.

Ordinarily that was as far as it went. He'd put the gun back and leave. This time, though, after the briefest reverie, he slipped the revolver into his pocket and scooped a few shells from the box. Then he left the barn, by the little door in the back this time, and started off across the fields toward the far north fence.

The day was heating up, and Denton was starting to sweat by the time he reached the crackling weeds at the edge of the property. Standing by the fence he dumped out the bullets that were in the chamber of the gun and slipped in some fresh ones—just in case fresh ones worked better. Then he snapped the chamber closed and, holding the gun in a tense two-handed grip, looked around for something to shoot. He took shaky aim at the first thing he saw—a squirrel poised on a bending branch. He pulled the trigger. The gun erupted in his hands. Next thing he knew it was lying in the grass at his feet, and he with it, and the whole sky was echoing like a bowling alley.

That scattered the wildlife, so he decided to start with a fence post, something that wouldn't move. But he couldn't hit that either. An owl, evidently roused by the noise, came banking out of a stand of elms and coasted within a few feet of him. Was that good luck or bad luck, to see an owl in daylight? Denton couldn't remember. He wondered, watching, if the owl could see him. He'd read someplace that owls can't see things that are very, very close to them, things that are right under their noses. Maybe he's not afraid of me because he doesn't even know I'm here, the boy thought.

He's not afraid of me because he knows I couldn't hit him with a cannon.

Something shifted in his gut, and he realized—the final indignity—he had to make a trip to the outhouse. Or as Mama Dillon called it, "the necessity house." He stuck the half-loaded gun back in his trousers and trudged toward home, trailing failure.

Ten minutes later he sat in the crapper, the door closed, the odor thickening, breathing through his mouth. Up in a corner he could see a spider, all busy little elbows, working its web; on the opposite wall a single green-bottle fly moved, rubbing its forelegs like a tiny connoisseur. Then through a crack in the planking Denton saw his mother come onto the back porch. She slung a bucketload of soap suds onto the rosebushes and went back inside. Soap killed the aphids or something, she said.

Bugs everywhere.

Denton sighed and took down the Sears, Roebuck catalogue from the chipped shelf at his elbow.

These days just about everybody had a Sears catalogue handy. In fact, plenty of farm families had a total of just two books, those compendia of wonders, the Holy Bible and the "wish book" from Mr. Sears—volumes it was easy to view as being in direct competition. After all, the catalogue paraded a solid twelve hundred pages of earthly delights, everything from plows to parasols, from city-style clothing to Dunbar's Patented Arch Prop for Flat Feet. Still, it made farmers feel like part of things. They could live out to hell and gone but even so, thanks to the catalogue, they could belong to the U.S.A.; they could share in the explosion of goods that was coming to be called the American way of life.

It also gave them unlimited bumwad. Lots of thrifty farm families used their catalogues for that too.

Denton was one of the very few who hated the Sears catalogue. He felt mocked by what he found there: the good life, minutely itemized. He sat thumbing its pages now, his mind a malarial bog crisscrossed by a few mosquitoes. Then he noticed something.

It was a two-page spread trumpeting the breakthrough of modern indoor plumbing. Sears was proud to announce that it could now offer a do-it-yourself water-closet kit, ready for installation in any home.

Leaning forward, Denton read more closely.

Why slog through wind, rain, and dark of night to a diseased and unmentionable location? "Our tank is highly polished and frostproof," crooned the catalogue, its copy sinuously woven around some densely detailed sketches. "It is fitted with heavy brass trimmings and a china push button, a slight touch of which releases the valve producing an explosive and powerful flush. The seat is made of highly polished oak, the bowl of the very highest grade of English vitreous earthenware. . . ."

And it was in the middle of reading this spiel, while sitting in the outhouse, that something in Denton finally gave way. He couldn't even take an up-to-date dump. With barely a conscious thought left in his head, he leaned down to the pants around his ankles and groped there for the gun.

The sound of the shot brought Allie to the kitchen window, just in time to see her son pitch half naked through the outhouse door. He fell onto his back and stayed there. She saw the bright blotch on his chest. With a cry she started outside—pausing long enough to shout to Louise to telephone the doctor—and an instant later was flying down the stone pathway to where Denton lay gasping on the ground.

TWO DAYS LATER southwestern Indiana was hit with crackling thunderstorms. Denton lay upstairs in bed recovering from his wound, watching the rain hurl itself against the windows.

Dr. Porter had gotten the bullet out and cleaned him up. Now the house was filled with a silence that swallowed every sound. Allie didn't know what to do next. The boy had admitted nothing—he had spoken barely at all—but her mother's instinct had told her immediately that it wasn't an accident. Should she pretend it was? Let him recover in the bosom of his family? Let him talk in his own time?

Maybe not. Maybe he should be seen by someone right away, some sort of mental specialist. But even to suggest that, Allie thought, might get him all wrought up again. Well, she would talk it over with Link. He would be here soon, tomorrow probably; in that letter he'd written her, he had said his job would keep him from visiting till July, but of course this business with Denton had changed everything. Allie had phoned Kentucky, and Link was catching the first train he could—just what she had wanted in the first place.

She tried not to feel lucky.

Now Allie was in the kitchen adding corncobs to the fire in

the stove while the rain beat at the house. Her daughter Marguerite sat nearby, elbows on the table, her face in her fists. As usual she was reading Nellie Popp jaw droppers from the daily paper. The doll sat propped against the sugar can, her legs straight out, with her perpetual whatever-next look.

Marguerite had just given her the details about a half-man, half-ape loose in New Jersey and was looking around for something else.

" 'Rats Feed on Hands of Corpse . . .' "

"Margie!" said her mother sharply.

"Okay," said the girl with a sigh.

Crossing to the counter by the sink, Allie began chopping squash with little whipstrokes. So much for the thrill of her pregnancy. If Denton had cracked up, she thought, she was at least partly to blame. Being so wrapped up in Ham, she probably wasn't giving her children enough attention. God only knew what was going on in their minds.

"Here's one!" Marguerite said. " 'Four Sisters Are Insane.' "

Allie looked up.

" 'Puckett Falls, Iowa,' " the girl proclaimed. " 'The record for insanity cases in this state was broken yesterday when Emma, Martha, Lizzie, and Mary Slater, maiden sisters, whose ages range from thirty-five to fifty years, were all brought before the county commission, charged with being insane.

" 'The sisters have complained that the community was conspiring against them; that by using spirit voices and gramophones, the neighbors were accusing them of being Negroes and otherwise humiliating them.

" 'The commission found the sisters insane. They have appealed to the district court.' "

Marguerite leaned over and babbled something confidential to Nellie Popp, while Allie stared at her daughter, strangely stricken. Of course she had told Margie, as she'd told everyone, that Denton's shooting had been a terrible accident. But did

Margie believe that? She seemed like such a sturdy little child, but a brother's attempted suicide, that could act on anyone like a slow poison.

Allie got supper ready while Marguerite wrung the paper dry of news: the maiden who had perished in flames, the baby carted off by an anaconda. Finally the little girl was closing up the paper.

"Guess that's it," she said. "Whoops!" She flattened it out again.

" 'DRIVEN INSANE BY CIGARETTES . . . Coffee and cigarettes were too much for twenty-five-year-old David Scofield of Chicago, who was committed yesterday to the lunatic asylum in Kankakee . . .' "

Allie threw down her cooking spoon and walked to the window, where she pressed the back of her hand against the cool of the rain-lashed glass.

13

L YING DULLY IN BED, Denton spent the first week or so of
his recovery engaged in a theoretical exercise: trying to dream
up a more humiliating suicide attempt. He couldn't do it. The
prize was his forever. Only the opium compound that Dr. Porter
was dosing him with for the surging pain near his right shoulder,
only this, Denton knew, was keeping him from feeling the exqui-
site shame of what he'd done in the very marrow of his bones.

Leaving aside for the moment the nakedness and the poop—
as if he ever could—Denton knew he was only alive right now
because he was such a bungler. The bullet had missed his heart
by six inches.

Under the circumstances this only made him feel worse. That,
and the fright that had been whispering through him ever since
he came to. What scared him was that he couldn't remember
deciding to pull the trigger.

Denton lay with a fixed glare now, trying to hypnotize himself with the design on the wallpaper. He barely heard the sounds of others moving through the house, the footsteps, the muted thumps, even his father's noisy arrival in the downstairs hall. Link came up at once and peered at the patient, fluttered over him (to the boy's mind) like an old maid, then disappeared. Denton didn't even react when his mother came tiptoeing in that night to tell him that she and his father had just been on the telephone with someone at the Five Oaks sanitarium, who would be coming in a couple of days to give him a sort of checkup.

At week's end, there he stood on the doorstep. Chubby, bald as a baby, Dr. Busby was an alienist, a staff specialist in mental disorders who had traveled down from Five Oaks some sixty miles by train. Allie's first impression, once she got him indoors, was that Dr. Busby might have been one of the patients sent to them by mistake. The way he sat squeezing his hands and looking about the parlor, shyly enthralled, his delighted stare when he discovered magazines on the tea table, and his immoderate gratitude for the snack she served ("Is this *cheese?*" he said), all suggested that the doctor hadn't been off the grounds of the institution in a very long time.

Still, he appealed to Allie, in a motherly sort of way—though when he dusted the crumbs off his fingers and opened his notebook, it gave her a palpable chill. Dr. Busby sat, pen poised, looking at them both expectantly. Nobody spoke. He snapped the notebook shut.

"You know what?" he cried. "Why don't I just run up and see the boy."

And almost before Allie realized what was happening, he was gone, springing nimbly up the stairs.

Ten minutes later he was down again. He announced that their son would be right as rain, subject to a full course of rest and treatment at Five Oaks. Allie was dazed at the lightning diagnosis. She and Link were both grateful, though. The way Dr. Busby stood there dabbing at his neck with a handkerchief, he looked even more relieved than they.

"Well," said the doctor.

Link asked if he'd like to stay for dinner. The children, he said, were off at their cousins' for the day. Dr. Busby accepted with an almost pathetic alacrity. This puzzled Allie further, but there was no doubt about it when the doctor sat down: if he'd been pleased with the cheese, he was plainly overjoyed to be looking at a full-course meal.

"So, Dr. Busby," said Link, reaching for the iced tea, "how long have you been working at Five Oaks?"

"Hm?" The doctor was gazing at his plate, utterly absorbed, as if he had just seen something move.

"How long have you been on staff?"

"Oh, years . . . Years and years . . ." Dr. Busby leaned over his dinner, giving his face a steam.

For the next half hour the alienist packed away the groceries, pausing now and again to look up at Allie with eyes of bright melancholy. He kept deflecting their questions about Denton as if opinions really weren't his department. On the subject of Five Oaks itself, though, he was very much otherwise, giving them a sturdy little lecture on its many fine features. It was a little unnerving, Allie thought, the way he went on and on about the place—the grounds, the staff, the cure rate—the whole time he was eating hand over fist.

"Yes yes yes," said Dr. Busby, munching, and slathering another biscuit, "an excellent place. More like a home than a hospital. And over time we'll do wonderful things for your boy. You see, at Five Oaks we believe in a regimen of fresh air and drugs. . . . Did I say drugs? Exercise. Fresh air and exercise. And drugs, of course, whenever possible. Necessary. Did you make this jam? It's delicious . . ."

That did it. After that all Link and Allie wanted was to get him out of the house. They had almost managed it: Dr. Busby was in the hallway with his briefcase in his hand, burbling to Link about the patient mix. Stealing glances at Allie while he talked. Itemizing her, she thought wearily. Shy men were always peekers. Go home.

"Anyway, what I'm getting to," Dr. Busby said, turning to include Allie in the conversation, "of all the kinds of folks who come for treatment, who do you suppose we see the most of? And I don't just mean our own establishment. The same's true in every asylum in Indiana." His pudgy face became pinker, oddly triumphant. "It's not the criminally insane or the hopeless alcoholics or the ones who think they're the king of Siam. Who do you think the largest group of mentally disturbed people is?"

"I have no idea," Allie said.

"Farm wives." The doctor's head bobbed vigorously. "That's right. More farm wives go crazy in Indiana than anybody else." Dr. Busby sighed with wonder, gave a big shrug, and then turned and went away. That's what Allie remembered, long after she had rid the house of him, and long after Denton had recovered from his wound and was out of bed again. She would think of all the women beaten down by farm life, by the loneliness and crushing labor. She didn't feel so fragile as to fear that she would join them, but it haunted her to know that they were there.

LINK AND ALLIE didn't send their son anywhere, as it turned out, and not just because of the distressing Dr. Busby. In the days that followed, Denton (perhaps shaken up by his visit) climbed a rung or two out of his funk. He talked, started feeding himself with his left hand, and even gave Allie an abashed smile. She felt cautiously relieved. Sticking him in an institution was the last thing she wanted to do.

But the question remained: What in the world could she and Link do for this bleak boy? Glum and underoccupied, Denton shuffled from room to room in his bathrobe now, like a ghost's understudy. And now that he was up and about, of course, he had to make trips to the outhouse again. Somehow in the tumble of events Allie hadn't thought of this before. Day after day, again and again, her son would have to revisit the site of the terrible act. Denton put a good face on it, but both of them knew she couldn't help watching him through the window as he made his way there along the path.

One afternoon Allie and Ham lay side by side in the Hales' bedroom. Link had taken Denton out for an airing over to Mama Dillon's, and the lovers had snatched the opportunity. They were resting together now, and Allie was worrying aloud about her boy.

She talked for a long time, till she ran out of gas. Then the lovers lay without speaking for a while. Allie studied the great frames of light falling on the thin quilt that covered them—red, indigo, aqua, rose, all fired by the sunshine.

"Why don't you have him come live with us," Ham said.

It took a moment or two for his voice to penetrate. Allie rolled her head to the side and stared at him.

"Honey, he's fourteen years old. He's ashamed. Having his mother hovering around him, worrying him to death, that's only going to aggravate things." Ham laughed with pleasure at her wondering face. "You watch, I can make something out of that boy," he said.

"That's what Dr. Busby told us," Allie replied. But once again Ham had rolled the stone from her heart.

So Denton Hale went to live on the Dillon farm. He needed no persuading at all. Embers of light came into his eyes the moment Allie proposed it to him, and before the week was out he was installed in the Dillons' best guest room. There on the wall he found a present to welcome him: a framed photograph of the Wright Brothers at Kitty Hawk, courtesy of Ham.

Link returned to Kentucky, which was a great relief to him. There seemed to be nothing left between him and Denton but an unconquerable awkwardness. As the two brothers-in-law shook hands, Link told Ham how sincerely grateful he was.

Before Link left town though, there was the matter of what to do about the Hales' outhouse. The whole family hated it, so they decided to tear it down. Link said he felt a little foolish, knocking down a perfectly good outhouse and then putting up another one out by the walnut grove. But even so, everyone was glad when it was done.

14

THE BABY, Allie and Ham's, was born in early February 1907. A day or two before, when it was plain that Allie was about due, Maggie showed up at the Hale house and took over. She sewed newspapers together and spread them out on the bed, and topped them with old sheets and muslin from her own attic. She shooed the hired girl out of the kitchen and made the meals. Allie, in dismay, kept telling her all this wasn't necessary, but Maggie wasn't listening. When she insisted on staying in the room for the delivery, Allie asked Dr. Porter for chloroform.

After the birth she had to spend ten days in bed since Dr. Porter believed, like most medical men, that it took that long for the mother's organs to slide back in place. So Maggie was still popping in and out, doing little things, trying hard to be a good sister. It was she who dropped Link a line two days after the baby's birth, letting him know the happy news:

Dear Link,

I know you will be pleased to know that the baby has come and that it is a fine big twelve-pound boy with black hair and it looks like my daughter, Dorothy. Allie says you need not hurry home.

Now the letter lay on his kitchen table.

Link sat by, a knuckle to his lips, lost in meditation. Finally he reached over, picked up the page and read it through again. Then he tossed it back, where it landed with a whisper atop the rest of his mail.

He lifted his eyes to the spear of candlelight burning loyally beside him.

"Twelve-pound boy . . . need not hurry . . ."

He wasn't agitated. His mind was only lightly engaged, the way it might have been by a word puzzle in the paper. He had been expecting the baby later on, that was all, in late March or early April. Allie had never quite said so, but he'd just assumed . . .

Maybe it was premature. Babies were sometimes. But Link had never heard of a premature twelve-pound baby.

He sat back, thinking more seriously now, trying to reconstruct his visits to Indiana the previous spring and summer. It was easy for him. He knew the various dates; he knew, within a couple of days, when he and his wife had had relations. Probably most men wouldn't have been so sure, but Link had always had a head for numbers, a shopkeeper's mind for details. At the distillery where he worked, it was his job to keep the accounts.

Not a jealous man so much as automatically precise.

Twelve pounds. That was a huge baby. His other five children had come in between six and nine.

Something came to his mind, it didn't find words, but it made him flinch like a cigarette burn. Then he got to his feet and

headed toward the bedroom looking for his old medical books—
the ones he'd bought when he planned to be a doctor. Maybe he
could find something to explain this.

S O BEGAN THE CAVE WINDS of fear and misery that
would last a full year and a half. In all this time Link never
spoke a word, not to Allie, not to anyone, about what was bothering him, even when it reached the edge of mania. *I'm not sure*, he
said to himself. *I don't have any proof. What if I'm wrong?*

He got his first look at the newborn when it was about three
weeks old, at the end of February, when he came to Elnora. Both
couples—Allie and Link, Maggie and Ham—were gathered in
the Hales' cozy bedroom, four giants looming over the gurgling
baby. Its big blue-gray eyes wandered, fixed on nothing. Link
touched its rubbery little cheek.

"He's got a head the size of a medicine ball," Ham remarked.

Allie, standing next to her brother-in-law, smacked his arm.
"That's not nice," she said. "You'll hurt his little feelings."

"Sorry," said Ham. He laughed.

"It's not exactly a compliment to me," she added.

"Or to me," said Link.

Allie looked over at her husband, who stood on the other side
of the bassinet. "That's right," she said. "Or to you."

They had dinner downstairs that night, the Hales and the
Dillons together, with all the loud talk and tableclatter of a happy
reunion. Ham regaled them with yarns he'd picked up here and
there from his constituents. He facetiously offered Link his old
job back. He also said there were a couple of good investment
properties he had his eye on and asked if Link might be interested in going partners.

"Are you going to talk business at the dinner table?" said
Maggie. She was on her feet clearing the plates. "Because if you
do, you won't get dessert."

"You're right, you're right." Ham sat back, big surrender, his palms at his shoulders. He was enjoying himself pretty well, even with Link there; what hypocrisy mostly requires is getting into a groove, and with Ham it was as much a habit now as getting up at five to do the milking. Link's mind was running on a couple of tracks. First, he was curious what these investments were his brother-in-law was touting. At the same time, he was wondering if Ham might be the father of the baby.

Of course, it had flashed through Link's mind that very first night he got Maggie's letter. Flashed through and disappeared. Link had no special reason to suspect him, then or now. He had never seen Ham and Allie in a single doubtful moment, and in the past couple of weeks he had thought about it hard.

Still, that baby. Why had Maggie written that it looked like her own daughter? No, newborns all looked alike; it was only women who thought otherwise. He glanced at his wife. Allie seemed a little wound up tonight, but then she'd always been bottled lightning.

His mind went on chattering like a telegraph key.

Back at the table, Maggie was passing out dessert, slabs of blackberry cobbler oozing a warm indigo sauce. ("I'd use a spoon with that if I were you," Ham told Link, handing a plate across.) Then Maggie crossed to the sideboard and came back with a small silver tray. On it were a chiseled crystal decanter of brandy and four thick-bottomed little glasses.

"Time we toasted the newborn," she said, "now that everybody's finally here."

Of course! Ham poured out the liquor, and they clinked glasses. "To Allie and Link" . . . "To the baby" . . . "To Number Six" . . . This was more like it. The way the light hit the liquor, and the smiles all around, were balm to Link's soul. Allie looked so beautiful to him then, so pleased and girlish, that for the moment he could only gaze at her with pale pride.

"Number Six. Sounds like we're christening a locomotive," said Ham as he set his glass down with a thunk.

"That's right. What in the world are you going to name him?" Maggie asked her sister. "It's three weeks, for heaven's sake."

"I was waiting for Link to get here," Allie said. Smiling, she leaned over and patted her husband's arm.

"Well, get on with it," said Maggie tartly.

"Ah yes, a name," said Ham. He pushed his lips out, looking thoughtful, as he leaned around refilling their glasses. "Five kids already, I don't know. You've used up all the best ones."

"Ice cream!" Maggie cried. "Good gracious, I forgot it! Who wants ice cream?"

The men raised their hands. She flung down her napkin and vanished into the kitchen.

"We could name him after my boss," Link said to his wife. "David Noble, at the distillery."

"Here's an idea," said Ham. "Why don't you name him after me?"

In the silence that followed he gazed at their faces, each in turn. "What?" he said.

"You want us to name him after you?" Allie said, barely on her voice.

"Why not?" he said. Maggie came in from the kitchen carrying bowls. "If you do, I might do something for him down the road. Honey," he said, addressing his wife, "I think they're fighting me here."

"What about?"

"He wants us to name the baby after him," Allie said.

"After you? Ham Hale?" Maggie shook it off like a wasp. "What a ridiculous name. What's the matter with you?" She sat back down.

Ham kept his smile, but his body stiffened. "My real name, darlin'."

"What? Albert Hamlet?"

"I was thinking along the lines of . . . Albert Dillon Hale."
Maggie looked dubious.

"Okay," said Ham, "what do you want to call him?"

"It's not up to me."

"That's right." He swung back around to the Hales as Allie
stared at him, transfixed. She felt as if she had never known Ham
before.

"A peacock's not enough for you?" Maggie said.

"So what do you say?" Ham was eyeing Link, all lazy good
nature.

Link, who hadn't spoken yet, still didn't know what to say.
But then he had the most remarkable feeling.

Later on he would feel like a rabbit hypnotized by a snake.
But at that moment, as he looked into the humorous warmth of
Ham's eyes, what Link felt was a rush of gratitude. With this
gesture, so utterly frank, so direct, Ham had exploded all fear. He
was offering love instead. Any other explanations went bounding
off into the woods.

"Sounds okay to me," said Link. He gave a long, tremulous
sigh. Then he turned to his wife. "What do you think?"

Allie had drawn erect in her chair, her body so taut it had the
look of great strength.

"I think it's a good idea," Allie said.

And so the baby became Albert Dillon Hale. They sealed it
with another toast.

15

LINK SPENT most of that summer back in Kentucky, except
for a couple of quick visits. The weevil of doubt crept back into
his heart, particularly regarding the size of the baby; those hands
looked as if they could strangle serpents. But his worrying was
buried by thousands of daily details, and by Allie's warm, wifely
letters from Indiana. If he was despondent sometimes, well, he
had always been despondent sometimes. Even he himself could
hardly tell the difference.

In late September, driven by sheer loneliness, he came for an
extended visit—a couple of months, he told Allie, possibly till
Christmas. Albert Dillon Hale was nearly eight months old now.
The night he arrived, Link slipped into the bedroom alone, crept
up to the crib, and peeked in. Just like before, the same gray little
ritual. But this time his first thought was: the baby was the
spitting image of Ham Dillon.

In the next breath he denied it. He told himself he must be hallucinating his worst fear. But that fat little face taunted him. Along with its blue-gray eyes and black hair (already the match of Ham's), there was something else in its expression now, a terrible touch of humor.

No, no, it was impossible. Link paced the room. He had crossed the bridge into hell now, and the bridge was burning: no longer could he call for relief on all those comforting memories from the early years with Allie; no longer get by in that hover-state between knowing and not knowing. Now he knew.

Still he insisted to himself he did not know.

Later that week, to celebrate Link's arrival, Ham took Maggie and the Hales to see the vaudeville show at the Teatro, the big legit house on Main Street in Washington. He appeared on Link's porch waving a newspaper buoyantly to show them the lineup of attractions: Prince Shaman the Persian aerialist, Signor Blitz and his spinning plates, the Tozer Twins, star after star, human, ca-nine, feline, flea, but the coup de grace, Ham told them, the ne plus ultra, would be the fabulous Cherry Sisters, a singing trio who confidently billed themselves as "America's Worst Act."

Ham had seen the Cherry Sisters before, so he knew just what to do. When Maggie went looking for him around five o'clock, to tell him they'd have to start for town soon, she found him out behind the house with a big basket over his arm poring through the compost heap for rotten vegetables. He looked as finicky as an Italian grandmother on market day, sniffing, squeezing, holding them up to the light. Maggie walked back to the house shaking her head.

A little while later the Dillons arrived at the Hales' house to pick them up, but when Ham got one look at Link, he sprang from the buggy. "No, no, no," he cried, and Link had the familiar sensation of being physically propelled by his brother-in-law, this time straight upstairs and into his own bedroom, where Ham stripped off Link's go-to-meeting coat. "You don't want to be wearing that," he said, and went rummaging in the closet. "Here!" He yanked out an old denim jacket. "Put this on. You'll thank me." Then he crossed to the window and called down into the yard, where Maggie and Allie were waiting in the buggy.

"Honey?"

They both looked up.

"Did you bring any towels?"

By the time they settled into their seats the Teatro was filling up fast. On a big easel in front of the curtain stood a poster board listing the attractions, which Ham scanned, fascinated, while muttering asides to his wife. Link peered about in the thick brown light, amid the growing cigar smoke and whiffs of garbage, watching people organizing and trading ammunition. Allie sat beside him and didn't say a word.

It was past seven-thirty now. The crowd began stamping their feet. A rumor was flashing around that the headliner, Prince Shaman, was pulling an Achilles, off sulking in his dressing room because of the Cherry Sisters, who not only upstaged him but also left him prey to the odd tomato.

But finally the gaslights that sprouted from the sides of the proscenium flared on; a disembodied arm reached out to snatch the easel. There was a cymbal crash from the pit. Then the fire curtain shot up and the Rossow tumbling midgets came rolling onstage like oranges. Ham leaned forward with a reverential face. Link looked mournfully at Allie's profile, then pointed his eyes at the stage.

For a while the midgets agitated his cornea, he didn't know exactly how long, but finally they retired and some cakewalkers came on. Then dogs of some kind. Obligingly Link joined in the gusts of laughter and applause.

At last somebody bowed and bounded off, the clapping died and the air filled with excited muttering. It was time for the last act before intermission. Link noticed Ham dragging his basket from underneath his seat.

There was another flourish from the pit band and then a tall figure in a yellow jacket and oversized red bow tie materialized from the wings. He stood at the lip of the stage down right, with his hands at his back, surveying the crowd with a look of boyish impudence. Behind him a large fishing net began to unscroll.

"Ladies and gentlemen!" he cried. "Good evening! On behalf of the beauteous, the celestial Cherry Sisters, America's Worst Act! Here tonight following their successful escape from Europe"—he held for the laugh—"and the finest theaters in Boston, New York, Philadelphia! The Cherry Sisters! Delighted to be performing tonight in Washington, Indiana!"

Delirium.

"There are just one or two things . . . thank you . . . one or two things I've been asked to put you in mind of before our sirens of song appear. First, for the benefit of those of you who may never have had the chance to enjoy these warblers in the flesh as it were, we ask everyone please to refrain from hurling anything whatsoever till after their opening number."

An eggplant missed his head by inches.

"Thank you very much." He bowed. "The Cherry Sisters rely on you absolutely. Second"—a tomato came rifling toward his body but, producing a tennis racket from behind his back, the young man whipped a forehand that sent juice and pulp spraying over half the crowd. "Second," he cried, louder, "and most sincerely, we ask that you refrain from throwing anything, and we mean anything, that you'd mind being hit with yourself. Thank you all for coming!" He bowed again and vanished stage right, chased by a few desultory vegetables.

Now the lights, which had dimmed, flared once more, and the Cherry Sisters made their entrance from the side, stepping daintily onstage behind their vast screen of net. One by one they turned and faced the roaring audience. They were perhaps not the youngest of women, but they were plump and pretty in the

Gibson style and dressed to the nines: plumed like musketeers, adorned with boas, gowned in velveteen. With royal hauteur they inclined their heads slightly while the barbarians adored them. Then they folded their hands and awaited quiet.

The middle sister, the tallest, nodded her head for an arpeggio from the pit. Then she lifted her head and emitted:

"I'm only a bird in a gilded cage, a beautiful sight to see . . ."

Link, jacked into a state of excitement by all the buildup, felt an astonishing sense of anticlimax. The girl's singing wasn't bad. It wasn't good either. She possessed the kind of fruity soprano to be heard in thousands of American parlors. Cautiously he checked the audience. They were poised like hunters, holding their fire.

She reached the end of the opening chorus without incident and started again at the top. That's when the other two ladies, their faces mournfully melodious, joined in, in competing keys:

"You may think she's happy and free from care, She's not, though she seems to be . . ."

They sounded like cats with their tails tied together. The audience cried out with pleasure.

" 'Tis sad when you think of her wasted life, For youth cannot mate with age . . ."

Next moment the air was a blizzard of rutabagas, eggs, tomatoes, squash—a merciless horizontal salad. Somebody lofted a live chicken, which landed squawking and flapping at the front of the stage, recovered itself with huffed dignity, but an instant later was sprinting for cover under the hail of pelting produce.

"And her beauty was sold, For an old man's gold, She's a bird in a gilded cage. . . ."

Anything hard or unripe bounced off the tight netting; everything else shredded and spattered. The sisters took it in the legs, the chest, the face, but sang right on, like martyrs in an opera.

Link glanced to his left. Ham was on his feet, firing tomatoes with murderous precision. Allie was flinging things with both hands. Maggie had a tube at her mouth firing grapes. Catching sight of Link, who was just sitting there, she rooted around in the basket and thrust a sopping peach into his hand.

"Go on!" she cried.

Groping up out of his seat, Link threw it, sort of, sideways toward the stage. He caught a fellow down front in the back of the head, but the man was so busy himself he didn't seem to notice. Maggie passed something else. Link threw that. The next time he took aim and produced a sudden bright stain on one of the trio. Then he dived into the basket.

He couldn't throw fast enough. When he ran out of things he began snatching them from other people and hurling those. And when the imperturbable Cherry Sisters, their faces and clothes in ruins, finally glided majestically from the stage, Link was still lunging around for things to throw. There was no telling how long he might have gone on if Ham hadn't stepped in and pinioned his arms.

A FTER THAT NIGHT Link's chief occupation was morbidly studying the baby. He watched it sleeping, watched it at play. Sometimes he got down on his hands and knees in front of it— blocked its way as it came slap-crawling across the carpet. Once he put a handkerchief on his head to hold its attention so he could study the little face better. Visitors thought him a picture of the doting father.

He was trying to fix precisely the resemblance between the baby and Ham Dillon—unless he was trying to do the opposite, as he often was, hunting its face for some resemblance to him to drive the goblins out of his mind. But of course the more he searched, the less he knew. He would stand over the crib fighting an impulse to grab little Albert and shake the truth out of him, while the baby looked up with his little wet tongue out, full of idiot trust.

Allie could see Link was in distress. Halfheartedly she asked him what was wrong. But she wasn't really interested. She'd been keeping up the pretense of being a loving wife so long, she was starting to bend with the strain. She struggled with herself over this, tried to dredge up a little saving hypocrisy. But she couldn't manage it. In spirit she was yoked to Ham now, and she had no stomach for this gloomy little man who kept showing up at the breakfast table with his kick-me face. Allie was so alienated she assumed, naturally, that all the estrangement was on her side. She knew her coldness must be troubling him, but she never seriously doubted her secret was still safe.

They squabbled. Link began to make oblique remarks and dark hints. "You're letting Ham and Maggie come between us!" he shouted one night as she was leaving to visit the Dillons; it was as close as he could come to an accusation, and even this left him out of breath. Allie looked down at him from the buggy, the reins in her hand, little Albert Dillon Hale snug in a basket at her feet. "You're getting excited over nothing," she said, and drove off. Link was at his wits' end. He tried everything to please her. After Allie told him one night, in an offhand way, that he'd look more manly with a mustache, he started growing one the next day. "It's nice," she said.

His one support in this dark stretch was his oldest daughter, Louise, now seventeen. Like a lot of girls who read novels and played the piano, Louise was a little too poetically anemic, a little too given to fainting spells. But she loved her father, not just sentimentally but sincerely; she honored his struggles in life in a way that others—Denton, for example—never had; and her Emily Dickinson manner masked an ever-watchful eye. She wasn't sure what was troubling her father, but she could make a cool guess. She had never forgotten coming home from school and finding her mother and Uncle Ham leaving the bedroom. Ever since, just looking at Allie quietly was enough to put her in a flutter.

Why, oh why, wouldn't her father confide in her? But it wasn't Louise's place to bring it up.

The only one who made an active effort was Ham. He didn't think there was any danger of discovery; after three years of adultery, it was practically the status quo. But he could see well enough that Link felt depressed and left out, and that wasn't good for anybody. One way or another, Allie kept bringing it to bed.

So once again Ham got Link out of the house. They attended meetings of the Masons together. Ham complimented Link on his new mustache. They shot pool.

Finally, in January, Link went back to Kentucky. He sat in the coach, listless, while the train pulled him out of town like a vaudeville hook.

16

MARCH 1908. Mad-sky season. The time of year when starlings would go tearing across the open sky, hit the brakes together, then wheel and shoot off in some other direction, here and there and back in a frenzy. Why they acted this way nobody really knew. Of course farmers had an explanation for it—they had an explanation for everything, just like the Greeks had mythology—but that didn't mean you ought to believe it. Allie stood at her window, gazing up at a flock of them caught in this lunatic zigzag, wondering what they were so frightened of. It took her a while to realize they might be enjoying themselves.

She'd been looking into the future of late—her future—and she was appalled by what she saw: the blank of a March sky. They had survived and endured; they loved each other; they had a child now, a year old. But Ham, with the roots of an oak, was not about to run off and leave his wife. Her sister. Though he was lying on the bed behind her now, he'd be gone again shortly.

She was so used to the dull ache of envying Maggie it was like an old injury that tells the weather.

"I listen in on that party line," she said.

"What?"

"I sit in the kitchen sometimes on that little stool. Just take the receiver down and listen to the gossip. I keep waiting to hear something about us."

"Better ways to spend your time," said Ham, who lay on his back under a sheet. He shifted and stretched one leg like a chicken wing. "We're family. We're supposed to be seen together. I've told you that how often?"

"You think everybody's stupid but you," she said.

Ham grunted. He wasn't in the mood for squabbling. All he wanted was to rest his head on this doubled-up pillow and let his eyes slide along the back of this woman, wrapped in a robe: his Austerlitz, his Waterloo. Her reddish hair a little browner now, a little browner every year.

"Come here, honey." He stuck out an arm.

She turned at the window, staring at him. "God!" she cried. "That smile. I see it in my dreams. Don't you ever . . . ? Or do we just go on like this for years and years till we all fall down dead? Is that your plan?"

"Aw, come on."

"Oh!" She brought her hands to her head. "Don't you get sick of it? Going around feeling like two different people?"

"I don't know what you're talking about."

She laughed at him. "Yes, you do."

"Well, well," said Ham, lazing. "There's gratitude for you."

"Gratitude?"

"Sure. Come on, honey, think about it. I saved you from . . ."

"Saved me!"

He knew it would make her pop like a firecracker. But then

he'd always figured that when a woman was determined to get mad, she'd get mad regardless.

"You saved me!" she cried. "And what did I do?"

"When?"

"What did I do for you?"

He could have said she'd saved him too, but he wasn't in the mood.

Allie crossed and sat on the edge of a chair, turned away from him.

"I am so ashamed," she said.

"Shame's good. Puts color in your cheeks," he answered. He had gone round and round with her about this for years, they'd talked about all the rights and wrongs six ways from Sunday, and it always came back to this with her, this goddamn self-punishing thing. Of course, it had its upside. There were times—especially early on—when her guiltiness had touched him, charmed him even, brought out a coaxing tenderness he didn't know he possessed. It still fueled the sex too, now and then.

But other times it just backed up like a drain.

"Sometimes," Allie said, "I think the only reason I let you come here is I feel guilty if I don't."

"What?"

They sat in silence.

"Saved me," she said.

"Honey—"

"How could you have married her?" Allie said softly. Then in a wild new tone: "How can you stand it, staying with her?"

"No, no . . ."

"Don't you have eyes? Don't you see how she acts? The way she treats your children? She's so cold-blooded."

"Cold-blooded!" Ham floundered up in the bed. "Is that so? Well then, just what would you call us?"

That stopped her. It was terrific. He'd thought this often enough before, and it was great to finally get it out. The thousands of lies he had told his wife and friends—and would go right on telling, if it meant he could be with this woman. . . . These past three years he'd learned a lot about ruthlessness. At least as much as he had about love. Amazing really, how the more his passion for Allie had grown, the more the temperature of his blood had dropped.

Aloud he said, "Why don't we stop talking about my wife?"

She raised her head, and he saw those beautiful gray eyes luminous with fear. He understood it. It was the same fear he had himself.

"Leave me," she said. She crossed to the edge of the bed, sat down beside him, and took his hand. "Please leave me."

He didn't say anything.

She leaned in and kissed his cheek. "Leave me." His mouth. "You have to." She pressed against him, kissing his face, here, there, a sad laughter mixed with her pleading. He slid onto his back. "Come on, precious," she said. "You can do it. I'll love you so much if you do."

TWO DAYS LATER Allie wrote her husband that she was selling their house in Elnora and returning to Kentucky with the children. She told him to be on the lookout for a new home in Nicholasville, something big enough for them all.

Ham was taken aback when he first heard, but he didn't protest. That was Allie: make the grand gesture and live to regret it. Well, maybe it would be a useful experiment. Meanwhile he could use the vacation.

He handled the sale of the house—which brought a six-hundred-dollar profit—and stored a promissory note for the money, along with some other financial papers of Link's, in the bank in Washington for safekeeping.

Meanwhile Link purchased a newly furnished home in Nicholasville on Broadway, a fine old street where houses hunkered in the shade of maple and locust trees. The family arrived bag and baggage on April 24, 1908. When Allie first wrote she was coming home, he'd had a great lifting of heart, and the day the whole crew came trooping up the front steps laughing and hugging him, it was everything he'd dreamed. The only sour note was the baby, Albert Dillon Hale. Link had almost managed to forget about him, but here he was again—bigger now, and still looking up with those alien eyes.

17

THREE AND A HALF months later, on the evening of Saturday, August 8, the only motorized taxi in Nicholasville came
sputtering through the peaceful, night-shaded streets, bearing its
last fare. It was past 11 P.M., so aside from the lights blooming in
one or two saloons there wasn't much to see. Even so, the passengers in the back seat both sat forward, peering out in opposite
directions as if they had never seen such trees or storefronts or
lampposts in their lives before. It was the first ride in an auto that
Ham and Maggie had ever paid for, and this somehow boosted
the interest of every object going by.

The taxi turned off the main road onto Broadway, a boulevard
of good-sized homes half screened by thick trees. Ham was taken
aback. They lived along here? He hadn't pictured the Hales doing
nearly this well. Soon the vehicle jolted to a stop in front of a

broad clapboard house with a number on it. Ham could see a dim glow behind the parlor curtains, but otherwise the place was dark.

He and Maggie got out of the car and headed up the walkway, followed by the taxi driver carrying some of the luggage and Maggie's hatbox. In the warm night the only sound was the sinister squeak of his shoes.

Ham knuckle-tapped on the frosted oval of glass.

The door was flung open. Link was there, the lower part of his face lifting his droopy mustache—he was probably smiling—and Allie right behind him, and alongside her Louise, their oldest daughter. The welcome was all hearty stage whispers so as not to wake the children upstairs. The men shook hands, the sisters hugged. Louise slipped eel-like in and out of her uncle's arms. Then Ham saw Allie stepping toward him out of the cloud of time. All of a sudden he remembered her: those vitalizing fingers pressing his shoulder blades, the miraculous way their bodies fit together.

Ham paid the driver. Then, under Link's guiding arm, the Dillons went inside.

IF IT HADN'T BEEN for Maggie, there's no telling when they would have gotten together. She had been the driving force behind this visit. For Maggie was a dreamer in her own steely way; just as she had devoted herself to Ham's grand public future, so regaining her sister's confidence had become another consuming long-term project. She was determined to succeed at it. Guilt over some of the recent past, nostalgia, loneliness, all these fed a rushing stream which might have stayed frozen up forever if Allie hadn't come to live in Indiana.

Their first afternoon together, a Sunday, the Dillons and Hales sat on the porch with jangling glasses of lemonade, catching little breaths of breeze and swapping news. Albert, the baby, sat on the floor in their midst, the soles of his plump feet touching, smacking two blocks together. Link kept glancing at Ham to see if he took any particular interest in the infant, but he didn't seem to.

Instead, lounging in a white wicker armchair, Ham talked merrily of politics. The 1908 presidential campaign was well underway—William Howard Taft, Teddy Roosevelt's handpicked man, against the windy populist William Jennings Bryan. Ham was mocking the Republican, Taft—not so much for weighing three hundred pounds as for trying to act as if he didn't. Just recently, before the assembled press, Taft had climbed aboard a horse to show off his riding skills and crushed the beast flat.

"Your man Bryan's going to have himself a tough time in this state," Link said. "A teetotaler in Kentucky's about as popular as nothing."

"Well now, you're a teetotaler yourself there," Ham said, with that wink. "Aren't you, brother?"

Link flushed.

"He's not talking about himself," Allie said sharply. "Link's got plenty of friends." (Loyal to Link! She'd surprised herself. But she was fighting a wave of hostility toward Ham for being there at all.)

"Sure, I know," said Ham easily. "Everybody likes Link. Sorry, brother."

Link waved it off. Though as a nondrinker working at a licensed distillery, he did brood sometimes about all the people who didn't like him—anybody who owned a still, and most members of the temperance movement.

The talk looped around to Ham's own political prospects. Link was surprised to learn that his brother-in-law, the perpetual golden boy, wasn't running for the state legislature after all; somebody had actually beaten him out for the nomination for Padgett's seat.

"Course, Padgett told me that day in Indianapolis there was some other bird might wind up with it," Ham said. "Somebody's no-account relative." He was leaning forward, elbows on his knees, toying with his glass. "At first they wanted to make him head of the Sweeping and Sprinkling Inspectors, stick him off where he couldn't do any harm. But it's like all these other dog-gone jobs now—they've all gone civil service."

"So he's running for office instead?" asked Allie.

"It's the only thing left if you're completely unqualified," Maggie said.

Ham gave a yawp of laughter.

"You're taking this pretty well, Uncle Ham," Louise Hale said quietly. She sat erect and severe, like a medieval icon, her thin body edged in sun. "I mean, I'd have thought you'd be disappointed."

"Well, as to that," said Ham, and he shook the last of his lemonade and took a rattling swig, "maybe it's all for the best. Padgett's telling me now he thinks I can wangle the congressional nomination in '10. Says he and the fellas will back me all the way. And I'll tell you what, if I make it to Washington, you've seen the last of this old boy."

Smiling at Louise, he caught Allie's eye. His grin stayed the same size, but lost its relationship to the rest of his face.

THEY'D TALKED about maybe going to the Blue Grass Fair up in Lexington, but when the moment came to start out, on Monday morning, nobody was all that keen. The cross-slop of emotions among them, all unspoken, the constant watchfulness, had combined to produce a curious failure of will; together, the four couldn't decide what they wanted to do. When they finally set out for a drive in Link's surrey, it was still with no sure destination.

The air was dusty and flecked with bugs, the sky the color of skim milk. Drawn by a sluggish bay, the vehicle rattled by stands of sunflowers, their heads bowed like supplicants in the heat; broad fields of hemp; patches of lemon-colored tobacco plants sprouting out of the cracked black soil.

Having lost a very brief struggle with herself—it was over by yesterday—Allie now wanted Ham. Craved him. Not quite like before: riding in the buggy she found her old, soul-filling passion for him reduced to a hard glitter, a kind of animal alertness while she tracked his every word. Her marriage, that was an unburied corpse. All summer (how in the world had she survived it?) she had watched Link grow more and more furtive and depressed, seen him come into full midnight flower . . .

They stopped in town to pick up cigars for Ham. As he bantered with the salesgirl behind the counter, Allie lingered unhappily a few feet away—just like that day at the charity booth, she thought, so long ago. Link hung in the doorway waiting for them both.

Finally, for lack of anything better, they wound up going to visit the E. J. Curley Distillery, where Link worked. Allie had never seen it herself. It was beautiful there. Tucked behind a screen of willow and sycamore trees, the buildings and work yards lay just steps from the sliding green sheet of the Kentucky River. Huge limestone cliffs rose along both banks, ragged with cedar and oak and yellow jasmine. Barges of coal and grain from upriver lay docked at the distillery wharf.

Maybe it sprang from all that impacted anxiety, from chewing his liver so long. But Link bounded out of the surrey in a burst of manic hospitality. This was his domain, his turf. First he pulled them over to the wharf to view the unloadings, talking all the while; then hustled them inside the mighty main building (made of rock hewn from the nearby bluffs, it was decorated with arcane carvings and the odd gargoyle, like something out of Sir Walter Scott) and on up to the second floor. He shoved open a giant door, and Ham and the ladies were stunned by the reek of boiling bourbon.

The fermenting room. Link insisted on giving a tour, though the women stayed close to the doorway with handkerchiefs to their mouths and their eyes streaming. Even Ham, who was interested, felt the perspiration jump to his face. Link lingered over every detail—the steaming copper vats, the hissing coal furnace, the rushing grain chutes, the sweat-slicked laborers—with a malicious enthusiasm which was doing wonders for his spirits.

Finally Allie turned and floundered down the stairs. Back outside in the cottony heat, she felt almost as much relief as if she'd stepped into winter. Soon Ham and Maggie followed, arm in arm. Link came last.

They began walking down the broad dirt trail toward the barrel yard. Ham dropped back alongside Link while the women went on ahead in their perpetual rustle of skirt, their blouses sticking damply to their backs.

Using his sideways grin, Ham remarked:

"Well, I think we've finally got that boy of yours on track."

Link didn't hear at first. The unfamiliar pleasures of spite had left him a little giddy. Ham had to say it again.

"Your boy Denton."

Denton! Link had actually forgotten all about him. "Oh, yes. How's he getting along? Not too much bother, I hope."

"No, no."

The two men trudged in silence past the gray slop tanks, where katydids shrieked in the grass, while Ham considered what to say next.

The most cutting thing he could think of was that Denton wished Ham were his real father. This was true. The boy had told him so, more than once.

But Ham couldn't very well volunteer that.

"I've been teaching Denton a few things," he said at last.

"Oh? Like what?"

"Oh, a little poker. How to shoot craps."

He had half hoped for some wild objection, but Link's strangled silence was good enough.

LONG PAST MIDNIGHT, Allie lay in bed, playing possum. The sheet was in a tangle at her feet, and a rude breeze was poking around the room, investigating her nightgown. Through the open window, past the restless trees, she could see a shimmer of lightning. There was no thunder, though. No rain.

Link lay sprawled beside her, sound asleep. Unless he was pretending, same as she.

The looks had started between her and Ham. Quick as a flash sometimes. They were playing hunter and the hunted now—though just who was who kept changing. What didn't change, what was only growing stronger by the hour, was the roaring in her ears that threatened to blot out all common sense, all care of consequences. She didn't know what she might suddenly do or say, and this was making her more and more afraid.

What was that?

A sound. Was somebody moving around out there? Maybe. Or maybe it was just one of those pops and creaks of a house in the middle of the night.

All at once, she couldn't keep lying there with her mind and body aflame and her lover somewhere in the house. She had to do something. Get some air.

Warily she disengaged her feet from the bedclothes and peeled herself slowly off the mattress. She checked to see if she had disturbed her husband, but he lay just as before with his mouth open, snoring lightly. The edge of his mouth twitched.

Step by step she stole out of the room and down the dark

hallway, fingertips to the wall. Whether she was moving toward something or just away from her husband, she didn't know.

At the end of the hall she glanced to the left into the dining room. Full of spirits with their shadow meals. She took another few steps and peered the other way into the parlor. In a deep chair by the window sat a man enthroned. Smoke rose from his motionless cigar, a pure stripe that finally broke and fluttered halfway to the ceiling.

She knew it was Ham, of course, though his head was covered in a hood of darkness and he hadn't spoken a word. She crossed a few steps to the mantelpiece, found the box of matches. Lifting it carefully to keep it from rattling, she extracted a match and struck a flame.

There he sat, the incubus at his ease.

"What are you doing up?" he said.

There was nothing special in his voice, nothing eager or romantic. She felt an unhappy pang.

"What are you doing up yourself?" she said. With the guttering match she lit one of the candles on the mantel. The light in the room became pearly, opalescent.

"Lot of bugs been smacking the screen out there," Ham said, gesturing toward the sleeping porch.

"So you came in here?"

No answer.

"What are you thinking about here in the dark?" she said.

It was the first time they had been alone together since his arrival, and Allie felt robbed of breath. She was trying to look at him, to gauge his eyes, but was distracted by the votive smoke from his cigar, the way it kept rising like incense to the ceiling.

"Oh, I'm just hatching a few plots," he said. "I get some of my best thinking done in the middle of the night. My, that's a thin little thing you've got on."

She flushed, embarrassed, and turned her body to the side.

Though why should she be self-conscious around him? He seemed to be making fun of her.

"*Why did you come here . . . ?*" she began, but he interrupted her.

"So you know who I got to talking to out at the distillery?" he said, still in the same easy tone. "The blacksmith there. Nice fella. He was asking me if I'd ever seen a mule get stuck in quicksand. I said no, but I'd seen a horse in it once. Whole different thing, he tells me. How so? I asked him. Well, sir, he says . . . Hey, Link."

Allie wheeled. Link stood just behind her, his hair matted, his eyes puffed and peering.

"What's going on?" he said. His voice had a night rasp.

"That's right," said Ham. "What *is* going on? I start off sitting here having a nice, quiet smoke, and all of a sudden it's Grand Central Station."

"I was just getting some cold water," Allie told Link as she took him by the elbow. "You want some? Come on, let's go back to bed."

Ham lifted his cigar hand and scratched his eyebrow with his thumb.

"Night, folks," he said.

THURSDAY, AUGUST 13. The Hale family, with Ham and Maggie, were in the dining room finishing supper. It was about six o'clock, still full daylight.

Silent and out of sorts, Maggie sat slapping the bottom of her spoon into her pudding. Just the way she used to as a child, half preoccupied, half putting her impatience on display. All week she'd been trying to make contact with Allie, break through to some real heart-to-heart talk. She hadn't been rebuffed exactly— if anything, Allie had been rather sweet to her—but even so

Maggie knew she'd failed. One after another she had watched her earnest overtures disappear into a cloud bank.

Setting her spoon on the place mat, Maggie said: "Well, I believe I'll go write a letter to the children."

"Use my desk," said Link. "It's got everything. There in the back study."

"Thank you," she said, and departed.

The remaining adults were left to their own meditations. Then Ham's voice cut through the gabble of the children. "So you making me pancakes in the morning?" he said. Allie's head turned. He was talking to her.

She colored. Link's eyes darted back and forth between the two of them.

"Oh, I promised Ham and Maggie I'd . . ." Allie wondered if her husband could see the mischief in Ham's eye; it was plain as day to her. "You know, honey, I used to make pancakes in Indiana when . . . You like them yourself . . ." Her voice died.

Pretty soon the meal broke up. Link went out to do a little weeding in the garden. It was a good time of day for yard work. The air was cooler now, the light hard as stained glass. His children lingered, face-deep in pudding, while Louise began clearing up around them.

Ham stood up, stretched mightily, and ambled off into the parlor. A few moments later, Allie rose and followed him. Louise, lifting baby Albert out of his high chair, watched her disappear.

Out in the yard, Link carefully spread newspaper onto the grass, then knelt down and began to pick and pluck among the weeds. He let the acrid narcotic of tomato vines fill his nose and lungs, a wonderful smell; it mingled with the odor of needlepoint pine sifting down from the overhead branches. In the nearest tree sat a blue jay, half hidden, squawking in moronic rhythm like a mechanical toy. Link kept trying to relax and gather his thoughts.

But his hands didn't seem to belong to him. He was seizing weeds as if they might leap out of his way.

When he dribbled some dirt on his shirt and then smeared it, he got into a fuss about that. Too eager to get outdoors, he hadn't stopped to put on his gardening smock. With a sigh he got to his feet and went back inside to fetch it.

The back hallway, which he entered from the yard, split at right angles. One led straight into the kitchen; the other hooked left and ran along a row of bedrooms. Link went down this second corridor to his own room, changed his shirt, tossed the soiled one into the closet, and returned to the hall. He was just starting back down the way he had come when he stopped, turned around, and went the other direction. Why, he didn't let himself formulate.

This way he would loop through the parlor, into the kitchen, and then back outside.

Coming through the archway, he discovered Ham and Allie in the center of the room, coiled in each other's arms.

They were kissing. Allie's back was to Link, her head raised, heels slightly off the ground as she stretched upward into the embrace. Ham's arms were lashed around the small of her back, pulling her body in tight. Only their jaws were moving.

The next instant Ham saw Link, dropped his arms, and stepped back.

"What do you call that?" said Link. A croak. But Ham was already crossing the room. He pushed open the screen door and went out onto the front porch, leaving Allie alone, white-faced. Link came up and seized her arm.

"You two haven't got me fooled a bit."

"Oh, Link," she said.

"Aren't you a nice pair? Breaking up two homes?" he said. He was fighting to speak, to breathe. What now? Plunged suddenly into the confrontation scene he'd so often imagined, rehearsed, and dreaded, he was sandbagged by a sense of complete unreality.

"How long has this been going on?" he said. Something else from a bad play.

Allie tossed her head with a ghost of her old defiance. "Some time," she said.

"This accounts for Ham's coming here. It's why you wanted to move to Indiana in the first place!" Link cried, still sounding like an idiot to his own ears.

Then: "I'm not the father of that child, am I?" he said.

"No," she answered. Just like that, with her nose turned up. For the first time the dizziness cleared and the anger hit him. Turned molten in his veins.

"*You*—" Then they both heard voices in the kitchen. He grabbed her arm again and yanked her away, into a little dressing room off the hall.

"My God, you—there's no name for you," Link spat. "How could you do such a thing?"

Allie said she couldn't explain.

"I'd rather see you dead in your coffin than acting this way. Well, you two won't get away with—" He caught sight of his own arm, as it clenched hers, vibrating.

"Oh, Link, don't . . . please don't do anything. Please, please. I'll take the baby and go away."

"What good will that do me?" It burst from him in a twisted groan. "You have broken my heart."

"Think of Maggie then," she begged, bright-eyed. "Our children's name, think of them."

With a roar Link pushed past her, rushed down the hall and into their bedroom. Allie followed. She watched as he fumbled his old revolver out of a box on the shelf, turned, and put the gun to his head.

He stood with the barrel against his temple, glaring at her, heaving breath. Allie stared back.

It was a test to see if she would try to stop him.

She didn't. Over the next several seconds he watched her eyes change, watched the horror in them clear away. Saw her daring him to pull the trigger.

He lowered the gun.

"Tell me how long," he said. "How long has this——?"

Allie's eyes wavered away. Through the window behind her husband she could see Ham on the front porch, sitting alone in a wicker chair.

"I said, *How long*——?"

The rage in Link's voice snapped her back to attention. He was pointing the gun, and for the first time she realized that he might kill *her*. Panic shot up into her throat.

"Has it been since that first visit of yours to Indiana?"

Trying to tell him to put the gun down, she couldn't speak. So she nodded. Then jumped with fear as Link flung past her and out the bedroom door, straight out onto the porch where Ham was.

It took Allie a couple of moments to gather herself. Then she took off after them.

When she reached the porch, they were gone. She looked all over. Finally, spying them in the side yard to the left of the house, she ran to the far railing.

At once she saw the glint of the gun. She couldn't tell if Link was waving it around, or trying to hold it steady enough to shoot, but every second it waggled and flashed. The lawn and trees lay covered in a deep-orange glare. She heard Link say: "You've broken up my home."

"Why, Link," said Ham. "I'm surprised at you." He sounded the same as always, real back-fence and easygoing. But his eyes were unnaturally fixed on Link, and away from the jumping pistol.

"I'm more surprised at you," said Link. Words were nothing now, just noises to make while they both stalled.

Ham snatched at the gun, but Link sprang back. "No, no!" he cried.

"Link!" shouted Allie.

Sounding supremely reasonable, Ham said, "Link, really, it's nothing more than what you saw."

"You're denying it?" Link yelped, and he leveled the gun at Ham's chest with both hands. Allie was off the porch now and running across the grass. She arrived at Ham's side breathless.

"Ask her," Ham said. "She'll tell you."

"She's already told me!" Link cried. "She's confessed to it, all of it, so you might as well too."

"Have you?" Ham asked her in a tone of surprise.

Allie could only look at him.

"Well, I suppose . . ." He shrugged. "You know," he said to her, "I would never have told anyone if you hadn't."

"Of course not," said Allie.

"You're a man of principle!" said Link.

Ham tried a cajoling smile. "Come on, Link," he said. "Let's talk this over. After all, we're Masons."

"*Masons! Masons!*" Link danced with rage. "A fine Mason you are! You've wrecked my home!"

"Stop it, stop it," Allie cried. "Both of you. Just come into the house now. For God's sake, remember the rest of the family." Any one of whom might step outside at any moment.

Ham said gravely, "Do Maggie and I have permission to stay the night, Link? That's all I'm asking. It's for Maggie's sake."

"You've broken up my home," Link repeated dully.

Just then came the screech of the screen door and Maggie came out onto the porch. Link, like a guilty man, jammed the gun into his pants pocket.

"Is everything all right?" Maggie said, coming up to the porch rail. "What's all the commotion?"

Link made some kind of noise and wandered off into the far reaches of the back yard, leaving the other two to come up with an answer.

THERE'D BEEN an evening jaunt already planned, a trip into town to see the flickers. But Link and Allie begged off, so the Dillons went without them. Louise Hale tagged along.

As they strolled down the sidewalk heading toward town, Maggie brought up the subject of Link again. "He's all het up about something," she said.

"He works too hard," said Ham.

"Are you sure that's what's bothering your father?" Maggie asked Louise. But the girl didn't look at either one of them. "You'll have to ask him yourself," she said. Then she flashed a look at Ham like a beam from a hooded lantern.

He smiled back at her emptily. Why was this girl so . . . ?

He left the thought unfinished, snapped it in two.

Back home, Link and Allie put the children to bed and finally sat down to talk. They didn't get anywhere. For her to be stuck in the parlor with this man while he whimpered and seized his hair was past enduring.

Around nine-thirty the Dillons and Louise returned, and everyone went to bed.

All but Allie. She sat up alone till very late, past midnight. When she finally tiptoed into the bedroom, she found that Link wasn't there.

Then she heard a rustling and knocking in the spare room. It was more of a storeroom really, with an old daybed in it. He was pacing, that's what it was—up and down, up and down. She lay on the bed and listened. It was hopeless trying to sleep with those footsteps.

But she became even wider awake when they stopped.

Now she heard other sounds coming through the door: the scrape of a chair, drawers opening and closing. Stealthy sounds, which only made them louder. She lay there trying to guess what he was doing. It was a game that helped distract her from one thought strung tight as an E-string: the outside chance he might burst in at any moment and shoot her where she lay.

Twenty feet away, on the other side of the door, Link had other things on his mind. He was plagued with new fears of his own. Using the top of a bureau as a makeshift desk, he was scribbling a candlelight note to an old friend of his, Judge James Denton deBekker—namesake for the Hales' oldest son—who had been the family lawyer for years. In this letter Link was asking deBekker to cut Allie out of his will right away, at once, since there was every chance "my wife may assassinate me in the night." He temporarily addressed this missive "To Judge deBekker in the event of my death" in case he didn't survive till morning; then he stuck the envelope into his pants pocket and collapsed on the little bed. But he didn't close his eyes. All night husband and wife lay like this, in adjoining rooms, wondering if each would kill the other.

ALLIE WAS UP by daylight. Louise got breakfast. The children came trickling in to eat, the Dillons appeared, and then Allie called Link to breakfast. When he didn't come, they started without him.

Maggie was more perplexed than ever by the weird atmosphere in the house. Ham had just told her they would have to leave today—twenty-four hours ahead of schedule—and still she didn't really understand why. All he'd said was that Link was overwrought with life generally and needed a rest. "So don't bother him with anything, okay?"

At last Link appeared in the doorway of the kitchen. Allie asked him if he wanted any breakfast.

"No," he said, "and it seems to me that there are some others in this room who wouldn't feel like eating either." Allie blazed a look at him, and he shut up. While the others ate, he paced aimlessly looking out the windows.

Then Maggie got up and went out to the sleeping porch to start packing. She was folding a blouse when she heard a tap on the doorjamb. It was Louise.

"Can I speak to you a moment?" the girl said.

"I suppose," said Maggie. She sounded short, more than she meant to. But Maggie was getting crankier by the minute.

"I was just wondering why you have to run off," said Louise, hovering in the doorway. She managed to be spectral even in broad daylight.

"Well," Maggie began, and then stopped, surprised to be asked. "To tell you the truth, I'm not sure why."

"I am."

"What?"

"I know what the trouble is. Would you like me to tell you?"

"I suppose so," Maggie said slowly. She was fantastically puzzled—not just by the mystery itself but by the girl's manner, which was fraught with portent. But then she had always thought Louise was a little peculiar.

Louise came onto the sleeping porch and sat on the edge of the bed. Then she looked up at Maggie and patted the spot beside her. Maggie sat.

Faltering for the first time, Louise finally looked her aunt directly in the eyes.

"This isn't exactly—"

"Hello there!" cried Allie. She filled the doorway, a little out of breath. "Anything I can do to help you pack?"

LINK AND HAM stood on the front porch talking.

"You've broken up my home," said Link for the third time that morning.

"Yes." Ham couldn't wait to get away. He was sorry for Link, sorry period, but that didn't make his whining any easier to take.

"How could you do such a thing?" Link asked mournfully.

Ham said that he was young and full of passion.

Link asked who was to blame.

"Both of us," said Ham, "but me more than Allie. I'm a man, so I'm stronger."

Tears began to seep out of Link's eyes. "My heart is broken," he said.

Ham waited.

"You have children to raise, so I'll let you go quietly, but we must never meet again." He looked up warningly. "You and Allie either."

Ham breathed a slow, silent sigh.

"All right," he said.

Link went back inside, where he found Maggie in the parlor. As they said their goodbyes, he suddenly gave a ratcheting sob. "You may never see me again alive," he said.

Appalled, Maggie shrank back. "I guess we shouldn't have come," she stammered.

"He'll be all right," Allie said. She had a steel grip on one of his arms. "He's just got the blues, don't you, sweetie?"

18

THE POT WAS LIGHT. Not for the first time. Ham kept forgetting to ante.

Back home in his own parlor, he was playing a little low-stakes poker with Denton and a couple of farmhands. They were surrounded by the usual detritus of men at cards: a cider jug forming a wet ring on the checkered oilcloth, a scattering of chips, ashes, stubby glassware. Once in a while one of the men would skreek back in his chair and go out to the porch where the bucket of cold water was, slosh a little on the back of his neck, and return to the game. Even with the door open, it was stuffy in here.

Denton liked poker. He liked the mathematics of it, the bump-and-dare, but most of all he liked steeping himself in this masculine silence: no talk, only the flick and flutter of cards, the chink of chips. "Raise you . . . I'll see that . . ." He'd never known anything like it. Poker was teaching him how men could socialize while keeping their mouths shut. They didn't even have to look each other in the eye.

A woman walked in, an invader—Aunt Maggie, carrying the mail. With a snap she placed a letter by Denton's elbow. "Came today," she said, and went right back out. She knew well enough the whole region was stuck in a brutal patch of weather; still, if the men really had to wait out the worst of the heat, as Ham said, before heading back out to the hay fields, she didn't see why they had to spend the time playing cards.

Ham glanced over at the envelope. The address was in Link's handwriting.

Denton seemed in no hurry to open it. This was typical. He never read any letter from his father right away. In fact, as Ham well knew, the boy might leave it sitting around all day.

"Nickel," said Denton. Chink.

It went on like that for two or three hands. Ham was aware of a tightening at his temples, but for some reason he couldn't get himself to tell Denton to open the envelope.

Finally the boy won a hand, which seemed to give him strength. Anyway, as the next hand was dealt he picked up the letter and slit it open with his thumb.

Ham got up and went over to the china cabinet, where he rummaged for something he couldn't seem to find. Then on his way back he stopped and hovered by Denton's shoulder, eyeing the single page. He tried to slap on a look of avuncular interest.

With a quick scan he couldn't tell much. The thing was written in pencil, in a crabbed and hasty hand—not like Link's usual prissy-student style. Ham caught the word *insurance*. Then his own name. Link was telling his son to get hold of the life insurance policy Ham was holding for the Hales. (Ham knew Allie was listed as beneficiary.) But was that all? There were two more paragraphs.

Reading, Denton glanced up at his Uncle Ham, who smiled

blandly and ambled back to his seat. He didn't think Link had spilled anything, but he wasn't certain. When he sat down, he stood right up again. "Deal me out," he said, and went through the front door and out into the yard.

The air smelled like a lion's cage: a mix of hay, manure, and dust. They needed a rain real bad. Ham came to a stop in the middle of the yard. The sun had flung his shadow onto the dirt in front of him, and soon he was lured into contemplating its details.

A little more than a week had passed since the blowup in Kentucky. A quiet week; no word from the Hales till now. Nothing. The diciest moment had come on the train ride home, with Maggie insisting to know once and for all what was the matter with Link. Ham, with the sigh of one finally admitting the truth, improvised a cock-and-bull story about Link's job, how it was hanging by a thread through no fault of his own—just more daggone government politics.

"Of course, he's acting like it's the end of the world," said Ham. "You know Link. He gets like a girl."

She nodded, thinking.

"Just promise me you won't say anything to him about it," Ham said. "It may work out, and in the meantime he doesn't want anyone to know."

"He told you," Maggie said.

"Well, actually, I got it from Allie."

"Allie told you that story?" Maggie said sharply. She turned abruptly to face him, and he shrank back just a trifle.

"Well, yes," he said. "She did."

Maggie looked out the window of the moving train and didn't say anything more.

"What's wrong?" he said finally.

"I just wish she'd confide in me," Maggie said.

In this way Ham had bought himself some time. The trick now was to secure Link's silence, now and forever. And Ham was optimistic; he thought he could pull it off. Together he and Allie would work on her husband—appeal to his decency, play on his weakness. Even after all this, Ham thought, Allie probably held the whip hand in that marriage.

Standing in the yard, he remembered kissing her again: those last seconds before they were discovered. The whole week had been circling around to that moment. He wondered if it would be their last embrace. Then he thought of her in the days just before that—her eyes especially, how transparent they seemed. From the first day he saw the hunger in them and the pleading too; half the time she was imploring him to leave her alone.

As he stood there staring at the ground, Ruth came skipping up and stood beside him. Her little shadow appeared next to his.

After a moment Ham looked over and pointed at it.

"You look like a big cookie," he said.

The child squealed with pleasure. "No, *you* look like a big cookie!" she cried, and pushed him.

NEVER ROBUST, Link dragged around now as if he were carrying thirty pounds of tears. He ate little and when he wasn't at work mostly kept to himself in the bedroom. Sometimes Allie would hear him through the door, sobbing. The children could hear it too, of course, but they didn't ask why their father was crying and they weren't told. They didn't expect to be. Parents didn't confide in children.

Link lost five pounds, ten, fifteen. He took to weighing himself, sometimes two or three times a day, morbidly tracking his own decline. The weeping did not let up. Worse, Allie never knew when he would come lurching at her for another heart-to-heart. She began to think her head would burst.

One thing he kept pressing her for was an account of the beginning: he wanted to know the details of how she and Ham became lovers. But Allie refused to tell. She wasn't sure why. Maybe she was hoarding the last of her treasure. "Oh, what difference does it make?" she would say, to that or almost any question. She denied nothing but added nothing.

Only Louise let him wallow in his grief. Because he begged for it like a bedtime story, she told him again and again about the time she had come home early from school and found Allie and Ham coming out the bedroom. The girl hoped for some solace for herself too, but Link didn't offer any. He was too busy rooting out everything she had ever seen or suspected about her mother, lapping up her words like some nourishing poison.

Meanwhile mother and daughter avoided each other, though sometimes their eyes met in the hall.

In September, desperate for sleep, Allie moved into the spare bedroom. She was hoping Link might finally settle down, but his misery only grew more extravagant. Late at night he would be poring through the Bible; she could hear the splashing pages through the door. And then his voice sometimes, barely audible: "Oh, Lord, I wish I were dead." Once he came bursting into her room just long enough to make her promise that if he died, she wouldn't go back to Indiana and break up Maggie's home. Allie promised, and he left.

One night she came awake to find him standing over her. With a gasp she flailed up onto her elbows.

"How can you sleep?" he whispered. He had the Bible in his hand. With impersonal strength he pulled her out of bed, forced her onto her knees, and then sank down beside her. They prayed together for a long time.

A night or two later, when he appeared again, she was half expecting him. But this time he wasn't carrying the Bible. Instead he had a written confession for her to sign. He told her to read it first to see if it was correct. She did.

"Give me the pen," she said.

He'd been thrashing about for a way to put a period to his suffering, to somehow cauterize the wound. But as he watched her scratching her name at the bottom of the page, he realized this wasn't it.

"How did it happen?" he moaned for the fiftieth time. "What made you do it?"

She handed the paper back to him with no expression on her face.

"You couldn't resist him. Was that it?"

"Yes," she said. "That was it." So this is penance, she thought. She preferred guilt.

Next morning Link took the confession and put it in a safety-deposit box in the Nicholasville bank, in care of his friend Judge deBekker. Along with it he laid the insurance papers Denton had mailed him. Link had crossed out his wife's name and made his five children co-beneficiaries. And on top of the policy he reverently placed a photograph of his wife and two youngest children, something he'd been carrying in his wallet. It had been taken in May 1905, just before Allie went to visit the Dillons in Indiana, when he knew she was still unstained.

On his way home he bought another gun.

THE FIRST ONE was gone. Together he and Allie had agreed they should get it out of the house, so he had given it to one of the guards at the distillery. No matter now. This one was better—a Smith & Wesson .32 caliber. A six-shooter made of blue steel, with a swing-out cylinder and a barrel half a foot long. He waited impatiently while the clerk rhapsodized about the self-cocking hammer and the rubber grip, then finally paid for it, with a box of cartridges, and made his way down the street reading the promotional literature: "This is S&W's latest creation. It is a revolver that is built for business. . . ."

Walking along, Link felt a lot better—anchored at last just having the gun in his coat pocket. But now that he had it, what should he do with it?

He played with the possibilities.

He imagined shooting his wife and shooting Ham, both singly and together. He tried to picture them dying this way and that. But these fantasies had a strange lack of energy, and before long his thoughts began to coagulate around suicide. Where would be good? He considered going to the graves of his parents down south in Somerset, and putting a bullet in his mouth there at the cemetery. But was that strong enough? Even in the bowels of his misery he kept casting about for the perfect gesture; the enormity of the wrong against him seemed to carry with it some aesthetic imperative, as if it were his job to come up with the right response. It was making him angry too. In his ravaged state, how was he supposed to make these decisions?

That night he lay awake, creating and discarding different death scenarios. Next day in his little office, making a mess of his work, he finally shoved aside the big ledger, brushed past the coils of flypaper hanging like streamers, and stumbled outside. Through the office window, his co-workers could see him striding feverishly up and down the dirt road. He would disappear in one direction, then a few minutes later go by heading the other way, then pass by once more, like a man continually forgetting something.

He was trying to form a plan, but as he marched up and down his mind was possessed with that moment he had walked in on the lovers. By now the scene had taken on the unstable colors of a hallucination, and there was a sound that went with it too: the noise of their kiss, hideously amplified. To steady himself, he tried to concentrate on his children. At least they loved him. Then he thought of Denton and, with a jolt of vertigo, suddenly felt as if he'd inherited the drive to suicide from his own son.

That evening, during dinner, he didn't say a word. The children were afraid of him now. Even Louise was beginning to feel oppressed by the tyranny of his self-pity.

But that very night, at last, the answer came to him.

He and Allie would commit suicide together. It was perfect. It was the only way to cap this nightmare. Not only would it put an end to his pain but—even better—Allie would be proving herself his again with her final act. If she died with him, the world would know she loved him best.

For once, instead of barging in, he softly tapped on the door of her room.

"What is it?" she said. He came in with a face like Christmas morning.

Sitting on the edge of the bed, he took her hand and told her his idea. They should jump off High Bridge together. This was a span that stretched three hundred feet above the Kentucky River, downstream from the distillery. People made day trips on the train just to see it. It was the highest bridge in North America.

Allie might have been more frightened if she hadn't been so disgusted. What revolted her most was the look of hope in his eyes.

She would never do such a thing, she said, now or ever. Who would be left to take care of the children? He didn't argue at all. She saw the light in his eyes fade and wink out. Humbly he apologized and left the room.

So that night he went to the bridge alone. It was around two in the morning when he set out, unstabling the horse so was not to wake anyone and then setting off riding at a slow, measured clop. He was filled with regret; it was so hard to abandon his dream. He kept imagining the two of them sailing through the air together, Allie's skirt whipping against her legs as they fell, their two bodies beginning to turn, slowly, slowly, then smashing into the water.

When he reached the bridge, he tied the horse to a bush and walked out onto the middle of the span. It was a balmy night. He could hear the whisper and gurgle of the water below, the stir of wind in the trees. Walking to the edge, he grabbed hold of a girder and gazed far down at the slippery shadows of the river. He crouched in the steel webbing, and felt the gun in his pocket clunk against a rivet. He looked toward the horizon, then up into a tornado of stars.

All he had to do was lean forward and let go.

He tried.

He couldn't do it. He tried again. Then he sat back moistening his lips. All at once he jerked forward but froze on the edge of that impossible space.

Clinging to a girder with one hand, he tugged the revolver out of his pocket and brought the barrel to his temple. He was weeping now as his finger rested on the trigger. Weeping with disgust at his own cowardice. He squeezed and squeezed till finally the gun went off with a bang that rocked the heavens.

Link still sat where he'd been, nesting in the bridge. At the last moment he had yanked away the gun.

DESPAIRING at being unable to live or die, Link finally went to see his doctor. Why he'd been resisting it, he didn't know, since for years he had flown to doctors with a whole host of complaints, and physically he had never been such a wreck.

"Doctor, I can't sleep," Link said.

"Just one moment, Mr. Hale," Dr. Carstairs said. He was at his desk with his head down, scribbling away at something.

Link shifted in the visitor's chair and waited. He liked doctors' offices. And of the many physicians Link had tried over the years, Dr. Carstairs ranked with the best. For one thing, when it came to administering jolts of electricity, he was the most liberal Link had ever found.

"You were saying?" Dr. Carstairs said as he signed his name to something.

"I can't sleep."

The doctor put down his pen and looked generically concerned. Then he got his first good look at Link. His eyes widened a millimeter.

"You've been taking the sodium bromide?"

"It's gone."

"What's the trouble?"

Weighed down with shame and sadness, Link couldn't bring himself to come clean. Without going into details, he said, a member of his family had committed a grave offense against him and the children, and his heart was broken. (At once, the doctor understood all.) Link didn't mention his brushes with suicide, but he did describe how he was slugging down bottles of opiated cough syrup at night and walking up and down in the front yard till he was ready to drop with exhaustion. "Unless I get something else to help me sleep," he said, "I'm afraid I'll lose my mind."

Dr. Carstairs appeared to take this in stride. Over decades he had honed the flat style of the professional nonalarmist, and now he ran the usual drill—peering into Link's ears and down his throat, tapping his knees, lifting and dropping the arms—with an air of practicality verging on boredom. But his eyes were busy. Then he sat back down at his desk.

"Have you thought of going to a sanitarium?" Dr. Carstairs said.

"A what?"

"Have you looked at yourself in the mirror lately? You're at least twenty pounds underweight."

"I don't know that I can afford—"

"I'd say it's imperative."

Link had never heard the doctor be so blunt.

They talked about the choices. Five Oaks? Out of the question. Link hadn't forgotten Dr. Busby, who had examined Denton after the boy's suicide attempt. Dr. Carstairs suggested Sterne's Sanatorium for Nervous Diseases, located in Indianapolis. Running a finger through a catalogue, he described its flowers and fountains and modus operandi: each class of patients to its own building; no intermixing. Even within each unit the patients were not allowed to speak of their troubles or symptoms to each other. This was to help keep everybody calm.

Link said it sounded lonely.

"Large and airy bedrooms. Electric lights." The doctor was still scanning the text. "They treat most of their patients with X rays," he said. "Though frankly I don't know much about that."

"Think it's worth a try?" asked Link.

"X rays?" The doctor thought it over. "Couldn't hurt."

"No, no," said Link after a pause. For once in his life he didn't feel up to high-intensity treatments and wanted something more benign.

"Well," said Dr. Carstairs, "if you're willing to spend the money, there's Battle Creek."

"I've heard of it."

"Do you know anything about Dr. Kellogg?" And Carstairs began to expatiate on Dr. John Harvey Kellogg, inventor of the corn flake and apostle of "biologic living." A bastion of vegetarianism and clean colons, the Battle Creek Sanitarium had been tops in its field for thirty years. Thousands of America's elite, from Henry Ford to the voluminous William Howard Taft, had gone there for treatment of such complaints as nervous exhaustion, coffee neuralgia, hyperhydrochloria, and executive stress. Simply stepping into the lobby, it was said, started the cure: a space half the size of a football field, dotted with Corinthian columns and banana trees, and kept at a constant temperature of seventy-two degrees. A string quartet was always playing, and Dr.

Kellogg himself, all in white, often bustled through passing out fresh fruit.

But what sold Link wasn't the promise of nut broth or live music. Shrewdly, Dr. Carstairs mentioned Dr. Kellogg's theory concerning "connubial relations": that they did irreparable harm to the human body. In fact, Kellogg was proud to say that he and his wife abstained completely—thus avoiding agitation to the nervous system, fluid depletion, and biologic shock.

For Link, who now thought of sex as pure evil, this was the ideal haven. He agreed to go right away.

It took a couple of days for Dr. Carstairs to make the arrangements. On September 9, Link withdrew $150 from the bank and bought some clothes—underwear and a new suit—and a suitcase. He stopped at the pharmacy for vitamin tonic and a sleeping medicine the doctor had prescribed. The next morning, a Thursday, he packed. Trying not to seem too eager, Allie helped.

Then Link took his little son Lewis and daughter Marguerite into their bedroom and prayed with them. "Remember," he said, "if you never see me again, that I love you." Scared, Lewis squirmed in his embrace.

Stopping by Louise's room, he told her to promise that if he died, she would tell Aunt Maggie the whole story. Louise promised.

Lastly he went into the kitchen to say goodbye to Allie. His mustache was gone. Sometime in the last ten minutes.

"I only grew it because you wanted me to," he said dolefully. "If you don't love me anymore, there's no point in keeping it." Helplessly Allie sighed. He had such a depthless capacity for melodrama.

"I don't expect to see any of you again," he said, and waited.

"Good luck to you." That was all she could manage. At last the door clicked shut behind him, and she could breathe again.

Toting his suitcase, he walked to the Nicholasville station and caught the late-morning train heading north.

1 9

COLONEL CHARLES MCDOWELL of Wilmore, Kentucky, owner of McDowell's Plantation Restaurant, was jouncing along with his eyes half open, lulled by the rhythm of the rails and the heat, when he began to think he recognized the back of a head. It rose from a seat several rows forward, damp and blond. He studied the scrutable ears. Finally McDowell unhinged his angular frame and made his way up the aisle through the thinly populated car. Stopped and politely craned forward. Even then he wasn't sure it was Link Hale, the man had changed so much.

Link looked up. He didn't say anything.

"Mr. Hale?"

"Yes."

McDowell identified himself. The two men had met more than once in a professional way, McDowell being a wholesale buyer of spirituous liquors. When Link still looked vague, the colonel took off his broad-brimmed hat. But Link didn't register the face. Or perhaps he did, and just didn't care.

After a couple of failed pleasantries, McDowell said: "Have you been ill, sir?"

"That's right," said Link. "I've been ill." When he didn't add anything to that, the colonel returned to his seat.

At Lexington both men changed trains for Frankfort. As he tried to climb the outside steps of the car, Link got dizzy and then fell backward—dragged down by the weight of the gun in his pocket. Together McDowell and the porter hauled him on board.

It was a long trip, and very hot. As the train churned west, Link rode alone with his head in his hand, his elbow on the vibrating window ledge. He was uncomfortable but at least he was sitting down. Spreading his thumb and forefinger across his upper lip, he remembered that he didn't have a mustache now. He had even lost track of his own face.

The train rolled by charred and wilted fields, mile after mile. This wasn't just a dry spell anymore. This was four weeks of high heat and no rain, leaving the whole of northern Kentucky and southern Indiana blistered by drought. Groves of apple trees were withering, and the corn was going brown. Pumpkins in the fields had turned inside out. Dry creekbeds were littered with dying fish. Farms bordering train tracks had been especially hard-hit, whole fields blackened by fires started by sparks belched from locomotives. As he stared morosely out the window, Hale passed an occasional fence post flickering with flame.

He could see how bad the dust was too, even at this distance. The newspapers had been publishing measurements. Even on main roads, they reported, it was drifting six inches deep. Horses sneezed, sputtered, and stumbled through the fog it made, and once in a while fell down dead. The horizon, when visible, looked like a long prairie fire with dense gray smoke; where the sun's rays caught it, it flared with wonderful colors like the aurora borealis. Nobody went out for pleasure drives anymore, and houses were closed tight as a drum.

Link's mind drifted again to a plan he'd been toying with: that he might stop off in Washington, Indiana, on his way to Battle Creek and draw the rest of his assets out of the bank. He still had some money there, mostly the fruits of small investments he'd made with Ham—more than a thousand dollars all told and a deed for forty acres of land. He had been figuring he would have Ham go to the bank for him, but right now he didn't feel like asking the favor. He didn't want to deal with Ham, didn't want to see him. . . .

Except for those vengeful moments when he wanted nothing more.

But those were just fantasies. Link would take care of the bank business himself and not go anywhere near Elnora.

Slowed by blowing curtains of dust, the train was just creeping along. By the time it reached Seymour, Indiana, it was more than two hours late, and Link had missed his connection for the northbound B&O. He got a hotel room near the train station and went to bed. Lying there in his usual funk—a mix of weariness and constipated rage—he thought again about shooting himself. He could do it now, here in this room. Fingering the gun, he began to compose a suicide note in his head, word by word, polishing for style. "I want to be buried beside my parents, the most noble . . ." He asked for a closed-casket funeral. The envelope would be addressed to Judge deBekker.

He picked up the gun and opened the chamber. Five bullets left. He remembered now: he had never replaced that one from the night on High Bridge. The memory of that failure—along with thoughts of his children—sapped him of any further will, and he lay for several hours with his hand on the revolver, slipping in and out of sleep, till the hotel clerk tapped on his door. He left Seymour at five in the morning on a train to Battle Creek. Once again he was planning to stop off in Washington.

. . .

HAM AND MAGGIE left the farm early after breakfast. To go for a drive on a workday was very rare, and this expedition—twenty miles by buggy to Washington, through all that dust—was going to be nasty. But that afternoon Washington was hosting a big political rally: Thomas Marshall, Indiana's Democratic candidate for governor, was coming to give a speech, and Ham Dillon—along with the other political pooh-bahs of Daviess County—would have a place of honor on the platform. The rally was scheduled to start at twelve-thirty. During the morning Maggie would do some shopping, while Ham did a little politicking of his own.

The trip to Washington normally took a couple of hours. Not today. Much of the way the Dillons' vehicle had to creep along through a false floor of dust eight inches deep. Maggie sat as far back as she could in the shaded canopy of the buggy, fretting about her clothes. She was dressed in high-throated white, top to toe, along with a big white picture hat covered in artificial flowers. Her very best outfit. Warm for the day, but she was determined to cut a figure.

Even with the dust, Ham felt first-class. A full month had passed since the unpleasantness in Kentucky. There had been no repercussions, nothing from Allie, no news at all. With each day that passed, the situation looked more manageable. Besides, in the past few weeks he'd been making a lot of hay politically. Arnold Padgett, now back in his old office on Main Street, had engineered things so that Ham would be sitting within a table setting or two of Marshall himself at the big Democratic dinner after the speech—a sure sign that Ham was solidifying his position as the heir apparent for Congress in 1910. To go with his light-colored suit today, Ham wore a boater and a bow tie with a slightly racy purple stripe.

Savoring his good spirits, he rode along with Maggie in a

comfortable, married silence. Not far out of Elnora they heard another vehicle heading toward them—heard it before they could see it. At last it exploded out of the dust fog a few yards ahead. The farmer, who wore a big straw hat and goggles, tipped his whip as he went by, and they turned to watch as his wagon rumbled by and disappeared again in the haze.

"Did you see that horse?" Ham said, grinning.

"What do you mean? What about him?"

"He had goggles on too."

LINK ARRIVED in Washington on train #5 about a quarter to eight that morning. He got off at a little gabled depot surrounded by workers' shacks and greasy spoons, shouldered his grip and walked north two blocks to the Meredith House. He remembered it from a couple of years ago, that day Ham frog-marched him along Main Street pointing out the sights. Link checked in, telling the woman behind the desk—a frail personage with pens nesting in her hair—that he might be in town a day or two. (He was thinking now he might rest up before heading on to Battle Creek.) Checking his bag, he went back outside without bothering to see the room. He kept the gun.

At the telephone exchange down the block he put in a call to Ham Dillon. There was no answer. A few minutes later he tried again. Still nothing. He kept asking himself why he was calling; this was exactly what Link had told himself he wouldn't do. But now that he was back in this neck of the woods, back at the very scene of his disgrace, something seemed to be driving him to it. For about an hour Link had the switchboard ring the Dillons' house every five minutes or so, till finally the hello girl snapped at him for wasting her time. On a day like this, she said, she had a thousand other things to do.

Hopping with agitation—his only form of energy these days—Link returned to the streets and walked up and down looking for a law firm. Any law firm. He was suddenly thinking of suing Ham Dillon. For what he wasn't sure, but there must be some legal grounds. After blundering up one street and down another Link found himself in a side alley and came to a stop. Looking around, he spied a goat in a back yard giving him the cryptic amber eyeball.

Link forgot about the lawsuit and hurried back to Main Street.

Now, at long last, he registered the hoopla all around. How could he have missed it? Signs were everywhere, plastered to fences and propped up in shopwindows: THOMAS MARSHALL HERE TODAY. He stopped and looked at one of the posters. Marshall, in his official photograph, had a spindly, professorial look, except for the thick flowing mustache that covered his upper lip. Link touched his own upper lip again. It was pearled with sweat.

He drifted up Main Street toward the Airdome, the open-air stage where Thomas Marshall was to give his speech. Along the way he passed knots of men braying about the campaign. Not noon yet, and the temperature had already passed ninety. He felt mesmerized by it all: the bunting and band music and baking heat. He saw women go by spitting dust off their tongues.

As he paused in a block of hot shadow, it occurred to Link that Ham Dillon might be in town. Ordinarily any person, even a public official, could go weeks at a time without visiting the county seat. But this was a heck of a big rally.

Link was thinking maybe he should make himself scarce.

He was heading back down the street toward the Meredith, just passing Neal & Eskridge's general store, when he spotted Maggie Dillon.

In the sunshine she was a blaze of white, her face shaded by the scoop of her hat, and she was peering into a store window not more than ten feet away from him. Link whipped around looking for Ham, but didn't see him. Then he went forward, retreated, and finally turned away.

"Link? Link, is that you?"

He stopped, caught like a burglar, and slowly turned around.

"Well, goodness gracious," said Maggie, approaching him. "I thought that was you."

Link couldn't find words.

"What's the trouble?" she said. "Is there something the matter? You look like . . . oh, my."

"My heart is broken," he said. Just like that.

She stared into his lugubrious eyes. "What do you mean?" she said testily. "What on earth are you talking about?"

"I'd rather not say," Link answered. "I didn't want to meet you in the first place."

"Fine," said Maggie. "Keep it to yourself."

At that Link's whole body sang with resentment. Maggie on her high horse. If she only knew.

And why shouldn't she? Why the hell was he suffering alone?

He asked her if she had ever seen anything wrong between Allie and Ham.

A dead pause. All around them others were whooping and carrying on.

"You're mistaken," she said.

Catching her arm, he pulled her through the swirl of pedestrians into Neal & Eskridge. Instantly the temperature dropped thirty degrees, and the sudden shift out of the street glare into semidarkness played tricks with their vision. When Maggie turned to face Link by the flour barrel, he was so sun-blind he could barely see her.

"Where is Ham?" he asked.

Maggie said he was here in town.

"Allie's confessed," he said. It felt so good to dish it out for a change. "This thing has been going for years. *Years.*"

"What has? What do you mean?"

"Ham is the father of that baby."

"What baby?"

He didn't answer.

Maggie made a sound. It was loud enough to cause a shopgirl in a nearby booth (topped with a sign, "Free Chase & Sanborn Iced Tea") to jerk her head up in alarm. She saw a woman in white unsteady and a man with his hands out, either helping or attacking her. The girl darted from behind the booth and caught Maggie herself.

"Let go of me," Maggie said.

She refused to sit down, though she did accept some free iced tea. Then the shopgirl retreated uneasily with the half-empty glass and, back at the counter, maintained close surveillance while the two figures kept up their furious dialogue. She wished she could hear the words. It was like a movie with no title cards.

Link was telling Maggie all of it in shards and fragments, the whole vile tale. His eyes were finally adjusting to the light in the store, and later on he would remember her slack, drained face back-framed by butcher's products: cans of meat stamped H. J. Heinz and Armour and a big glass jar of pigs' feet. There was an odor of talcum powder coming from somewhere. When she finally stopped interrupting him, he went on stammering out the story. She seemed so unresisting, he couldn't have known she was fighting an impulse to take him by the throat.

At last she cut him off.

"You've got to leave town," she said. "Please, you absolutely have got to go. Before Ham turns up." When he seemed to hesitate, she gritted her teeth and pleaded. For the sake of the children—all nine of them, nine innocents . . . (Something else was flashing through her mind too: a horrible scene in front of Ham's important friends.) Link could go straight to the station, catch the next train out. As she talked, she kept glancing out the window of the store.

Once she thought she saw Ham and cried out.

"All right," Link finally told her. "For the children's sake I'll go away." Just saying the words made him feel stronger—strong for the first time in weeks. Magnanimous and noble. He began to make some little speech appropriate to the occasion. But she interrupted him angrily.

"Just go, for God's sake," she said.

Link paused, then leaned in and kissed her on the cheek.

"I've always had the greatest respect for you, Maggie," he said.

With that, Link turned and left the store, heading east up Main Street. A moment later a vision in white appeared in the doorway looking after him. Many an onlooker would have thought it a sentimental scene.

Just then, at the west end of town, gubernatorial candidate Thomas Marshall was arriving in the Washington train station on the eleven-thirty from Evansville. The Citizens' Band struck up a Sousa, and on both sides of the tracks homemade signs began pumping the air.

Link barely heard. Back slogging through the sun again, he wasn't aware of much but the buffeting he was taking from a mass of people as they began streaming, against his line of march, down to the station to greet Marshall. Doggedly he struggled on, slightly uphill, colliding with one person after the next.

He had taken fewer than twenty steps when he looked up and saw Ham. His brother-in-law was no more than five or six feet away, heading along the sidewalk straight for Link, on his way to the train station like everybody else. Ham had his coat over his arm, his straw boater pushed back on his head, and was gabbing with a friend.

Someone dodged between Link and Ham, and Link lost sight of him for a second, but they kept moving toward each other. Finally Ham glanced up, and a look of recognition appeared in his eyes.

He took the first bullet in the abdomen.

It folded him over. Then he veered, straightened, and began a stumbling run through a stripe of shade into the middle of the street. His feet slipped on the streetcar tracks as Link, still standing at the curb, extended his arm and fired again at Ham's back, splintering his right collarbone. There were three more shots—*pop, pop, pop*—and wounds exploded on his left arm.

Bystanders, who had thought it was a joke at first, finally began to move. But Maggie was faster.

With the sound of the first shot she was running forward, close enough to see the red smack of the bullets.

"My God, why did you do it, why did you do it?" she screamed, staggering in her thick dress after Ham, who reached Carnahan's store on the far side of the street and, after gaining the doorway, disappeared inside. Maggie followed. Tom Lascoulie, the young farmer Ham had been walking with, was the first to seize Link by the arms.

"What the hell are you doing?" Tommy cried.

"Damn him, he broke up my home," Link muttered. He didn't make any effort to get away, but stood quietly at the corner of the street, holding the empty gun, barrel down.

"Isn't somebody going to arrest me?" he said.

But a policeman was already on the way, hustling up a side street from city hall. Deputy Theodore Wallace, who was hefty, arrived out of breath, his cheeks the color of raw steaks. "What is it? What is it?" he gulped. Lascoulie turned his prisoner over to Wallace, who snatched away the gun and searched him. He found no other weapon, but an unusually large sum of money: almost $150. "Don't squeeze my arm so hard," Link said as Deputy Wallace hauled him away, a small but noisy crowd swarming around them. He felt so light-headed, Link almost believed he was being borne along as their hero.

HAM SAT in a little wooden chair toward the back of Carnahan's. All around him were buggies on platforms and bags of fertilizer, and closer in a circle of at least a dozen people, including Maggie on her knees. He was streaming blood but fully conscious.

In two or three minutes a doctor appeared, and the folks fell back. Methodically Ham explained where he'd been hit, how deep he could feel the bullets. He didn't groan or flinch. His only sign of distress was the sound of his breath whistling through tight lips.

The first doctor was followed by a second, a third. Together they decided that most of the wounds were messy but not dangerous. Only the one in the stomach really concerned them. It had punctured his left side just below the waist, lodged deep in the tissue—and nobody knew quite how to get it out. Though Ham didn't say so, this was obviously the wound causing most of his pain.

At last a cot was brought in and he was stretched out upon it. Maggie stayed close by, assisting when and how she could, holding Ham's hand, cooling his brow. She almost insisted on getting blood on her dress. What few tears she began to shed dried on her lashes.

There were hundreds of people surrounding Carnahan's store now, stuck outside, but even with the doors barred they were still a problem: so many bodies at the front window blocked the light, and made it hard for the doctors to see. They were trying to decide which bullet to go after first.

Meanwhile the procession for the Honorable Thomas Marshall had started up Main Street, accompanied by the boom and splash of band music. Ham could hear it as it went by, and even tried to note the tune, but the fight to keep his own breath regular overpowered everything, even the big bass drum. As he lay in the cool of the store, a sopping rag against his stomach, he listened to the cheering crowd pass by and then, minutes later, he heard the faraway sound of an orator in full cry. Marshall? No, somebody introducing him. The roar of the crowd came and went, as soft as the sea. As the bullets were extracted one by one and dropped, *plink,* into a pewter dish, Ham concentrated on Marshall's voice. He couldn't distinguish the words, but he rode the sound of it, felt an almost languorous pleasure every time the voice peaked; this was always followed by the boom of applause.

If the size of that crowd disappointed the candidate (and he was heard complaining about it on the way to dinner), it wasn't only because of the gawkers at the store. Another multitude had followed the fortunes of the shooter—trailed him from the scene of the crime to city hall. There one Dr. Henry Herr, in the midst of a pop-eyed throng, examined Link's face and eyes in the manner of a horse trader and announced that he was sane. The mayor ordered Link taken to jail.

When the afternoon papers hit the streets, Marshall's speech was an afterthought.

HAM DILLON SHOT DOWN ON MAIN STREET
BY HIS BROTHER-IN-LAW H. L. HALE

So ran the banner headline of the *Washington Herald.* People snatched for copies because, though rumors had flown all afternoon, there was still no hard information about what had happened and, more important, why. In taverns, designated readers were standing on bars and reading aloud:

"Without a word of warning, H. L. Hale of Nicholasville, Ky., pulled a .32 caliber Smith & Wesson revolver out of his pocket and began shooting at Ham Dillon in front of Whetsell's shoe store a few minutes before Friday noon. Five shots were fired and all the bullets took effect on Dillon. . . ."

The ambulance carrying Ham had to weave its way around the crowd outside the newspaper office in order to get out of town. Still conscious, he was taken to the home of Joseph G. Courtney, one of the local doctors who'd been working on him, installed in a big bed downstairs with a fat nest of pillows, and displayed to the press. Dr. Courtney announced that he and the other consulting physicians now expected Mr. Dillon to recover. The doctor cited the strength and health of the patient and the small caliber of the bullets.

He cautioned, however, that Ham wasn't out of the woods. That fifth bullet, the peskiest, remained buried in his abdomen, and to perform this operation a specialist from Evansville had been summoned. Soon after, Dr. Gilbert arrived on the 7 P.M. train.

Once again Ham described just where he felt the bullet and bantered a little with the doctor. Then at 8:30, Dr. Gilbert gave him chloroform and made the first of three incisions. A clump of other doctors assisted, all leaning in to study his technique. By ten o'clock the operation was over, the bullet was out, and Dr. Gilbert—his sleeves still rolled up and his collar spronging off his thick neck—was giving a press conference.

The shot had fractured a rib, he said, and grazed the intestines, but caused no damage to vital organs. "In all probability," he went on, sipping a large brandy, "Dillon, if he survives, will owe his life to that rib. It slightly changed the course of the bullet. Sometimes the difference between life and death is . . ." Gilbert held up a thumb and forefinger, nearly touching. He added that in these cases there was always the risk of blood poisoning from peritonitis, so the patient would have to be watched carefully for the next two or three days.

Ham slept decently that night, and next morning was sitting up eating broth. Maggie wanted to clear the room, but he said no, no, he liked the company. People kept asking him what had gotten into Link Hale.

"That's exactly what I've been asking myself," said Ham. "It just passes my understanding. I guess he went a little crazy. Why, Barney! Where the Sam Hill have you been keeping yourself?"

Of course there were rumors whipping around town now

about a love triangle. Nobody knew for sure, but it seemed like a real good guess. But even so, this was still Ham Dillon they were talking about. The vast majority simply refused to believe that a man they liked and respected so much would ever do such a thing.

So pretty soon—partly inspired by Ham—there was a countersurge of rumors that Link Hale had a history of mental problems. The last edition of the paper that night reported that he'd had a nervous breakdown.

HIS HANDS tight on the rust-flaked bars of his cell, Link was calling out for the sheriff. He kept yelling for the latest on Ham's condition. Finally Deputy Wallace came ambling in from the office. He pulled a newspaper out of his pocket and, standing in a blotch of light in the dim corridor, read aloud:

DILLON PASSES QUIET NIGHT; CHANCES ARE FOR IMMEDIATE RECOVERY

" 'Owing to the physical strength of Dillon and his being accustomed to free outdoor life his system was able to stand the shock of five bullets ploughing through his flesh without any disastrous effects. . . .' "

"Five times and he didn't go down," Wallace said. "You can't shoot worth a shit, you know it?"

"He's not dead? Thank God," said Link. "I didn't want to kill him."

Deputy Wallace, with a phlegmatic swipe at his mustache, sauntered over to the prisoner and stood on the other side of the bars.

"You didn't intend to kill Ham Dillon?"

"No, I was trying to stay away from him. I did everything I could. Something just—"

"You told Doc Herr you shot to kill. You said so at the city hall. At least a hundred people heard you."

"I didn't say I *came* to kill him!"

"Well, now," said Wallace. "That's a little fancy for me."

He left Link on his knees praying aloud to God for Dillon's recovery.

IN MIDAFTERNOON Ham grew restless and feverish. Peritonitis was taking hold.

Around the death couch were gathered family and a few close friends: Maggie, along with her father, Arthur Thompson, just arrived from Ohio (and in a daze; the others had to move him around like a piece of furniture). Mama Dillon was there. Ham asked his mother to pray for him.

"Put your trust in the Savior," she said. She'd told her husband, Wesley, the exact same thing when he'd been lying there wanting that apple butter.

"Mother, I am trusting Him," Ham said, a little peevishly. (As Dr. Courtney's wife later remarked: "Dying puts some of them in a bad mood.") "I may not have lived as carefully as I should," he added, "but I've never lost my faith."

Maggie shooed everybody out then, even the doctors. "Just five minutes," she said. Then she pulled a chair up close beside him. Ham turned his head to her. He seemed to be blinking against a stinging wind.

"Hi, darlin'," he said. "Where are the children?"

"On their way." She took his hand. "Why did he do it, honey?" she said.

He only gazed at her, didn't answer.

"Whisper it to me," she said. She leaned forward, struggling to keep her broken heart together, steeling herself for the reply. But as a good Christian, she knew nothing else mattered now but for him to confess his sin at last—to make a clean breast of it to her and to his Creator.

"I don't know why he shot me," Ham told her. "I wish to God I did."

At 8 P.M. he lost consciousness. Soon after that he died. The local paper gave it the full treatment. "Fighting for every breath, using all his physical strength and mighty will power to combat the awful approach of the silent death angel, Ham Dillon slowly slipped on and across the dark river at 8:15 Saturday evening after one of the most heroic struggles for mastery over the monster that has been seen here in many a day."

Link Hale wasn't told right away. A doctor attending the prisoner said the news should be withheld overnight in hopes that Link could get some sleep. But even full of medication, Link was kept awake all night. There was an unusual amount of mean noise in the streets—shouting and the occasional smashing of glass.

PART THREE

"Sin has many tools, but a lie is the handle which fits them all."

—Underlined in Ham Dillon's copy of *The Autocrat of the Breakfast Table* by Oliver Wendell Holmes. In the margin Ham wrote: *good.*

2 0

IT WAS LIKE a little shovel blade driving into his sleep. Twice, three times. The meowing of a cat. When he finally came awake, Link found he was lying flat on his back. Then gradually, as his slow-blinking eyes adjusted to the morning's shabby light, he began to realize there was something strange about this place.

Not that he was in jail. He expected that.

He was in the wrong jail.

Coming onto his elbows, he peered all around the cell. He saw blackened walls and, through the one barred window, low roofs and chimneys. It came back to him then. About three in the morning he had jerked out of a light doze to find the sheriff of the Washington jail standing over him, and the next thing he knew a couple of deputies were pushing him out the back of the building. That low-life bunch in the streets, the shouters and glass breakers, hadn't gone home Saturday night even after the bars closed. By two o'clock they had collected at the scene of the crime, looking for bloodstains by gaslight and passing a bottle around, mourning Ham Dillon with that sentimental reverence of vice for virtue. Crouched behind a barrel, Deputy Wallace didn't take long to decide they were about two drinks away from storming the jail.

So the sheriff rousted Judge Houghton, got an order to relocate the prisoner, and in two shakes Link sat slumped in the predawn, creaking and swaying on the local train headed west to Vincennes. Now here he was in his new quarters at the Knox County jail. It was a big cell with other cots, but he was alone in it. A new guard was on the other side of the bars, his chair tipped back against the wall and his hat on his face.

Link wondered if he was still on suicide watch. For some reason it seemed an important thing to know.

Shhh. Shhh. Scraping sounds, getting nearer: somebody shuffling down the hall with sandpaper steps. Link stood up, and the prison cat, still meowing, slipped up close and began to curl around his leg like a barber pole.

It was the Vincennes sheriff bringing some breakfast on a tray. He unlocked the jail door one-handed with a lot of clanking, which didn't bother the sleeping deputy any, then came in and set the food on the table. Link looked for steam coming off the food and didn't see any.

"Can't say it's good, 'cause it's not," the sheriff said. "Maude don't put herself out on Sunday mornings, 'cause all we've got here ordinarily are drunks, and they can't taste nothing. They're all downstairs," the sheriff added. He was white-haired and pink-eyed.

"Thank you," said Link. But instead of coming to the rough wood table, he sat back down on the bed. "Could I see a newspaper?" he asked.

"Why not," said the sheriff. "I told 'em I'd take good care of you." He started off, then came back. "Got a nickel?"

After he was gone, Link tried to lie down again, but the blanket was scratchy and moth-eaten and the heat of the day had started creeping in. He was breathing something, disinfectant. So he got up and went to the window. The bars, about three inches thick, looked fresh-painted and gleamed black as tar. He tested one with a finger, then rested his head on them and looked down into the quiet street. A man on horseback was sloshing through the dust. Link remembered the dust now. There was nobody else in sight. It was Sunday morning, so all the stores were shut.

Then he realized he heard a lot of yakking from somewhere, someplace close, the high fireworks of women's voices.

"Here you go, friend," said the sheriff. Link walked over and the sheriff shoved the rolled newspaper through the bars. "Don't worry. Eight to five they spelled your name wrong anyway." A woman's shrieking laugh cut in from the left. Link flinched.

"That's Adelaide," said the sheriff sociably. It was pretty plain he liked to jaw. "She's next door at the firehouse." He listened again. "Yep, that's her. I know every one of 'em."

"The firehouse?"

"By their voices, I mean," added the sheriff. "I know all them girls by sound. I'm not saying nothing else, okay?" He winked.

"What are women doing in the firehouse?"

"Why, that's Madame Miranda's place. You never heard of it? The girls and her have the top couple of floors."

"You have a house of . . . ?"

"Yep. House of shame right next door! Anybody gets out of line"—the sheriff snapped his fingers—"we're there." His face got all serious. "Listen, I might as well tell you right now. No-body ever escapes from this cell. You want to know why?"

"Why?" said Link.

" 'Cause of the peephole."

Link came forward and took the newspaper, then turned and started back toward his bunk.

"Want me to tell you where it is?" the sheriff called.

Sitting heavily on the edge of his bed, Link found the story about the shooting in the center column of page one.

"SHOT DOWN LIKE DOG . . .

"Hamlet Dillon, trustee of Elmore Township, Daviess County, and one of the best-known politicians in southern Indiana, was shot down upon Main Street about 11:30 A.M. Friday by his brother-in-law H. L. Hale . . ."

The jolt of seeing his own name sent the words mumbling onto his lips.

". . . a revenue agent who arrived from Nicholasville, Kentucky, that morning with the evident intention of killing Dillon . . ."

Link slammed the paper into his lap. "That's not so!" he cried.

"Oh now, don't let nothin' in there upset you," said the sheriff, idling on the other side of the bars. "The papers get things balled up all the time. Besides," he added as he moved off down the hall, "it ain't like you won't get the chance to tell your side." He stopped. "Okay, boys!" he hollered, and three or four reporters came boiling through the door.

ALLIE SAT in the parlor of her home in Nicholasville. There was nobody else in the house, except Marguerite, upstairs in bed with some little fever. Pleading sick herself, Allie had shooed the rest of the family off to church.

From her chair she could see through the open doorway to the box phone on the kitchen wall. The receiver still hung straight down on its cord, the way she had dropped it just past dawn.

Winters in Indiana Allie had gone sleigh riding to the sound of distant telephone wires singing in the wind. She seemed to hear that same singing now.

Ham skittered in and out of her mind: Ham alive, Ham dead. He wouldn't stay dead, so she couldn't grieve. Or wouldn't, not yet. For now she clung to shock like a life preserver. Besides, remembering an often-absent lover or a dead man, there didn't seem to be much difference.

A little while ago she'd heard someone creeping around on the front porch. But he'd gone away again without knocking. Allie knew it was that boy from the newspaper. She'd spotted him hiding behind a tree across the street. He'd never make a reporter. No guts.

Only a month ago Ham had been sitting in that chair. Right there, in the middle of the night. Casting his spider's spell. Why?

Maybe something in him, some imp of conscience, finally wanted to be caught.

No no, that was silly. Guilt had always been her department, hers alone. Or if not . . . Well, she would never know now.

"Ma?"

Allie swung around. Marguerite was standing in the entryway in a short nightgown, one leg cocked like a flamingo. She was eight years old now, pinch-faced, brainy. Still a big reader of tabloid terrors. What would it be like for her to find her own name in the paper?

"I thought I heard somebody on the porch," the girl said.

Allie didn't answer right away. She was trying to take a mental photograph of her daughter on what felt like their last morning together. "You shouldn't be out of bed," she said at last.

Marguerite drifted to the window and looked out. "Who's that?" she said.

"I said go back upstairs, young lady."

"What are you going to do?"

"I have to write a letter."

"To Daddy?"

"Yes."

But it wasn't so. Sitting at the kitchen table, Allie spent the next hour pouring out a letter to her sister—even though the whole time Allie kept picturing her feeding it into the stove unread.

Accurately, as it turned out.

THAT AFTERNOON Ham Dillon's body was carried out of the house on Williams Street, loaded into a horse-drawn ambulance, and driven back to his own home in Elnora. After that people came streaming through the door to pay their respects.

Ham was in the parlor, laid out real nice; everybody said so. He was dressed in his best dark suit ("Warm for the weather," Mrs. Dupree whispered, "though I don't suppose it matters") and rested on a mortuary board that was wrapped in crushed purple velour. Candles burned at the four corners. Miss Halsop, the Mud Pike pianist, sat on a stool beside the body with an oversized hymnal, fanning flies away.

It was late now, past midnight, and very quiet save for the low wash of voices from those maintaining the vigil. Not even the clocks were ticking; Maggie had gone through the house and stopped every one. A little while ago she had finally put Harold and Ruth to bed (like dutiful farm children, they had been beside her for hours—not catered to, expected to cope), and now Maggie sat by a half-open window, an untasted cup of beef tea in her lap. People still came up to speak to her. She let them talk till they were finished and then watched them go away.

Her grief was so enormous it felt like apathy. Of course she was bone-tired now. She knew her sorrow would come back later all rested up, in rolling tides, maybe forever. She glanced over at the corpse. Mrs. Wampler was bending over Ham, wiping his face with a moist rag. Taking special care with each eyelid, to make sure they didn't cake up.

For Maggie, gazing at the dead face didn't stir much in the way of memories; it seemed to freeze memory altogether. But she decided it didn't matter. Just who was she trying to conjure after all? The man she had thought he was until the day before yesterday? What was the point of that?

Nobody else seemed to remember him either, at least not out loud. She had never been to a wake before where so few people mentioned the deceased. Two men nearby were talking about the weather. Maggie listened without bitterness. To farmers the weather was a subject of infinite nuance and bottomless interest.

The next thing she noticed, the moon had moved. She lifted her dazed head and looked around the room. Mrs. Wampler had displaced Miss Halsop and sat in mute attendance by the bier. Other people clustered here and there. The opiated smell of hot peaches was drifting in from the kitchen.

Maggie wasn't sure if she'd been dreaming or thinking. What had been floating in her mind? She was going to destroy all her photographs of Allie. That was it.

LATE THE NEXT MORNING—it was Monday now—a proud citizen of Elnora appeared, strutting around a bend in the road. He wore a black suit and hat, with white gloves, and had a bright white apron tied around his waist. He carried a naked sword too, the hilt in both hands, holding it aloft like a torch. The empty scabbard slapped against his leg as he advanced in a modified goose step.

Eventually another man appeared behind him, identically dressed, but without the sword. He bore a large book open on a black cushion.

After him came the body of Ham Dillon. He was in an open

coffin now, pillowed in flowers, and jostling along in the back of Mr. Gill's best hearse. It was made of iron, polished to a high sheen, and embossed all over in a Victorian fantasia of wreaths and vines and curlicues. Black horses pulled it. Two diamond-shaped headlamps framed the driver's head.

Flanking the hearse, and spilling out behind, were the rest of Ham's brothers in the Masonic lodge, all wearing their white aprons and gloves and solemn black suits, mixing now among other members of Elmore Township, male and female, both riding and walking. A horde of mourners moving with unnatural slowness, in deference to both the deceased and the everlasting dust.

Others got to the church first. By the time the cortege arrived at the Mud Pike, the building was already filled. People spilled out the doors, across the lawn, and onto the road, shifting and curling like penned cattle trying to make a path for the hearse. There were about two thousand people all told—some just curiosity seekers, of course—but Ham Dillon had a big reputation in these parts, and in death it had grown even bigger. Why, he would have been governor, people said. Many schools were closed for the day in his honor, and the funeral audience was filled with children.

"Our brother is gone, not to return. Never again will he join us in song or sport, or in the quiet joys of honest labor. He will never laugh again, or carry his children on his back!"

Reverend Aspinall was preaching the sermon.

"And how suddenly was he snatched away from us! Swept in an instant out of this life. Oh, how many things enter into our souls and unseal the fountains of our grief!"

Marcus Ragsdale, the pharmacist, cried out and wrung his hands. Everywhere there were pockets of sobbing.

"Yet has he no message for us?" cried the minister, raising his voice to reach the people out of doors. "No message, even now? His lips do not move, and yet we seem to hear them speak. And if we draw close—nay, closer yet—and incline our heads to his, perhaps we can hear what he has to tell us:

" 'PREPARE TO MEET THY GOD.' "

This sent a dark thrill through the congregation. For forty minutes the reverend carried on this way, invoking Ham with a kind of pitiless sentimentality. It wasn't till he was almost at the end that he struck a strange note—at least for those alert enough to catch it:

"Yes, he was cut down by lightning out of a clear sky. A death so sudden, so random, does it not seem to us poor mortals the most solemn and divine mystery? Over these past few days I have heard many say so. And yet . . . Painful though it may be at this awful time, I cannot neglect to denounce the rashness, the blindness, that in any manner risks all that is dear in life—that carelessness which may plunge loving hearts into grief that can never fully be assuaged.

"But now, forgetting to blame him, we only regret his fate, and amid sincere sorrow bid him farewell, farewell . . ."

It hung there for the rest of the service, that unpleasant whiff of a notion that Ham had dug his own grave. Some left the church muttering that it was grossly inappropriate (especially since there was nothing known yet, just a few rumors). But that was Aspinall for you: moral to a fault.

Into the warm and windless day the coffin emerged, borne aloft by six teachers employed in Ham's schools, the pallbearers he had requested shortly before he died. Then came the Dillon family, amid a tide of Masons, passing through a double line of flower girls along the path—supersolemn little girls, most of them, though one or two eyed each other and squirmed with guilty glee.

As the coffin was reloaded into the hearse, the Mud Pike's

requiem bell in the tower began to toll, registering the age of the deceased.

. . . nine . . . ten . . .

Mr. Gill, the undertaker, was dusting out the interior of the pallbearers' wagon, flapping at the long seats with his handkerchief, still in a bit of a dither. He had rented the wagon yesterday to a family for a picnic—standard practice, but they'd taken their sweet time returning it, not till the service was underway.

twenty-nine . . . thirty . . . thirty-one . . .

And that was all. Only thirty-one strokes. At every funeral that last tone hanging in the air always seemed to have the most unearthly vibrations. But especially when it came so soon.

It was a six-mile journey to the Walnut Hill Cemetery, which lay on a knoll just north of Odon. The enormous mass of people moved along the hot road behind the joggling hearse. Inside rode Maggie, with Ruth right alongside her. The little girl's knees were touching a bank of wild roses that lay squashed up against the coffin. Maggie stared ahead, her eyes as stony as an Irish wall. Ruth looked out the little window. They were passing a field of cornstalks, white-gold, clacking in the dry breeze. Here and there she saw cows gleaning in the ruined fields. The thick saccharine of flowers filled her nose and lungs.

She would hate the smell of wild roses for the rest of her life.

THE FIRST EVENING Ham Dillon spent in the ground, Link sat alone on his jail cot in Vincennes with a couple of the latest newspapers and his Bible.

Q: Did you intend to kill Dillon?

A: Is he dead? God knows I did not want to kill him. When I met him face to face my temper overcame me and like a firebrand the memory of the past misdeed of his came across my mind and in an instant I began shooting. . . .

"Like a firebrand . . . ?" Could he really have said such a

thing to that reporter? It didn't sound like something he would say. Or something anyone would say, outside of a book.

Well, he wouldn't have to go babbling to newspapermen now, just to have someone to talk to. His old friend and mentor, Judge James Denton deBekker, had arrived from Kentucky that afternoon and taken charge of everything. He brought optimism and energy and, even better, a plan of attack. He announced that Link's defense was going to be temporary insanity. He also offered the support and best wishes of mutual acquaintances back home, not to mention the whole state of Kentucky, while he sat flicking at bits of debris with the end of his cane.

It was the first cheering face Link had seen since long before the shooting, and he was grateful for it. But now that deBekker was back in his hotel, the prisoner was losing heart again. His friend's presence seemed to have polluted the air with memories of Kentucky life, which only made him more forlorn.

Link looked around at his cell: at the window, barred and shuttered, at the initials and raw remarks scratched in the walls. He had never dreamed he would find himself in such a tank of shame and depravity.

There was no chance of sleep, not yet. Madame Miranda's firehouse girls were still whooping it up next door. It was immoral, illegal. Why didn't the authorities shut them down? Or make them be quiet anyway? But the deputy, who was playing solitaire on the other side of the bars, hadn't even lifted his head.

Trembling, Link snatched up his Bible and pawed his way to Revelations:

". . . And I saw a woman sit upon a scarlet-colored beast, full of names of blasphemy, having seven heads and ten horns. And the woman was arrayed in purple and scarlet color, and decked with gold and precious stones and pearls, having a golden cup in her hand full of abominations and filthiness of her fornication . . ."

Link cried out.

"And upon her forehead was a name written, MYSTERY, BABYLON THE GREAT, THE MOTHER OF HARLOTS . . ."

He moaned again, and read and rocked and whimpered.

At last the deputy rose, stretched, and ambled along the corridor and down the steps, into the main office, where the sheriff sat.

"You know our friend upstairs?" the deputy said. "I was thinking maybe we ought to take that Bible away. It's starting to upset him."

2 1

WHEN THE SHERIFF'S WIFE finally pulled out Link's good suit, it had been satchel-mashed nearly a week. She smoothed it out for him as best she could, and fussed and flicked at it once he got it on. Somebody put a soft crush hat on his head. It was tan like the suit. He had never seen it before. Then, wedged between a couple of guards, he rode the train back to Washington to be arraigned for murder.

It was Thursday, three days since the funeral, long enough for the local hotheads to simmer down. There wasn't much danger he'd get strung up now, unless he got it with all the trimmings, after the trial. The guards didn't even bother with handcuffs. Wan, drawn, he entered the county courtroom and made his way down the center aisle with an old man's shuffle. Several dozen pairs of eyes followed him, on the lookout for signs of guile or madness.

DeBekker was waiting for him at the defense table—extending his arm in welcome, as if Link were late for a party. Gazing around, Link noted with a spark of resentment that he didn't recognize anybody there. Finally he looked up into the large, eroded face of the judge.

Then, without preamble, magistrate Hilary Houghton began to read aloud the grand-jury indictment. It charged that the prisoner, age forty-three, born in Pulaski County, Kentucky, did "feloniously, purposely, and with premeditated malice, kill and murder Albert H. Dillon, by then and there, feloniously, purposely, and with premeditated malice, shooting at and against, and thereby mortally wounding, the said Albert H. Dillon, with a certain deadly weapon, called a revolver, then and there loaded with gunpowder and leaden balls. . . ."

The judge had a nice rich voice. Link closed his eyes and felt its vibrations in his face and chest.

" '. . . against the peace and dignity of the State of Indiana,' " said the judge, and stopped.

Link said he was not guilty—"by reason of transient mental defect," deBekker added—and Houghton set the trial for mid-November. That was it. Link was escorted back to the brick jail on Walnut and Third by Washington's chief deputy Wallace. The prisoner did not say much along the way. Once he lifted his head to ask if he'd be put in prison stripes now.

Deputy Wallace let go a squirt of tobacco juice in the dust. "Well, I suppose that's up to you," he said. "Some of them wait till they're convicted."

THAT SAME AFTERNOON Maggie Dillon turned up, by appointment, at the law office of newly retired state senator A. J. Padgett, a.k.a. the Potbellied Stove—the man who had taken Ham to dinner in Indianapolis little more than a year ago. Padgett's offices were located, as they had been for thirty years, at the top of a one-flight exterior walk-up, a short distance up Main Street from the murder site.

She climbed the steps with a slow and conscious dignity. Every day she woke up to the same set of facts: she had discovered that her husband was sleeping with her sister and then, the next moment, seen him assassinated in the street. How would she ever get over that, the cataclysm of that fifteen minutes? Though there was something in Maggie's personality that probably didn't want to. Whatever else happened, from here on she was going to keep her eyes on the truth—in other words, the worst in people.

She hadn't come alone. Thumping up the stairs behind her came a young man who had been turning people's heads all the way up the street, the reason being he was just about the spitting image of Ham Dillon, deceased.

Even Padgett gave a start when he first laid eyes on him.

"This is Dennis," Maggie said. "Ham's brother. Have you met?"

They hadn't. After everybody shook hands, Padgett circled the visitors a little warily as they settled into their chairs, then shot a glance at his impassive assistant, Eberhardt. A pale, high-domed young man, his scant hair brushed back like guitar strings, Eberhardt was standing at the front window fussing with the shade. If he drew it up to get some air, the room became a box of light.

"Fan?" Padgett asked Maggie, as he seated himself.

Smearing aside some papers, the attorney uncovered a little pile of palm fans on his desk, a wide oak slab mounded with correspondence, books, amber pipe stems, and ashtrays. Out of the clutter a telephone rose like a black daffodil.

Maggie shook her head no, shifting a little in her heavy mourning dress. She had a little bag in her lap that gave off dark sparkles. Dennis reached forward and took a fan, then slumped back, working it.

"Well, I'm sorry as I can be about this whole thing," Padgett said to Maggie. "I thought a lot of your husband."

"Thank you," said Dennis, when Maggie didn't speak.

Up close, Padgett could see now, Den didn't look quite so much like his brother. He looked thinner, more pinched, and his eyelids drooped. Looked as if he'd taken some punishment. And so he had: for nearly two years Den had been down in Durango, Mexico, humping along some get-rich-quick scheme involving a copper mine. Start of the summer he'd finally come dragging back home. Padgett cut another look at his eyes. They were red-rimmed, from either drink or weeping.

They made a weird pair all right: Maggie in high-gloss mourning with a cameo at her throat and this mutant ghost of Ham. Padgett wondered why she'd brought him along. Then the answer came to him out of the blue. Maggie was hemorrhaging with sorrow and—unfortunately—using Dennis as a kind of tourniquet. She wanted him around because he looked so much like her dead husband.

"So how can I help?" Padgett said. Although he guessed that too.

Maggie said she wanted to hire him to prosecute Link Hale.

It wasn't that wild a proposal. Folks did this type of thing from time to time—the ones with money anyhow—on the theory that there was no reason to trust a run-of-the-mill county prosecutor with a really important case, any more than there was to settle for a court-appointed defense. In fact, it was downright silly not to do better when you could, and Maggie wanted the very best now. She wanted Link dead. She didn't say that, not in so many words, but Padgett could feel it coming off her like a dark heat. Link Hale had killed her husband in front of her and a hundred others, and now it was his turn to hang, preferably in the public square. She would be taking Allie's husband away from her too. It was something.

Padgett ruminated, flipping a finger against his lips. Then he called over to his assistant.

"Gene! Pull me down that copy of the *Register.*"

"What for?" said Dennis. Since Ham's killing he'd gone around like that, half insulting everybody.

"Why don't we see how the state bar rates Mr. Laughlin. Could be you're not giving the county prosecutor his due."

Maggie gave a little snort.

Eberhardt went over to the high bookcase and, leaning close, made a microscopic study of the titles, as if he were analyzing cave paintings. At last he selected one and sat down with it at his desk. Then he pulled out an enormous magnifying glass and began searching out the name of Laughlin. Eugene Eberhardt was slowly going blind. He had the brains for a much bigger career, but had fastened himself to Padgett's coattails as the only realistic thing to do.

Padgett leaned back and laced his fingers behind his head. He always liked watching his associate use that magnifying glass, especially on a lawbook. Eberhardt seemed to be ferreting out loopholes and legal nuances nobody else could spot. Padgett had him do it in court sometimes to impress the jury.

"Here it is," Eberhardt said. At a nod from his boss, he began to read aloud: " 'EDGAR LAUGHLIN, Odon, Daviess County: He possesses perhaps few of those brilliant, dazzling, meteoric qualities which sometimes flash along the legal horizon, leaving little or no trace behind; but rather has those solid and more substantial qualities which shine with constant luster, shedding light in dark places with steadiness and continuity. . . .' "

Eberhardt looked up.

"In other words, he's dull as a butter knife," Maggie said.

Padgett laughed.

"Well, maybe not altogether. You ever seen that buck on his wall?" Laughlin had been elected county prosecutor largely because he was a clubbable oaf who also happened to be the best hunter in north Daviess County, from deer on down. He had the eyes of a hawk and the ears of a new mother. It was said he could pick off a tree frog with a pistol at seventy-five yards.

"So what?" Dennis burst out. "What difference does that make?"

"Settle down," said Padgett.

"It brings the bile to my mouth, the way—"

"They're going to plead him insane, you know," Padgett remarked, turning his attention to Maggie. He tossed down his fan and picked up a panatela, crinkled it fondly in his fingers, then leaned across his desk to his cigar cutter. This was in the shape of a miniature guillotine; engraved on the front was the legend DO JUSTICE TO YOUR CIGAR. "Temporarily insane, I should say. Not responsible. You've heard about this?"

"Of course."

Padgett punched down the guillotine and the tip of the cigar dropped, headlike, into a tiny silver bowl. "Want my advice?" he said, looking up at her.

Maggie didn't say anything.

"Support that plea," Padgett told her, and sat back. "Maybe he'll spend some time in the birdcage. Maybe not. Either way, if I were you, I wouldn't be taking this to court."

"Why not?" Dennis said.

Still fingering his cigar, Padgett used his other hand to scrabble out a newspaper from the mess on his desk. He squinted down at it.

" 'It is drawn from very reliable authority,' " he read, " 'that Hale thinks Dillon is the father of the two-year-old in Hale's household.' "

"You're not going to smoke that thing in here, are you?" Maggie said.

Padgett raised his heavy eyes to hers, then ran his tongue under his lower lip. "I suppose I'm not," he said. He set down the cigar, stood, and moved to the window.

"I know perfectly well what I'm in for," Maggie said.

"Don't see how you could," Padgett answered equably, "unless you've been through a public scandal before. Your whole life's gonna get picked over by a bunch of jackals, me included, once you lay this out in court. It won't do your children a bit of good, and your husband's reputation, as far as I can judge, will go up in smoke like a Hindu sacrifice. But on the other hand, if you support an application . . ." He stopped. Down in the street he saw two buggies parked side by side, each with an elderly party at the reins. Buggy whips in hand, they were lashing at each other with awkward rage. One of them began to crumple under the rain of blows. People were running up.

This goddamn heat.

"You were talking about my husband's reputation."

"Aside from which, there's no guarantee of the outcome," said Padgett as he ambled back to his desk. "You may think you'll get justice, and maybe you will. But you put yourself at the mercy of a jury or any other twelve-headed animal, chances are you'll get hurt." He sat.

"None of this matters to me," Maggie said.

"Not your husband's good name?"

"Well, that of course." But there was something in her eyes. He wondered, for the first time, if she wanted revenge on Ham too.

"You're sure about that?" he said.

"Listen to me," she answered, leaning in and grasping his arm like a sibyl. "I didn't come here to convince you I loved my husband. I came because this man murdered him. He came all the way from Kentucky to do it. *He even told me so.*"

"He did?"

"Right there in that store. Those very words. We got into an awful commotion about it—that salesgirl must have seen. I thought I talked him out of it, but . . . Mr. Padgett, if that isn't cold-blooded murder, why don't you tell me what is."

"I'm not saying you don't have an argument," the attorney said slowly.

"An argument?" cried Maggie. "I've got the truth!"

"Well, when it comes to the law," he said, "sometimes the truth is just one more thing in the mix."

"Look here—" said Dennis.

"Goddamnit," said Padgett. He snatched up his cigar, lit it, and brought it to life with noisy kisses. Only when smoke was tumbling in the corners of the ceiling did he finally draw a satisfied breath. "All right. Now I'm gonna lay all the rest of it out for you, every other reason I can think of for you not to proceed, and then if you still want to go ahead . . ." He didn't finish that thought. "One." He raised a fat thumb. "You've got the unwritten law against you. The one that says you mess with a man's wife . . ." Dennis gave an incredulous squawk. "It ain't on the books, son, but it's holy writ to more people than you may think. Two. Mr. Hale has never been in trouble with the law before. In fact, from what I hear they have to throw him out of church to lock up. You get a good defense lawyer going with all that, accompanying himself on the violin—"

"Look at her," said Dennis quietly. "Just think about what she's been through. Can't you do the same for her?"

Twenty minutes later his visitors were gone, and what was left of Padgett's cigar lay smoldering unregarded in the big brass ashtray. The attorney himself sat slumped and silent. He noticed a dried stain on his tie and began chiseling at it with a thumbnail.

"They got problems," he said at last, brushing off the tie.

"Who does?" said Eberhardt.

"The defense."

"The defense? What do you mean? The way you were banging away just a little while ago, I thought they couldn't lose."

"Hellfire, I was trying to talk her out of going ahead."

"You mean you think you can win?"

"Look, if you hose away the horseshit, just what exactly does their side have to do? They've got to contend that Hale put a revolver in his pocket and left home. Traveled almost twenty-four hours, taking three different trains. Finally got off in the very state and county where the man he hated most resided—and shot him by accident."

"Spur of the moment."

"Either way. They've gotta say it was fate."

Eberhardt laughed. "That's pretty Greek."

"Right. The Oedipus defense. I was a helpless plaything in the hands of the gods."

All this while Eberhardt had his legs up on his own desk, doing eye exercises: watching the tip of his index finger as he brought it toward the end of his nose. Over and over again.

"You know, there's something funny about Mr. H. L. Hale," Padgett said, slouched so far down in his chair now his voice was mashed in his throat. "Here's a man never touches a drop of whiskey. Doesn't smoke. And what does he do? Gets himself a job at a bourbon distillery smack-dab in the heart of tobacco country. Now what kind of an individual does that?"

Eberhardt was still following his finger. "Just don't make him sound crazy," he said.

"That's the fight, right there," Padgett said, and sighed. "Them and us both, we'll have to dig up every head doctor from here to North Christ."

"Well, if it's all such a pain in the ass, why did you take the case?"

That was the question all right, and Padgett still wasn't sure he knew the answer. The trial was going to be a hog wallow, as far as he could see, and he didn't feel an overpowering drive to be a part of it. That's why he had gotten out of politics: it had gotten so he couldn't walk into the capitol building without his moral compass spinning like a roulette wheel. The friends he'd sold out for the greater good, the greater good he'd sold out for his friends . . . It added up to a lot of regrets. Not to mention the money.

Those orphan bundles of cash he'd taken in practicing the so-called art of compromise. He didn't like remembering what a good home he'd given them.

So why get mixed up in this hometown opera? Well, he remembered Ham Dillon. He had really liked that boy. But Padgett knew there was more to it. He wanted to believe that in this corrupt and self-excusing universe there were still one or two commandments left: a list of unpardonable offenses, no matter how short. Murder being one of them. Putting five bullets into a man on the public street, that was an absolute wrong—no equivocations, no excuses—and by shouting it down in front of a jury, in the sheer physical exercise of that, Padgett hoped that maybe he could sweat out a few bad memories.

He held his pudgy hands up in front of his face. " 'Will they ne'er be clean?' " he muttered. Then: "Goddamnit." Slamming a hand into his trouser pocket, he fished out a dime and dropped it into a Mason jar on his desk. Every time he quoted Shakespeare now, he cost himself a dime. There were twenty or thirty in there already.

"If you ask me, he had it coming," Eberhardt said.

"Who?"

"Dillon."

"You think so?"

"Sure. That's a hell of a way to deceive your wife."

"Maybe so," said Padgett. He thought about it. "Of course, Mrs. Dillon may have helped him out some."

"What do you mean?"

"Maybe she deceived herself."

2 2

" A LITTLE SLIGHT up front," deBekker said. "Looked as if
he could carry his weight, though. Big knees. Breedability."
He tapped his cigar. "A good Hail to Reason ass."

He rattled his glass at a passing waiter: "Once again, sir," he
said.

A couple of the newspaper boys leaned forward and added
their own before the tray disappeared; then their host went on
with his languorous descant on the top yearlings of last season
back home in bluegrass country. DeBekker had invited a few of
the press over for a chinwag at his hotel, and they were all tucked
together now in a plush corner of the lobby. The Hyatt Hotel was
the fanciest rendezvous in Washington. The rugs were thick, the
mints were thin, but even money couldn't hide from the mean-
ness of a hot day. The potted palms were turning brown at the

edges, and the big sand ashtray near the defense attorney's elbow was overhung by a stubborn cloud of grit.

Still, James Denton deBekker, in spite of his shining brow and the rosettes of broken capillaries on his cheeks, maintained an air of perfect coolness. He had practically been born in this pose. A pillar of the backwoods gentry, deBekker had been trained in Kentucky colonelhood as rigorously as any other career soldier, and now, well past the age of fifty, wore the manner so easily it almost passed for the man. His face fit the part: he had a nose like a can opener and a luxurious silver mustache; it was only on rare occasions—some gleam of anxiety in his eyes—that one might have guessed at a more awkward spirit within, one both imprisoned and at the same time grateful for the cover.

Right now deBekker was gassing about horseflesh because that's what these newspaper fellows expected. If you were a man, you had to be able to talk to men (his daddy had called it the first law of life), and if you came from Kentucky, you had to talk horses, especially if you wanted to make your way in politics. Just like the men around here talked coal or baseball.

"Well, now," deBekker said, rotating a big antebellum smile. These Indiana boys looked to him like a gallery of grotesques. "If I might turn for just a moment to what brings me here to town . . ."

"You're still paying, right?" said the man from the *Democrat*. He had bright eyes and very small ears, like a wolverine.

"Ha, ha," said deBekker.

"I been wondering about these famous Kentucky manners of yours," another reporter said. He had a broad shelf of forehead and eyebrows like hanging gardens. "We been here half an hour, and you still haven't praised the enterprise of our men and the grace and beauty of our women." He glowered a second, then started to haw-haw. DeBekker laughed again. Back home the men of the press were nothing more than a large, friendly dog that did tricks for a biscuit. This was hard work.

"Sad business, isn't it, boys?" he said, rolling his cigar on the lip of the ashtray. "Very, very sad. Course," he added collegially, "I don't suppose many of us would show to advantage if our private affairs were being di-ssected for the de-lectation of the public."

"So what's the dope on your client?" the wolverine said. "Still pretending he went nutty?"

"Well, now," deBekker began, "I don't know that——"

He was cut short by the arrival of the drinks. The men sipped and sighed.

"Mr. Hale's not pretending anything at all," their host resumed. He went on to paint his client as a man who, now that the fit was passed, sincerely regretted the incident yet was somberly at peace with himself. This was a lie. In fact, when Link wasn't slumped in the corner like a bag of soiled laundry, he was radiant with misery. He wouldn't stop tormenting himself with readings from the Bible—Cain, Job. Worst of all, he was starting to believe he was guilty.

"You know, I was always jealous of him," he'd confided to deBekker that morning. "Always, not just about Allie. I've been thinking about it a lot, and if I'm honest with myself . . ."

"Well, now, no need for that," said deBekker, with an airy wave of his cane.

"And yet deep down, I think I always believed . . . this'll sound ridiculous . . . that I was the better man. That's funny, isn't it?" said Link lugubriously. "I've sinned ten times worse than Ham Dillon ever did."

"Perhaps you were God's agent," said the lawyer smoothly. "The instrument of His divine wrath. You ever look at it that way, son?"

Apparently he'd have to save this boy not just from the gallows but from himself as well. DeBekker had always liked Link in the old days, looked upon him with a kind of condescending admiration during the stretch Link worked for him in the state tax office. They weren't close friends—naming his firstborn after deBekker, that just showed Link Hale's boundless capacity for sentimental gestures—but for years deBekker had been a mentor to him, a steadying hand. And when he heard about Link's troubles, and how he was being held captive on foreign soil (which was exactly the way folks back home viewed it)—well, call it noblesse oblige or maybe upholding the honor of Kentucky, but deBekker felt duty-bound to help him. Felt, perhaps, that he was the only man who could.

He had already done one smart thing: bringing on William Gardiner, a partner in Washington's preeminent law firm, as co-counsel for the defense. With his white Vandyke and fifty years' experience, Gardiner was a sober and principled man routinely referred to as the "Nestor of the southern Indiana bar." Strategically it was imperative, as deBekker knew, to have a local icon like this on their side.

DeBekker had written to Clagg too, back in Jessamine County, Kentucky. Clagg was a good lawyer. In small doses anyway. You had to make judicious use of Clagg.

"You trying to tell us Hale wasn't angry as hell at Ham Dillon?" the beetle-browed reporter said. "He back-doors your client for three and a half years . . ."

He sure as hell did, deBekker thought, the fumes of bourbon in his nose. He let them reach all the way to his aging and alien heart. "Why, I wouldn't deny for one moment that his wife's dishonorable behavior put Mr. Hale on his back legs," he said. "But you know what they say, boys. 'Anger blows out the lamp of the mind.' "

It went on like that for a while. DeBekker offered the newsmen home-fried boilerplate about Link Hale the family man and sober citizen. Finally he paid the bill and, with elaborate graces, guided his stumbling little herd out the door of the hotel.

From there they headed down Main Street together to the barbershop. Outside they found a host of slack-jawed faces at the window, staring in. Inside, Mr. Mayhew, the barber, awaited the arrival of the press, with a lathering cup in one hand, a badger-hair brush in the other, and a calliope of colored bottles behind him. There were two guards in the shop as well, keeping an eye on Link Hale, notorious murderer, who was shackled to the big horsehide chair. The coverage of this event would later carry headlines like the following: "September 23: Hale Is Shaved."

23

THE SIDE LOT was a crazy quilt of buggies and buckboards, most of them not so much parked as abandoned, a crush that spread all the way down the driveway and out into the street. Dobbins, mares, mules stood with their heads grazing the sides of neighboring vehicles, or communing nose to nose; when an animal snorted, another tossed its head in reply. Farther down the block, riding horses were tethered along the rail (and to each other when the rail ran out). A line of bicycles lay spilled along the fence.

Up the rise beyond stood the county courthouse, a broad brick building matted against the squirrel-gray sky. In the tower a gusting wind was bullying the heavy bell, and creaking the branches of the big naked elm that stood near the courthouse steps. Bits of trash frolicked over the lawn.

It was Monday, November 23—the start of Thanksgiving

week—and in this panorama of beast and buggy only one human soul stirred, a boy about ten years old. He had wedged himself almost flat to the ground beside the town pump (which stood directly downhill from the courthouse) and was busy carving something into the side of the water trough.

Pausing, he crooked his head to look up at the sky. Touched his face. Yanked himself, with both hands, high enough to peer over the rim of the trough. There were prickles on the surface of the water.

He looked skyward again; then at the first hard fling of rain he leaped to his feet and took off down the road like Paul Revere.

Inside the courtroom, whole rows of heads turned to the half-opened windows. Even Arnold Padgett, who was just building up steam in his opening argument to the jury, had to cock an ear. Since Ham Dillon's death two and a half months before it had rained exactly once in Daviess County, one poor piddle. But this rain was different, it was gathering force, and the people crammed into the courtroom yearned toward it, smelled it gratefully on the wind like dogs.

This audience numbered about a hundred and fifty, not counting the standees still shouldering for space against the back wall. A thigh-high rail with a swinging gate divided them from the principals, who were deployed across a long, low platform constituting the field of battle: defense left, prosecution right, at large oak tables. There was a line of makeshift desks along one wall for the newspapermen, and bleachers for the jury opposite. Miss Fish, the court stenographer, had a mesh bag of her personal chewing apples at her feet, and upstage center sat Judge Hilary Houghton, a jurist of long experience and unquestioned rectitude, whose Johnsonian ugliness even made drunks blink. Behind him, up near the ceiling, an allegorical painting ran from wall to wall. What it was an allegory of was open to debate, but everyone agreed it had all the right ingredients—smoke, banners, landscape, and a female in flowing gauze.

Padgett pulled his eyes from the rain-streaked windows and checked the jury. Undistracted, they were still giving him the same dutiful, marble-eyed stare. Even so, it was exasperating to have his rhythm busted up this way. He had already been interrupted in his opening argument once before—a full week ago. Rolling along, not twenty minutes in, Padgett had noticed one of the jurors starting to flip back and forth in his seat. It was such an oddly familiar motion—the spasms of a repentant sinner on revival night—that for several seconds everybody just stared. Then they realized he was having a heart attack. That set off all kinds of commotion, and it had taken days to get things back on track, with a new face in the jury box.

So naturally Padgett felt a little snakebit with this rain. Especially because he was convinced that the faster and harder he could drive this trial, the better chance he had to win. It was vital to keep the outrage over Ham Dillon's murder fresh.

Padgett gave Judge Houghton a weary look.

"Anybody who's got things to tend to because of the weather, get on out of here," the judge demanded, "and I mean right now."

A few peeled off. Then Padgett, squaring himself in front of the jury, got back to business.

"The unwritten law!" he boomed. "I say again, it is your sacred obligation as jurors to expel and expunge this phantom from your minds and hearts—the dark and bestial notion that a man is justified in killing another if the provocation goes . . . *or he fancies it goes* . . . to the sanctity of his home. There are nations on this planet, gentlemen, that are governed by unwritten laws. Nations whose citizens cower beneath the whips and whims of the despot. But not here! In the United States of America we the people regulate ourselves by no unwritten laws, no invisible legislation, but only by those laws which have the stamp and seal of our duly elected representatives, and to which every single one of us is equally subject. These laws, and only these, have any place

in an American court." Thumbs hooked in his suspenders, Padgett rested his palms on the mudslide of his belly. "And I say to you now, watch the defense carefully in this regard. Be as vigilant as the owl, be as wary as the deer. For they will try to persuade you that there is this shadow law—not by direct argument, that they dare not assert, but by insinuation, by intimation, by . . ." With his right hand Padgett suggested the wriggling of a snake. "Do not be seduced! For it is this man"—and now he was pointing straight at Hale, who sat slumped behind a bottle of cough syrup and a spoon—"this man here who has traduced and exploded the sanctity of the American family. He has slain not a stranger, not an acquaintance, but his own brother-in-law (his *brother . . . in . . . law*—consider for a moment, gentlemen, the awful weight of those words), and by this deliberate act of foul murder, this violation of the most fundamental *written* law our society knows, brought as much grief and havoc to the Dillon home as if he had wired it with dynamite . . ."

Padgett could thunder and volley this way, and sincerely too, while at the same time his actor's brain was tuning his performance and judging his grip on the crowd. He didn't have them quite in hand yet. Rain aside, there were still the whisperers here and there, ladies mostly, not settled yet, craning their necks for a look at Maggie, or furtively pointing out other principals in the case. Padgett could guess every word:

What about Mama Dillon? . . . Not coming. . . . Not coming! . . . She couldn't bear it. But see, there's Ed Watkins, you can bet your bottom dollar he's bringing her back reports. . . . Ed Watkins! Now what do you suppose he knew? . . .

Where's Denton? . . . Who's that? . . . The Hales' oldest boy. See, there's Louise, Arthur, Marguerite. Oh, look, they're letting the littlest play right down there on the floor. . . . Where? . . . There, by the defense table. . . . Not the actual baby, surely? . . . Oh, not that baby, good heavens. That's Lewis Hale. . . . Lewis? He's legitimate? . . .

Meanwhile other spectators, mostly men, were still musing over the lineups and figuring the odds. Whatever the moral and legal issues involved, however they felt about Ham Dillon, here was an interstate contest (Indiana v. Kentucky) that fired their sporting blood. For the home team: Padgett, now leading off; Eberhardt, his assistant, toying with a magnifying glass on the table; and Edgar Laughlin, champion hunter and part-time county attorney, who seemed to be studying the jury with a one-eyed squint, the kind he used when he raised his .30-30.

"And I emphasize premeditated!" Padgett cried. "For eighteen months, a full year and a half, Lincoln Hale nursed this serpent in his heart. He never took his concerns to his wife, as a frank and honest man would. He never asked counsel of any friend. No. Instead he slowly compiled a list—a secret list of the wrongs done to him, real, imaginary, he counted them, this career bookkeeper, he totaled and retotaled. And at last he thought to himself: What shall I do?

"Today we know all too well what he did. The task before you now, you twelve, is to decide what name his dreadful act deserves. Murder? Manslaughter? Should Lincoln Hale hang, should he go to jail, should he walk out that door scot-free? To determine that, you must hold in your minds, gentlemen, not just the shooting itself but every creeping action of the defendant's leading up to it . . ." His battle-pride mounting, Padgett went on to paint scenes like hallucinations: Hale buying the second revolver, the one he kept a secret from his wife; Hale riding the train all the way to Washington, Indiana, with that revolver in his pocket— three trains, in fact. . . .

"Can you not see it, gentlemen," Padgett roared, "how stubbornly, how remorselessly this defendant stalked his victim?" He had them now, he knew it: the jury, the crowd. "For more than twenty-four hours that individual seated there, a man by nature both timid and violent, moved in one straight and undeviating line that brought him at last face to face with his prey—whereupon, on the instant, he emptied every bullet in his revolver into Hamlet Dillon's defenseless body. There was no parley, no discussion. No chance for Dillon to speak a word. Consider all this, gentlemen, and when you do, you can only ask yourselves one thing. Not: Was this crime premeditated? The only question is: Could anything be *more* premeditated? . . ."

By now the veteran trial watchers and handicappers could see that Padgett was getting in some smart licks. But would he prevail in the long run? The defense team hadn't been heard from yet and (except for the little cadre of Kentuckians who formed a rooting section of their own) nobody knew much about them. DeBekker, the lead counsel, had a provocative ease about him, lounging with his long legs crossed at the ankles, the way he probably enjoyed his juleps. William Gardiner, folks knew him of course. But it was hard to judge him coolly. Padgett's only rival as a legal demigod in Daviess County, he brought so much respectability to his act of treachery in helping the defense that his own neighbors were left floundering between awe and contempt.

And then there was Clagg. Small, fierce, and old as creation, he had milky blue eyes and jowls like drape curtains, as well as a certain lurid glamour thanks to a rumor circulating about his service in the late war. Word was that Clagg had not only fought long and hard for the Southern cause, he had refused to come in after Appomattox. Instead, he spent a couple of extra years darting back and forth across the northern Tennessee border sniping at occupying Yankees and booby-trapping their encampments. Giving this up at last, he had studied for and passed the Kentucky bar, his declared interest in the laws of the United States being solely and purely to subvert them. To Clagg anything the government sought to accomplish was ipso facto worth thwarting, and on this foundation he had built a powerful name for himself as a defense attorney.

"Finally," cried Padgett, "as to this claim by the defense regarding the defendant's mental state at the time of the murder. This plea, this ploy, this act of desperation.

"I would remind you first *that it is not the burden of the prosecution to prove the defendant sane.*" He looked several jurors in the eye, one by one. "Our sole and entire responsibility is to prove that this man committed the crime charged against him, a fact we will shortly make plain to the meanest understanding. You, the jury, must assume the defendant was sane unless the defense can prove otherwise—and that, as you will see, is a burden too heavy for even Atlas to support.

"However," said Padgett with a sigh, "since they will do their utmost, you may be sure, to obscure the facts of this case with a lot of flapdoodle and flummery provided by so-called experts on the human mind, it has been only prudent for us to recruit some medical and psychological testimony of our own. For now," he said, crossing to the prosecution table, "you need only remember one thing." He picked up a leaflet. "This," he said, "right here, is a copy of the 1908 Indiana Statutes on Insanity. 1908. This year. I'd like to read you a little something." He thumbed. "Here we are. Gentlemen, this is the comprehensive, the overarching question—*the question above all others*—that doctors in this state must ask themselves when they judge a possible case of insanity:

" 'Is, or has, he or she been, and to what extent, noisy, profane, obscene, restless, destructive, filthy, cheerful, silent, seclusive, dull, epileptic, syphilitic, scrofulous, phthisical, hysterical, choreic, deformed, intemperate, deaf, mute, blind, lame or paralyzed,' *and if you behold the defendant,*" Padgett cried, pointing suddenly at Link as if he were a purse snatcher, "you can see that this man before you, Hardin Lincoln Hale, is manifestly none of those things! Except perhaps silent in the face of this awful tribunal! For he knows, gentlemen, the same thing you and I know. An evil heart does not make a diseased brain!"

The crowd released a great collective breath as Padgett sank to his seat, yanked out a handkerchief, and mopped his throat and neck. He had been speaking for more than three hours—an aria as much as an argument—and since the defense's opening statement wouldn't be heard till later on, when they began to present their own case, for now the vibrations from Padgett's mighty oratory claimed the courtroom undisturbed.

Sipping ice water, the prosecutor made a show of scanning his witness list. He was tossing sweat like a mill wheel, wishing he could switch right now to his afternoon shirt and drawers, when he happened to glance up and see Allie Hale.

She was sitting at the far end of the front row, near the defense table, hemmed in by a box of files. A little out of the way, but how on earth could he have missed her? He must have been the last person in court to notice.

She was wearing full widow's weeds. Black bonnet and dress, locket: the whole shebang. In fact, her attire—his eyes flew to Maggie on the other side—almost exactly matched her sister's. Really, you wouldn't turn your hand over for the difference. Dueling widows. It was unbelievable.

"Mr. Padgett?"

"Yessir. Sorry, your honor."

But even as he called his first witness, and watched him mumbling the oath, Padgett still felt as if he'd taken a blind-side punch. What the hell was in that woman's mind? And what would she say on the stand? Allie Hale was slated as a defense witness, so presumably she'd be trying to take the blame, trying to soften things for her husband. But in that getup? The real widow must already have seen her. He almost winced to think of it, the arctic depths of Maggie's rage.

THE BAILIFF moved along the far wall with a pole, closing high windows against the rain, while Dr. Bryson Gilbert, the surgeon from Evansville, testified to the cause of Ham's death.

"So in plain terms," said Padgett, after the doctor had ticked off all five wounds, "Ham Dillon actually succumbed to the bullet in his stomach?"

He died, said Dr. Gilbert carefully, of blood poisoning: "That is to say, the bullet carried septic poisonous matter into the tissues."

"But it was that first shot that ultimately killed him?"

"That's right."

"A bullet from this gun?" said Padgett, lifting a tagged revolver from a side table near the bench.

"Well, I'm not really—"

DeBekker called from the defense table. "We concede that, your honor. That's the gun."

Padgett gave the defender a courteous nod and then handed over the witness.

After a long, deliberate pause, deBekker rose. Then he eased around the table and strolled toward Dr. Gilbert.

"Doctor, did Mr. Dillon, in your presence, ever say why Mr. Hale had shot him?"

Dr. Gilbert considered. "I heard Dillon say that he couldn't think of any reason at all."

"Anything else?"

"I believe he said Mr. Hale must have gone crazy."

"Objection!" from Padgett.

"That's all," said deBekker, gliding back to his seat.

First blood. DeBekker had struck quick as a cottonmouth. Padgett was on his mettle now.

Next in the witness box was Rita Brazelton, one of the hello girls at the Washington telephone exchange. She was a serious-faced maiden with Victorian ringlets.

"Mr. Hale came into the office about ten-thirty," she said.

"On the morning of the shooting."

"Yes."

"And what did he want?" said Padgett.

"He asked me to place a call to Mr. Dillon in Elnora."

"Did you succeed?"

"No. There was no answer."

"So he went away?"

"Well, no, he didn't, not at first. In fact, he kept after me and after me," said the witness with a modest blush. "I must have tried eight or ten times. Finally I told him I was too busy handling other calls, what with the big political rally and all. Well, I mean, for goodness' sake, the man wasn't home!"

"So he was very persistent in trying to track down Mr. Dillon."

"Objection."

"Overruled."

"Mr. Hale was very persistent?"

"Very persistent, yes, he was."

Padgett returned to his seat, and deBekker came forward.

"Good morning, Miss Brazelton," he said.

"Good morning," she replied, eyeing him the way she might a dubious gentleman on an ill-lit street.

"Tell me this. When Mr. Hale was standing at the counter there in the telephone office, did you have an opportunity to observe him at all?"

"Yes, I suppose. More than I wanted."

"How did he appear to you?"

Miss Brazelton furrowed her brow and looked out toward the rain. "I don't know what you mean," she decided.

"Did he appear . . . well rested?"

"Actually he told me that he hadn't been sleeping."

"Do customers usually share this kind of personal information with you?"

"Customers make all kinds of remarks to me."

"They do?"

She hesitated. "Men do."

"What about Mr. Hale's appearance?" deBekker said, as a delayed flush of color touched Miss Brazelton's cheeks. "How did he look that morning?"

"How did he look?" She shrugged. "Not very good."

"You're saying he looked odd?"

"Objection."

"All I know is he was very determined."

DeBekker was through then, but before Miss Brazelton could depart Padgett rose again and called a question to her. "Miss Brazelton," he said, "I haven't been getting much sleep myself lately. Preparing for this big trial and all. How do I look compared to the way Mr. Hale did that day?"

"I don't know. I suppose about the same."

"And what would that be?"

"Not very good."

Laughter. Padgett sat down. After glancing apprehensively at the judge, Miss Brazelton smiled too.

Next Padgett began to present a chain of eyewitnesses to the crime. There was an eager rustle in the audience as the first of these came forward. Frank Dixon! He was the one who ran for the doctor. . . .

2 4

Y ESTERDAY'S DOWNPOUR had left behind an odd warmth
in the air—a surge up near fifty, like a last flick of summer's
terrible tail. So the trial's second morning brought a throng to the
plaza outside the courthouse even larger and rowdier than opening day's. In addition to the main herd now forcing its way
through the double-front door, there was a thick scattering of
hawkers, idlers, children, and other obstacles. One man was selling brooms and brushes, another was flogging a Homeopathic
Anti-Sin Pill ("Works on swearing too!"). A third fellow, surrounded by hang-jawed out-of-towners, was demonstrating the
eight distinct vocalizations of the owl.

There was some jostling on the main steps below, and then
the crowd there parted like the Red Sea to let Allie Hale ascend.
One glance at her black bonnet and the midnight dress that

peeked below her coat was enough to show she was dressed the same as before. Surrounded by three or four of her children, she mounted the steps keeping her eyes fixed on the courthouse door, while the whispering that had been so fierce yesterday started all over again.

Whispering, and some sputtering too. For a woman to appear in mourning for her lover while she sat near her husband in court was almost enough to disarm outrage, and leave some of the busiest flapjaws in town blinking like chickens in her wake. Why had she done it? To Allie herself it was plain enough, to a point anyway. The unbridled defiance of her spirit, from the time she was a girl—climbing that tree to face down the thunderstorm, holding up the blood-spattered hen to the heavens, even marrying Link, for that matter—still surged in her, and if her obstreperous independence had brought on the greatest griefs of her life, it had been her salvation as well. In the face of the present catastrophe, her first instinct was to flaunt her confession at the world.

She did not blame Link for anything now. The great aftershocks of the murder had put an end to that. Allie would testify in his behalf, do her utmost to save his life. But she would do it without renouncing her love for the man she had lost. Contrite—indeed, ready to take on any humiliation—she was still determined to wear her shame with pride.

Since the first wild wonder of the idea, of course, it had turned out to be a bitterly hard thing to pull off. There were times, under the feral eyes of these hundreds of strangers (and some not strangers, but whose eyes she no longer recognized), when the mourning she wore seemed to burn her like Medea's cloak. But there were times it felt bleakly beautiful too, natural, exalted even: almost a wedding dress.

At the least, appearing in it gave her the sensation of driving wolves back with a torch.

. . .

ONE THING Allie had forgotten to prepare herself for was the eyewitness accounts of Ham's murder. The prosecution offered them up one after another—the blood, the cries, Maggie staggering up the street. Allie listened with dread fascination. Now and then she glanced across the courtroom at her sister, but she never caught Maggie's eye. It was odd, Allie thought: her relationship with her husband was a twisted wreck, yet it remained a relationship still. Not so with Maggie. Between the sisters there was nothing, not even memories.

The eyewitnesses said much the same. (Edgar Laughlin, the easygoing county prosecutor, handled most of this testimony since it wasn't much harder than running sheep through a gate. The expert testimony, Padgett knew, was where the battle would be joined.) Tom Lascoulie, the farmer from Odon who had been walking with Ham that morning, identified Hale as the gunman and described Maggie wailing and stumbling through the crowd. Zeg Shufflebarger, Will Kennedy, Charles O'Brien all backed him up. They described popping sounds, some yelling, Ham bleeding like St. Sebastian in the shop doorway before he disappeared inside. Some of these details had appeared in the papers, some not.

"He look crazy to you?"

Laughlin asked everybody that. Houghton let him do it too, even though deBekker objected repeatedly. ("Don't tell me about Kentucky!" hollered the judge. "In this state you don't have to be an expert to have an opinion!"—a pronouncement that brought approving murmurs from the crowd.) Every eyewitness said no, Hale didn't look crazy, or else they couldn't tell. "The man was very pale," said one primly, "but I couldn't see any storms raging in his breast or brain."

Meanwhile Padgett leaned back analyzing the testimony as it

clicked along. So far so good. After ten weeks, it was vital to air out the brutal details again, to rekindle the outrage over Dillon's death.

"He said what?"

"He said, 'He busted up my home.' "

"Then what?"

"Then I took him to jail," Deputy Wallace said.

"This was what," said Laughlin, "maybe five minutes after the shooting?"

"If that."

"And he seemed of sound mind to you at that time, Deputy?"

"Seemed okay to me."

"Seen a few crazy folks in your time?"

"Seen a few."

"Your witness." Laughlin sat down, and deBekker stood up. He wore a bemused expression, as if he were marveling anew at the infinite comedy of life. Padgett had seen this look before and was getting leery of it.

"Sound mind, you say."

"Yep."

"But you're not an expert in the field of mental health."

"Don't claim to be."

"Deputy, let me ask you this. Later that night, when you finally left Mr. Hale in his cell to go to bed, what was he doing exactly?"

"Doing?"

"Was he in any particular physical position?"

Slowly, with a thick thumb and forefinger, Deputy Wallace traced the big horseshoe of his mustache.

"He was on his knees, I think."

"You think?"

"He was down there on the floor."

"Doing what?"

"He was praying."

"Could you hear him? What he was saying?"

Deputy Wallace gave a minute pause. "Yep," he said. "He was praying for Ham Dillon to get well."

Came time for lunch, the people who hadn't brought something to eat beat it out of the building in a hurry. Then the others began flowing toward the door. Waiting near the witness box for the path to clear, Padgett found himself standing close by deBekker. Just behind him was the rest of the defense team and Lincoln Hale.

"Well, sir," Padgett said, genially addressing deBekker, "hope you weren't trying to prove just now that praying to the Lord is a sign of insanity. That won't get you far around here."

"I thank you for your good advice."

Link Hale leaned forward and tugged at deBekker's sleeve. "You know, I promised I'd talk with the editor of the Evansville paper," he said, "back at the jail. Shouldn't we be getting over there?"

"Don't you worry, son!" Padgett called out. "If people think they can make money off you, they'll eat shovelfuls of shit!"

"Don't talk to our client," Clagg snapped, and raising both hands in mock surrender, Padgett moved away.

IN THE HALLWAY outside the courtroom, Allie spotted her son Denton and began shouldering her way toward him through the throng. They hadn't seen each other in months, and since the murder he had not even answered her letters. When he caught sight of her now, arm outstretched and calling his name, the boy blanched and skittered down the stairs to get away.

Allie stopped, and her shoulders sagged.

Early that morning, not long past dawn, she had made a secret pilgrimage to the little white house where Ham died. First floor back, that's what she wanted to see; where the deathbed was. But the female troll at the front door wouldn't let her in. Allie wheedled, but the woman said she was sick of gawkers. Then her eyes narrowed.

"Are you *her?*" she said.

Something in that gaze made Allie, for once, lose courage. "No," she said.

The woman studied her some more. "You're just a born liar, aren't you?" she said, and closed the door.

Now Allie stood in the courthouse hall as the last of the crowd trickled down the stairs, the same way Denton had gone. She felt desolate, utterly abandoned. Then she turned and saw Ed Watkins.

He was standing at the far end of the passage by himself, fumbling pistachio nuts out of his coat pocket, munching, dribbling shells. Ed. Her heart flooded. All through her high-wire love affair with Ham, she had often thought of Ed as a sort of good-luck charm. It wasn't just that he was the one person who traveled between the Dillons' and the Hales' every day. Way back when, he had done his own odd but important part as fill-in father to Ham. There were so many things she'd always wanted to ask Ed, all those eager, silly questions about what Ham had been like as a boy. But of course she never could. Instead she would stand at the mailbox sometimes talking to Ed about nothing at all, knowing she was making him late, overpowered by a need to keep him there.

She walked toward him now down the almost empty hall.

"Hello, Ed," she said.

Ed dragged his head up and looked around. He didn't seem to have noticed her before. "Hello there to you," he said.

"How have you been?"

"Oh, I'm getting pestered to death," Ed returned with an air of great satisfaction. "First this one outfit, the H. E. Hellser Company, they come after me wanting me to sell their mailboxes to my customers, and now I got two other concerns after me to try their mail wagons. All of them promising this and that and the other. Don't give a man a moment's peace."

"You sound very popular." She was grateful he wasn't shunning her.

"And as if that ain't enough, now there's these automobile agencies started coming around, telling me don't listen to those mail-wagon fellas, they're old news, you want to be sitting at the wheel of the twentieth century. So I took one of them salesmen out on my route and I said to him, 'Son, have a look at that road there. How many holes you see? Go on, count 'em up. And then you come back and take another look next time it rains. And then you multiply that whole mess out by twenty-four and a half miles. Till these daggone county officials get some more graveling done, I believe I'll stick with my oatsmobile."

Allie was so pleased to listen. Until she realized with a sinking heart that he might be talking to anyone at all like this, friend or stranger. His eyes offered nothing: no hint of a bond between them, no special history, no glimmer of sympathy or reproach. And he'd always been this way, she thought. So sociable, yet so remote. It was a little creepy when you thought about it.

Suddenly she felt as if her mourning dress were a clown's suit or a Halloween costume.

"Hey, Mama." Marguerite came up and curled her hands around the black lacework on her mother's arm. "Don't you want something to eat?"

2 5

"GOOD MORNING, Doctor. How are you?"

"Healthy as a heathen," said Dr. Herr.

Dr. Henry Herr had a round, stubborn face and wore a boutonniere: two baby pink roses held together with tinfoil. He was Padgett's first psychiatric witness, the doctor who had publicly examined Link Hale right after the shooting, in Washington's city hall.

He described taking Link's pulse that day, checking his face and eyes and so forth, and declaring him sane on the spot.

"And you asked him questions during the course of this examination?" Padgett said.

"Yes."

"Such as?"

"What's your name? Do you know why you're here . . . ?"

"And he answered correctly?"

"Every time."

"Did you ask him why he had fired his gun?"

"Of course."

"And what did he reply?"

"He said, 'I was trying to kill him.' "

"You're certain."

"He said it clear as a bell. Fifty others heard him too."

"Yours."

DeBekker approached the witness.

"Doctor, during your examination of Mr. Hale, testing this and that, I believe you tipped his head back? Looked inside his mouth?"

"Yes, that's right."

"What were you looking for?"

"Swollen tongue. Possible signs of hydrophobia."

"So you checked him the way one would a dog, say, or a horse."

"I don't know. I'm not a veterinarian."

"Really?" said deBekker. "You surprise me."

Dr. Herr's face turned a faint violet.

"Now," the attorney continued, "as to this infamous remark of the defendant's, 'I was trying to kill him' . . . Can you tell us in what tone of voice he expressed this sentiment?"

"Objection," said Padgett.

"Dr. Herr is an expert," deBekker said, "in interpreting human behavior. At least according to the prosecution."

"Oh, go on and answer," said the judge.

"What was his tone of voice?" said Dr. Herr. "I'd call it . . . flat."

"He wasn't boasting."

"No."

"Though come to think of it," said deBekker, gracefully musing, "I suppose he might have been boasting."

William Gardiner, at the defense table, looked up.

"If as you say," deBekker continued, "his tone was . . ."

"Flat," said Dr. Herr.

"Flat, yes. Uninflected, neutral. *'I was trying to kill him'* . . . Why, under certain circumstances a man can brag in that sort of voice, can't he?"

"I suppose," said Dr. Herr.

"And by the same token," deBekker went on, still following this butterfly of thought, "he might be conveying something different, isn't that so?"

Dr. Herr didn't answer.

"Regret, let's say. To pick an example. *'I was trying to kill him.'* Yes. Or shock perhaps. *'I was trying to kill him.'* Dismay. *'I was trying to kill him'* . . ."

"Your honor, please!" cried Padgett, bounding up.

"Why, he might be expressing anything at all . . ."

"That's fine!" Padgett shouted. "Now how about Hamlet's advice to the players?"

"Knock it off," said the judge. "Both of you."

Herr was followed to the witness stand by Dr. MacGregor Porter of Elnora.

"You're a general practitioner, a family doctor, right?" said Padgett. He was still a little flushed.

"Yes."

"And you have treated various members of the Hale family?"

"Yes, I first went to their house in the winter of 1906 to see their son Arthur. He was in bed with croup." Dr. Porter couldn't help glancing at Allie as he spoke, for he still remembered that night: the rack and rasp of the boy's coughs, the beautiful fever in her own eyes as she hovered there in the doorway.

"Have you treated Mr. Hale as well?"

"Yes, fairly often while he was living here in Indiana."

"For mental problems?" Padgett asked.

"No, no. He had some physical ailments."

"Such as?"

"Minor muscle spasms, anemia."

"And when did you last treat him?"

"Three days ago, in jail."

"What for?"

"Stomach trouble."

"So you've had professional contact with Mr. Hale over a period of some two and a half years. That is, during the period when he was supposedly having such terrible difficulties."

"I've seen him off and on, yes."

"Has he ever, in all that time, seemed insane to you?"

Dr. Porter kept his eyes away from Allie. "No," he said.

"He's perfectly normal?"

"I would say so. I wouldn't call Mr. Hale the happiest man alive, but yes, he's in the normal range."

"Even though he's suffered from a number of physical ailments."

"Yes."

"Can physical problems all by themselves cause the sufferer to become gloomy? Agitated?"

"Yes, often."

"He might have trouble sleeping?"

"Yes."

"In other words, such behavior isn't necessarily a sign of mental disease."

"That's right."

Dr. Porter felt a little queasy. He wasn't lying. But he was doing his bit to hang Allie's husband.

To everyone's surprise, the venerable William Gardiner rose to cross-examine. It was the first time Gardiner had taken a witness.

"Dr. Porter."

There followed an oceanic pause, during which Gardiner seemed to be meditating on something, possibly the vastness of the universe.

"You're not a specialist in mental disorders, are you?" he growled at last.

"No."

"But you're a medical man of wide experience."

"If you want to put it that way."

"In your experience does insanity run in families?"

"Run in families?" Dr. Porter gave a mild laugh of surprise. "No, I wouldn't say so."

"It doesn't."

"Not usually, no."

Gardiner stood in the middle of the room massaging his Vandyke. Everybody waited.

"You treated other members of Mr. Hale's family. I believe you told us that."

"Yes, that's true."

"Were you ever called to attend his oldest son?"

"His son?"

"Denton Hale."

Dr. Porter felt a warning flush through his body.

"Yes, I did. I came to see Denton."

"More than once?"

"Yes."

"Why was that?"

"He was injured."

"In what way?"

"He'd been, uh . . . He'd been shot."

"I see." Once more Gardiner's mind seemed to circle the globe. "Self-inflicted, was it?"

A sudden movement of protest from Link at the defense table caught many people's eyes. Others were searching to see if the boy himself was in court. Yes, there he was.

Denton sat toward the back, squeezed between two strangers, prickling with shame. He worked his thighs slowly, like pincers, against his clasped hands. From her own place several rows away, Allie watched him, stricken.

"I'm sorry, am I speaking too softly?" Gardiner said. "I was asking if the wound was self-inflicted."

"Yes, it was."

"Can you tell us the circumstances?"

Padgett objected finally, but Judge Houghton overrode it, and Dr. Porter had to go on and recount in stark detail how Denton had shot himself in the chest and fallen through the door of an outhouse.

"And when this accident occurred. . . . But I suppose I'm using the wrong term. It wasn't an accident, was it?"

"I don't know what you mean."

"The boy shot himself deliberately in an attempt to take his own life, isn't that right?"

"He never said so."

"But based on the circumstances, discussions with the family, the angle of the bullet as it entered his chest, that was your conclusion, wasn't it?"

"Yes."

"But he's all right now? He's been all right ever since, hasn't he?"

"As far as I know, yes."

"Tell me something, Doctor," said Gardiner. "Is it possible that the boy was temporarily insane—just for that moment or two, when he pulled the trigger?"

PADGETT STILL HAD several more psychiatric witnesses to shake out of his sleeve, and from now on they were all specialists in mental health. He called one Dr. Wall, an alienist who ran a sanitarium in Champaign, Illinois, and the author of a book on the subject of impulsive insanity. Distinguished-looking in a cadaverous sort of way, his cheeks pitted like the moon, Dr. Wall testified with morose certainty. "Impulsive insanity cannot exist," he said, "where a person has a reasonable motive for his action."

"And there was a motive in this case?" Padgett said blandly.

"From what I understand, there was a motive as big as a house."

"But what about a case where— Well, let's make it a hypothetical. Suppose a man was right on the verge of killing another. Say he grabbed a gun and chased his quarry out into the front yard. And let's say that at the last moment, the very last, he was deterred by the pleadings of his wife . . . ?"

"Yes?"

"Now if this man, a full month later, shot and killed his victim after all, would that be impulsive insanity?"

"Well, of course not," said Dr. Wall. "It's all the more proof the killer had ample time to think it over."

Others followed Dr. Wall—a Dr. Samassoud, a Dr. May—who promoted the same view. Dr. May gave Padgett fits with his academic bob-and-weave ("Well, in effect yes, but on the other hand, somewhat no . . ."); overall, though, the prosecutor was well satisfied with the drive of the psychiatric testimony. Late Wednesday he brought it to a climax with his grandest witness yet.

Dr. Allan Upchurch was from Boston, an alienist with his own clinic and a national reputation. Goaded by some notorious murder trials of the recent past (that of Czolgosz for shooting President McKinley; Harry Thaw's for the killing of New York architect Stanford White), Dr. Upchurch had developed a bee in his bonnet about the growing use of the "temporary insanity" defense, and he had taken to traveling about the country trying to stamp it out. It was a fad, he maintained, a fraud on the court and a gross abuse of justice.

Not only was he an expert's expert in his field; he was also a big-gun intellectual from the East, and that alone, Padgett knew, would likely make him a powerful persuader. Goggle-eyed, high-shouldered, and sporting an olive-colored checked suit, he nevertheless possessed a certain beaky charisma. When he took the oath with genuine dignity and self-assurance, the random titters stopped.

Padgett walked him through his credentials for the jury, then got to the matter at hand.

"What is your view, Dr. Upchurch, of this term 'temporary insanity,' or 'emotional insanity,' as it's sometimes called?"

The doctor settled himself like a nesting hen. "My view," he said, "is that 'emotional insanity,' as it's commonly understood by the public, is a phantasm and a canard. In plain words, there's no such thing. Any self-respecting alienist wouldn't give it the time of day."

"Why not?"

"Because it's absurd to imagine that a man can be sane one instant, insane the next, and sane once more a moment later—the moment immediately following the commission of a crime, as is usually alleged. It's simply an attempt to provide an excuse, ex post facto, for impulsive bad temper, cruelty, and a readiness to take the law into one's own hands. It's a notion stolen from bad novels—"

"I see. Do you—"

"—and then polished up by unscrupulous lawyers," Dr. Upchurch went on, "in order to—"

"Yes, yes," said Padgett hastily.

"—in order to arouse false sympathy with criminal violence. It's a hoax. All genuine insanity is the product of prolonged gestation, and those who say otherwise . . ."

Nodding, Padgett raised a hand to steady his witness, who was saying all the right things but with a little too much fizz. Dr. Upchurch fell silent, his breath making vapor puffs in the air. Temperatures, which had been seesawing as Daviess County balanced on the brink of winter, had plunged overnight, and today cold curled through the shut windows and pooled about the floor. Many of the spectators in the ill-heated courtroom sat with their coats and boots on. Clagg, over at the defense table, had tied a red kerchief around his bald head and looked like an old pirate.

"Let me ask you this," said Padgett at last. "If those who claim they were insane for an instant, a few seconds, whatever it might be . . . If they aren't insane, what are they?"

"What are they?" said Dr. Upchurch with relish. "Frankly, I've found that those who plead temporary insanity are usually among the more refined, the more elevated criminal types—if you'll pardon the antilogy."

"Of course."

"An individual like this has a simply outlandish conception of his rights in society—a misplaced vanity, an egotism of mythological proportions. If he ever feels he has been wronged, he immediately casts himself as the injured hero."

"Can you give an example?"

"A husband who shoots another man on his wife's account."

"Ah. And typically how does a scenario like this develop?"

"An egotist such as I've just been describing neglects his wife, ignores her tastes and inclinations, and then suddenly he's surprised when she takes up with someone else. After brooding over his lost property—for that's just what he considers her—and fearing the criticism and ridicule of the community, he kills the other man, usually in some melodramatic fashion, while taking care to save his own skin."

"We've been hearing the word *depression* from the defense . . ."

"Pooh," said Dr. Upchurch. "What is depression after all but morbid self-involvement? It's egotism, that's all, a funereal form of egotism."

When the time came at last for his cross-examination, Dr. Upchurch seemed to welcome it. Perhaps a little too eagerly. He flicked his tongue as deBekker approached, and Padgett, who was congratulating himself on the direct testimony, felt a touch of unease.

DeBekker stopped and cocked his head. "You said something about unscrupulous lawyers . . ."

Dr. Upchurch huffed. "Well, some are."

"Over at the defense table we were wondering if you might be referring to us," said deBekker. He wore his perplexed look.

"I don't know a thing about your personal ethics," said Dr. Upchurch crisply. "You may be a perfectly upstanding individual."

"In other words," said deBekker, "it is possible to offer a legitimate defense of temporary insanity."

Dr. Upchurch frowned. "Misguided, that would be the best construction I could put on it. Misguided, or desperate."

"Desperate?"

"Emotional insanity is a last-ditch defense. Lawyers with nothing else to offer sometimes try to use this pseudoscience to mystify ignorant juries."

Padgett winced.

"Oh?" said deBekker. "You think juries are really that easy to delude?"

"To delude, or perhaps, rather, to lure into a sort of unconscious conspiracy to defeat the truth. Sometimes, I'm sorry to say, jurors in these cases are really looking for a rationale, for any excuse whatever to acquit the defendant—if they have some idea that the person he killed deserved it, so to speak."

"So you're saying that jurors prejudge these cases."

"Objection!" bellowed Padgett, rising.

"On what grounds?" said the judge.

Padgett sat down.

"Can you tell me a little more," said deBekker, at his most oleaginous, "about how this collusion between the defense and the jury takes place?"

"Well, there's a readiness to . . ." Dr. Upchurch gathered

himself. "You see, public sympathy with these cases depends upon the dramatic skill with which the husband, and the agents acting in his behalf, present his story. He has to appeal to the degenerate tastes of the public."

"Degenerate?"

"Unfortunately Americans are fast becoming pigs at the trough of popular entertainment—that is to say, lurid books, magazines, moving pictures—an appetite which is fed every day by the depraved tone of the public press. . . ."

"The public press today is depraved?"

"In large part, absolutely."

"The kind that, say, these gentlemen write for?" DeBekker indicated the line of newspapermen at their desks along the wall.

"And this is exactly why," cried the witness, barreling on, "lawyers should not be permitted, with the aid of disreputable members of my own profession, to invent spurious forms of insanity and inject improbable dramatic elements purloined from sensational fiction. The alleged insanity of any defendant should be settled by a commission of alienists, not passed on by an ordinary jury at all."

"I see, Doctor," deBekker said, pausing with his palms together at his lips, as if in prayer. "A jury, even if it somehow, miraculously, manages to resist prejudging such a case, still is not really equipped to decide it."

Padgett sat listening with his forehead resting on the palm of his hand.

SOMEWHERE DEEP in his testimony Dr. Upchurch seemed to realize he had lost the crowd. He apologized to those he had offended (virtually everybody) and blamed the strains of a long train trip. Padgett patched him up some on redirect.

Still, the doctor was nothing like the knockout blow the prosecution had hoped for. All the better then that Maggie Dillon appeared for her testimony next morning looking perfect: regal, tragic, a martyr's queen.

Gently, as if leading her into a wading pool, Padgett drew from her the story of her close acquaintance with Lincoln Hale going back twenty years, starting with the days he taught both sisters in the one-room schoolhouse in Kentucky. Padgett painted her as a trustful girl back then, Link as her guide and tutor. (When this same man killed her husband years later, was it not like a father betraying his own child?) The prosecutor cast Hale as an outsider and opportunist—a man who, after worming his way into the bosom of the Thompson family, had moved to El-nora in the vain hope of cashing in on Ham Dillon's connections.

Link found it very strange listening to all this: an endless story about a man he half recognized. Instead of getting angry, though, he slid off into sentiment. Those weeks when he and his family first came to Indiana, when they were living with the Dillons—how lively and cozy that time now seemed. He'd seen too what a fine parent Maggie was. Once she had told him that the best favor she could do her children was to remember they'd be dead someday, that it was her job to make sure they went to heaven. She had starch.

At last Padgett brought Maggie around to the day of the shooting. Eyes front, like a soldier, she described running into Link Hale that Saturday morning, and how he had tugged her inside the general store. Padgett wished she would look at the jury.

"He was dancing around something, I didn't know what, but finally he broke down and told me."

"Told you what?"

"About my sister—his wife—and Ham."

"That they had become intimate?"

"Yes."

"And how did you react?"

A silence. "I don't remember."

"You were given a glass of iced tea, weren't you?"

"Yes, that's true."

"What else do you remember?"

"He told me he wasn't going to take it lying down. I remember that clearly."

"Did he say what exactly he intended to do?"

"Yes," Maggie said, her eyes blind and burning. "He said he was going to kill my husband."

"Those words?"

"Virtually those words. I had absolutely no doubt what he meant."

"What did you do?"

"Well, I was very frightened. I begged him to go and get on the train, not to cause any trouble. I could hardly . . . I was still trying to . . . you know, I didn't know what to say. Finally I said, 'For the sake of the children, yours and mine, for their sake, please, please stay away from him.' "

"And then?"

"He didn't say anything at first and then . . . Then he said all right."

"All right?"

"He said not to worry, that he wouldn't do anything to hurt me or the children. That was when . . ." She paused.

"Yes."

"That was when we saw Ham."

"Where was he?"

"We saw him outside, a-way up the street. Neal & Eskridge's has that great big front window, and you can see more than a block. . . ."

"You're certain it was he?"

"I know my husband."

"And you're certain Mr. Hale saw him as well?"

"Of course. I pointed him out, and he said to me, 'Yes, you're right.' "

Padgett glanced at the defendant, who was watching the testimony with widening eyes. "Go on."

"Well, as I say, I saw my husband first, and I began to get very agitated again. I knew he was coming there to meet me, and I was just pleading with Link to go away."

"What did he say?"

"He gave this big sigh and said, 'I promise.' Then he kissed me." Her fingers wavered to her cheek. "I saw him glance out the window again, and then he said . . ." She faltered. "He said, 'I've always had the greatest respect for you, Maggie.' And then he left."

"Which way did he go?"

"He turned right, heading east up the street toward Ham. My heart went into my mouth, I was so surprised he'd gone that way. For a moment or so I couldn't move at all, and then I ran to the doorway and looked up the street. And that's when he shot my husband."

Padgett led her on through the events of the next few minutes and hours, and finally to Ham's last breath. She wanted Link to hang, he knew, more than anything else in life. But she wasn't projecting any vengefulness. She never lost her great stricken dignity.

"What has life been like for you since the shooting?" he said at last.

"I have to object to that," said deBekker from his seat.

"I don't see why," said the judge.

Maggie touched her temple. "I have headaches. I have to lie in the dark for . . . Dr. Porter comes."

"And your children?"

"My children are just fine," Maggie flared.

Padgett ended his questioning solemnly delighted. She had been a perfect witness: Niobe without the tears. During deBekker's cross-examination, which ran most of the afternoon, the prosecutor felt easy enough to let his mind drift ahead to some of the defense witnesses coming up.

He was half watching, half dreaming in this way when he realized that deBekker was asking the same question for the third time.

"You're saying that you and Mr. Hale saw your husband through the window of the store."

"Yes, I—"

Padgett stood up. "She's answered that already, your honor."

"You're right. I'm sustaining that."

Padgett was sinking back to his seat, wondering why deBekker seemed stuck on the point, when he caught a look at Maggie's face. Her eyes were flat and impersonal; they reminded him of eyes he'd once seen in the slit of a door at a private club. Nobody noticed as far as he could tell (had deBekker?), but Padgett wondered for the first time if Maggie was lying.

2 6

ALLIE WAS REMEMBERING HAM.

He was lying naked on his back—buck naked, Greek naked, with the quilt thrown to one side. They were quiet together.
A fly, making a slow, drunken loop around the room, finally shot
out the window.

"How does it feel to be overburdened with natural advan-
tages?" she said.

He laughed aloud. "As the sideshow manager said to the
freak." But his smile faded when he turned and saw something in
her eyes. A sort of sad envy.

"I was over at John Boggs's place the other day," he said at
length. "Talking politics. We're getting on fine. That new wife of
his comes into the room. He seized up. Just a little, but I saw it.
That's kind of an obstacle when you're trying to get a man to put
his confidence in you."

"You've got them afraid for their women?"

"It happens once in a while. I don't know what they think I'm going to do, carry them off like some damn Cossack."

Allie lay toasting in the sunshine, considering.

"What are you thinking?" he said.

"Gentlemen of the jury," James deBekker said, and Allie changed worlds.

The Kentuckian stood, with florid authority, in the open space between the lawyers' tables, surveying the jurors as if he were a distinguished visitor in a cemetery and they were so many headstones. When he spoke again, his voice, touched with the honey of the South, had an elegiac ring.

"Where can a man find sanctuary?" he began. DeBekker could still set young girls' hearts aflutter, especially when fortified (as he was now) by a couple of jolts from his pocket flask. "Sanctuary from what? you ask," and he went on to say what: the punishing tempo of modern life, the rise of science and the machine, the scream of steel, the jangle of the telephone, the cankerous and degraded lures of the city, the trampling of the simple joys and the old ways . . . Finally the slow toboggan of his rhetoric brought deBekker right back to his starting point: Where could a person find sanctuary? This time he had an answer.

"The home! The home, gentlemen. We have church, of course, our priceless communion with Christ, but day in, day out, do we not find our dearest earthly refuge in the faces around our own fireside—and especially in her whom we have chosen to share life's journey? The cheering smile, the tender touch, the milk-white arm stealing round our shoulders, as we recombobulate ourselves by the fireside at the end of a long day . . ."

Somebody in the crowd let go a tremendous sneeze. A thick cold, presaging snow, was leaking in through the windows today. But the audience wasn't restless. It wasn't just that the Kentucky contingent (bigger now, Padgett saw) was silently urging deBekker on; everybody there was well accustomed to oratory covered in frosting, they were practically connoisseurs of it, and so had almost infinite patience waiting for the cake. Thus they hung with deBekker through his encomiums to this and perorations to that. They hung with him too through the interruptions caused by a periodic banging in the ceiling. The winds had turned vicious over the weekend and sent tin shingles from the courthouse roof sailing around the streets. Now workmen, muffled and gloved, were up there making repairs.

"You know, back a ways," deBekker said at last, "I believe I said that the sacred American home is our only refuge on this earth. Now I have to acknowledge that in the case of Mr. Hale here I made a slight error. He found another sort of refuge. He took refuge *in his own doubts.* Doubts that his own dear wife and his own brother-in-law could be capable of such monumental treachery. He just plain couldn't believe it. And he hung on to those doubts, clung to 'em with both hands, for a good couple of years. Now that's a sad state of affairs, you might say, and so it is—sad indeed when a man starts telling himself, like that old stage Negro, that maybe his wife's honest, because, well, at least he ain't had the ocular proof. It's a sad thing. But it's a human thing. And then! To see that proof gradually taking shape . . .

"What proof am I talking about? Not the day he walked in and caught 'em red-handed. No, sir! I refer to the silent mockery of that *baby!* Every day growing just a little bit bigger, looking just a little bit more like Mr. Hamlet Dillon. Now you might say the baby was only circumstantial evidence. But I remind you of the words of that famous Yankee Mr. Henry David Thoreau, when he suspected his milkman of watering the milk. 'Some circumstantial evidence is very strong,' Mr. Thoreau said, 'as when you find a trout in the milk.' That baby, gentlemen, was the trout in the milk."

DeBekker's voice had softened to a sonata of melancholy. Allie sat quietly in her corner. For the first time since the start of the trial her eyes were moist with tears.

"Even then Mr. Hale resisted," the defense attorney went on. "Even then he fought the facts. On the fatal day itself, when he stood with Mrs. Dillon in Neal & Eskridge's store, Mr. Hale was doing everything in his power not to perpetrate, but to prevent catastrophe."

Padgett slipped a look at Maggie, who sat stiff as a ship's figurehead. The loyal Dennis had hold of her right hand.

"For when he left that store, gentlemen, and walked up Main Street, it was not with the intention of shooting Ham Dillon. How do I know this? Because it was impossible for Mr. Hale to have seen Mr. Dillon through that store window, as the prosecution has alleged. Impossible. And we will prove it."

The defense began calling witnesses about 3 P.M.

LINK HAD NO IDEA before he was such a fine fellow. All the testimonials being heaped on him now seemed almost as unreal as the prosecution's abuse. First came a slew of depositions from residents of Kentucky, and a few from Elnora too, testifying to his good character: morality, sobriety, good citizenship. William Gardiner, second chair for the defense, read them one by one in rolling tones. When he cleared his throat to begin the ninth or tenth, Padgett rose and suggested to the judge that everybody got the idea; the prosecution was not contesting the defendant's previous good conduct. Judge Houghton mulled this over long and slow, his face working a little, like a largemouth bass. "No, we'll take a few more," he said finally, and Gardiner piled on some more descriptions of the defendant as "a model husband" and "an ideal man."

At first Link felt like a spirit listening to the eulogies at his own funeral. Then gradually all the unfiltered praise began to have a tonic effect on him. How many souls had rallied to his cause, some little more than names to him. For the first time in weeks he began to feel the dawn of hope, a stirring of anger toward the prosecution. He deserved to live. He wanted to live.

Late Tuesday morning the defense called its first substantive witness: Dr. Fayette Carstairs, Link's personal physician back in Nicholasville, Kentucky. Dr. Carstairs wore his office face. Clagg, the unregenerate old rebel, handled the questioning for the defense.

"Originally you treated Mr. Hale for what?"

"Pen paralysis."

"Pen what? Talk louder, Doctor!" Clagg barked. "They're still hammering on the roof."

"I treated him for pen paralysis. Cramps in the hand."

"Was that the only thing wrong with him?"

"No."

"Well, what else?"

"He showed a variety of symptoms."

"Did they point to a particular condition?"

"Yes."

"Well, what?"

"Neurasthenia."

"What?"

"Neurasthenia!"

"What's that?"

"Well," said the doctor, growing expansive, "it's a new sort of disorder that's arisen just in the past decade or two, mostly here in the United States. Actually we ought to be a little proud of how many cases there are, because you might say it's an indicator of advanced civilization—caused by the general movement in our society now away from physical labor and toward mental labor. Naturally it's more common in offices than in outdoor work. More common in men than women because men are required to use their brains more."

"Can it lead to insanity?"

"In extreme cases."

"What are the symptoms?"

The doctor sighed. "Oh, there's quite a list. Tenderness in the scalp, teeth, or gums. Abnormal secretions. Chills, heat flashes, morbid fears, headaches, dilated pupils, palpitations . . ."

"All right."

". . . dry skin, yawning . . ."

"Yes, thank you. What about depression?"

"Well, see, medically depression is considered a subset of neurasthenia. It has its own set of symptoms: dyspepsia, constipation, abnormally large appetite, abnormally small appetite . . ."

"Insomnia?"

"That too."

"Sounds serious."

"Oh, yes," agreed the doctor. "Fortunately we've come up with some new ways to attack it."

"And what did you prescribe for Mr. Hale?"

"Well, I started him off—this was about a year ago—drinking several glasses of hot water when he first got up in the morning, followed by calisthenics. Eventually I put him on the Whitely Exerciser, which is—" The doctor arranged his hands in various places in the air. "It helps with morbidness. We topped that off with electricity."

"Electric shocks?"

"Mild ones. You see, the human nervous system is like a galvanic battery. Certain times of the year, especially fall and winter, and certain times of day, late morning and early evening, are high in what we call positive energy. These are also the occasions when the neurasthenic personality is most susceptible to attacks of nerves. So naturally, those are the best times to apply the charge."

"Not dangerous, is it?" said Clagg.

"No, no. The current's fairly weak. And we use very localized electrodes. We can target say, this area, up near the armpit. The cheeks, the nose, orifices such as . . ."

"And Mr. Hale received the full range."

"Close to it, yes. Over time."

"Were you prescribing drugs for him at the same time?"

"Sure. For a while he was taking a mixture of antipyrine, an analgesic, and sodium bromide, a sedative. Then every once in a while I'd add a mixture of small amounts of arsenic, strychnine, and quinine. It stimulates the blood."

"How did Mr. Hale respond to these treatments?"

"Pretty fair. He was a good patient. Very docile. But then late this summer his condition deteriorated sharply. He wasn't sleeping at all. The circles under his eyes were blue-black. I switched him from his usual bromide in the evening to scopolamine, which is a form of belladonna, but even that . . ."

"Did he tell you what was upsetting him?"

"He wouldn't tell me anything concrete."

"But you decided he was in such bad shape he ought to check himself into a clinic, right?"

"A sanitarium, yes. I suggested Dr. Kellogg's, in Battle Creek, Michigan. I urged it in the strongest possible terms."

"In fact, wasn't Mr. Hale on his way there when the shooting occurred?"

"Objection."

"All right, all right." Clagg turned and snapped at his witness: "What about it, Doctor? When he pulled the trigger was the defendant sane or insane?"

"I would say without hesitation that Mr. Hale was of unsound mind."

Clagg finally surrendered the witness, and Padgett shot up.

"Doctor, about this recommendation of yours that Mr. Hale should pay a visit to Battle Creek. That's not an asylum is it?"

"No."

"It's a place where people go to relax. Play tennis, maybe lose a little weight . . ."

"Well, it's more than that."

"Among the people who have spent some time there . . ." Padgett fluttered through notes. "Upton Sinclair, Henry Ford, Thomas Edison, Admiral Byrd . . . I don't suppose you'd call them insane?"

"Of course not."

"Mr. W. H. Taft. That name . . . Why, wasn't he just elected President of the United States?"

"Dr. Kellogg's establishment offers special—"

"The new President of our country isn't insane, is he?"

"Not to my knowledge."

"Or threatened with insanity?"

"I don't think so."

Padgett let go a breath of relief, just for the folks in the front row. "Now. As to the various diversions offered at Dr. Kellogg's establishment, I have here somewhere—ah—a list of some of those featured within the past year. Let's see. Fiddle concerts, sleigh rides, Bosco's World of Magic, the Celestial Hand-Clapping Jubilee Choir, the Baxter Boys and their trained dachshunds, Mr. D. J. Donovan—he brought along his banjo . . ."

"What's the question here?" shouted Clagg.

"The question is," Padgett shouted back, "how about sending me, Doctor?"

DeBekker at the defense table raised a finger, like a bidder at an auction. "Yes, I'm sustaining that," said the judge.

Padgett took a moment to collect himself. He felt very good. After those dragging hours of character witnesses, not to mention the chewing doubts he had now about Maggie's testimony, he had a lot of energy to burn, and he meant to use up some of it making a steaming heap out of this witness.

"Mr. Carstairs . . ."

"Dr. Carstairs," said the witness stiffly.

"Doctor. Sorry. Do you consider yourself in the mainstream of medical thinking today, Doctor?"

"In most areas. In one or two I like to think I'm on the frontier."

"The frontier or the fringe?"

"Objection."

"In the year or so before you sent the defendant off to this recreational facility, did you ever see him when he was not under the influence of some drug?"

"What's that?"

"Well, it seems like you spend an awful lot of time with your head in the medicine chest. Now this scopolamine. According to the physicians I've been talking to, scopolamine produces what they call twilight sleep, hallucinations . . ."

"Only in enormous doses. Otherwise it's perfectly safe."

"Arsenic, strychnine. Same thing? Don't they produce delirium, delusions?"

"Only if . . . Drinking too much milk is bad for you. I never prescribe—"

"Oh, come on, Doc. I'm surprised you don't have writer's cramp yourself, all the prescriptions you sign. Now these bromides you had him on. They produce, I believe, a condition called 'bromism,' whose symptoms include skin rash, constipation, headaches . . ."

"Now look here—"

"Weren't those some of the same symptoms you were treating him for? Sure you weren't chasing your own tail there, Doctor?"

"I was not." Dr. Carstairs didn't say anything else. He was turning visibly inward, his shoulders creeping toward his ears.

"Let me put it this way, sir," Padgett said as he moseyed closer, "since it's pretty plain you gave the defendant enough pills to cure the original thirteen colonies, how can you possibly judge whether he was legally sane or not? In fact, aren't you the last person in the world we ought to be asking?"

By the time the cross-examination was over, the witness was breathing through his teeth. Tossing his pencil onto the table, Padgett sat back with a fat smile of satisfaction.

Clagg stood up.

"Dr. Carstairs," he said, "let's say, just for the sake of argument, that the prosecutor is correct. Couldn't the accumulated drugs you gave the defendant have rendered him legally not responsible?"

"What?" The doctor stared.

"Isn't it possible that—"

"No, it's *not* possible! I am a one hundred percent fully licensed—"

"Now don't get all—"

"Your honor!" Padgett cried, arms out as if to embrace the wide world. "Shouldn't somebody pull these two off each other?"

At last Clagg sat down, and Dr. Carstairs started to leave the witness box. Padgett interrupted him.

"One second, Doctor."

The witness froze, then sat back very slowly.

"Defense counsel was a little rough on you there," said Padgett. (Eberhardt snickered.) "So just to make sure we're a hundred percent clear. Is there anything you gave Mr. Hale, any form of treatment, any prescription at all, that you haven't also given dozens of other patients?"

"No," said the doctor. His face was whipped, angry.

"And all these other people, who took the same medicines, has any one of them committed a murder?"

"No," said the doctor. "Not to my knowledge."

"Thank you for traveling all this way to be with us today."

2 7

AFTER DR. CARSTAIRS' TESTIMONY, Maggie pulled the children outside for some fresh air. She often did this during breaks in the trial, mostly to dodge the commiserators and well-wishers who shot toward her every chance they got. All those long-faced hand squeezers. Women in particular. The worst of them, she thought, were coarser than any man: not bothering to introduce themselves, full of brute sympathies, as if their common experience of Women's Lot were a free pass into her confidence.

One of them had Maggie pinned now. She stood holding Ruth by one hand, Harold by the other, while a frosty-faced female described in detail the tragedies of her own life. The children were bundled against the bitter chill. Maggie had made Harold's snowsuit just last month out of a coat of his father's. While the talking went on, she watched a horse nuzzling through the spun-sugar ice on the surface of the trough.

"I can't feel my face," said Ruth, looking up at her mother.

Maggie noticed the woman's hands—rough, chapped, exposed to the cold. She was impervious to feeling of any kind, apparently. The flesh had grown over her wedding ring.

But then, Maggie realized, this gabbling stranger could have been anyone; she might have been the most delicate angel of grace. Maggie still couldn't have accepted the comfort. Not since her testimony.

"Well, it just goes to show one thing," the woman said. "How important it is to be ready when God whispers your name." Noticing Harold, it seemed for the first time, she bent down and put her nose two inches from his. "Will you be ready when God whispers your name?"

IN THE CRUCIAL DEBATE over Link Hale's sanity, the defense sent four of its own alienists to the stand. Each had his personal angle on the case: that is, though all agreed Hale had fired his revolver in the throes of an "irresistible impulse," they differed in some of the long words they used to explain it, as well as in exactly how long the defendant had been legally incapacitated. ("Quite a legal battle took place between the attorneys here," the *Herald* reported, "trying to establish just where a man ceases to be sane and becomes insane.") One witness stated the defendant's "brainstorm" began while he was packing his suitcase, another that he became unbalanced on the train, another that Hale was technically insane only in those few seconds he was pulling the trigger. DeBekker, naturally, kept emphasizing the areas of agreement among his experts; Padgett chipped and chiseled at the differences. Finally, after a day and a half of this knotty and fractious testimony, deBekker topped it off with a Dr. G. P. Scudder—not an alienist, as the witness explained, but a "scientist of the inner life" at the Waller-Hynes Laboratory of Psychology in Belle Plain, where he conducted experiments in the "physiological effects of the emotions." Dr. Scudder propounded the theory that Link had been driven temporarily insane by an excess of katastates in the bloodstream.

"And what are katastates?" deBekker said.

"Well, you see . . ." Dr. Scudder paused and gave a little laugh, as if sharing some arcane medical joke with himself. "In the human mind," he went on, "positive emotions, pure thoughts, the higher truths, all these engender what we call anastates. Their function is to cleanse the brain and the blood and to help keep the entire organism in harmony with its environment. On the other hand, evil feelings—fear, rage, and so forth—these produce poisons we call katastates, which in extreme cases so infect the blood that they destroy the ability of the organism to cope rationally with the world."

"I see. You're saying then that at the time of the shooting the defendant . . . ?"

". . . no doubt suffered a crippling inundation of katastates."

"Thank you very much, sir. Your witness."

Padgett stood up.

"Katastates, hunh?"

AFTER DR. SCUDDER, the shoe dropped. Miss Julia Kane, an employee of the Neal & Eskridge general store, was called by the defense. Miss Kane was a tallish girl, rather pretty, who had clearly devoted much thought to what she would wear for her big day in court, for she was adorned like a duchess, with all the very best treasures of her closet and bauble box. Her dress—it was almost a gown—was Lincoln green with Elizabethan balloon sleeves. Somebody had slaughtered a flock of grackles for her hat.

Ham probably used to flirt with her, Allie thought, watching her go by.

While Miss Kane planted herself like an orchid in the witness box, defense attorney Gardiner dragged out a large chart of the interior of the store and set it up on an easel. The chart had a lot of numbers and dotted lines on it, marking windows, doors, angles, distances.

DeBekker was more courtly than ever as he started to question Miss Kane—not so much in deference to her own loveliness, perhaps, as in homage to the anticipated beauty of her testimony. Together Miss Kane and the chart were going to brand Maggie Dillon a liar.

The witness, with a touch of hauteur, identified herself as the salesgirl closest to Link and Maggie during their agonized talk just before the murder. In fact, said Miss Kane, she had brought Mrs. Dillon some iced tea when she looked wobbly and hovered nearby in case she might need further assistance.

"Now," said deBekker, "we have heard testimony"—he didn't have to say whose—"that the defendant recognized Mr. Dillon through the front window of the store and went out to intercept him. Is that what happened?"

"No, it's not."

"How do you know?"

"Because it's impossible."

"Really?" DeBekker feigned surprise. "And why is that, young lady?"

Miss Kane showed why on the chart.

Guided by her, deBekker moved a pointer here and there, gradually building to the conclusion that from where Link and Maggie were standing at the time, neither they nor anyone else could have seen up Main Street, only more or less directly across it.

"I see," said deBekker. He was drinking in this information the way he did most of the testimony from his own witnesses, with a kind of bogus fascination, probably to encourage the jury. "So the two parties were standing about here . . ."

"Further left," said Miss Kane.

"Here?"

"Yes, there."

DeBekker laid the pointer flat on the chart. "That still allows a line of sight up the street, doesn't it?"

"Not that day."

"Oh no?" DeBekker stood back and frowned. "Why not?"

"Because," said Miss Kane with a touch of asperity, "that day we had most of the shutters on the main windows closed, it was so bright outside. To keep out the glare."

"Preventing . . . ?"

"Preventing anybody from seeing east up the street."

DeBekker tested her like a melon, squeezing her testimony here and there. She was perfect. There was no way, she said again and again, Link Hale could have seen Ham Dillon through the window.

Padgett looked at Maggie. She was sitting very still.

"Thank you so much for your help today, Miss Kane, in straightening out this bit of confusion. Your witness." And deBekker subsided serenely into his chair.

Padgett approached the witness slowly, in a sort of hanging crouch.

"You're aware that Mrs. Dillon herself contradicted you in her sworn testimony?"

"I can't help that," said Miss Kane, brushing her velvet dog collar with finger and thumb.

"How long have you been working at Neal & Eskridge?"

There was some unproductive waltzing, as Padgett groped for a line of attack. Miss Kane kept insisting Link couldn't have seen Ham Dillon out the window. The third or fourth time she said it, she added, "Mr. Hale would have had to step way back."

Padgett got a look in his eyes like a cheetah spotting an ante-
lope across the veldt.

"Step back, you say?"

"Yes."

"How far back?"

The witness considered. "Four or five steps."

Padgett nodded. "How do you know he didn't?"

"I—"

"Were Mr. Hale and Mrs. Dillon the only customers in the
store that day?"

"No."

"Busy day, wasn't it?"

"Yes."

"Practically pandemonium in town, as I recall, what with Mr.
Marshall coming in to give his speech."

"I know what I saw."

"I'm sure you do. But the question is, do you know what Mr.
Hale saw? Now in the middle of all this whoop-de-doo there in
front of the store, when Mrs. Dillon looked like she might pitch
over, you went running off to fetch something, didn't you?"

"Not running off."

"You didn't go off to get her iced tea?"

"Two steps."

"Two steps?"

"Five steps."

"Well, if you went five steps, Mr. Hale could have gone five
steps, couldn't he?"

"He didn't have—"

"Could he have gone five steps?"

"No."

"You had to get the tea? Dig out the ice? Pour it out of the
pitcher? What were you looking at, the tea or the defendant?"

"I was looking at both," Miss Kane insisted.

"You saw Mr. Hale every second?" Padgett popped a gasket

finally, mostly because he knew in his gut she was telling the truth. Maggie had lied to him. Him first, then the world. The odd thing was, the discovery had actually fired his combative instincts. Miss Kane was going to pay for this.

"No," she said with brittle dignity. "I didn't see him every second."

"So he might have moved. It's possible. You know, that was a terrible hot day," said Padgett. "Bright as a furnace too. All of us here remember how it was, Miss Kane. And what it was like inside too. Kind of gloomy? Maybe a little hard to see. Then you take that dust drifting in from the street . . ."

"Mr. Eskridge had the floors oiled every day. To keep the dust down."

"You telling us you never got any dust blowing into your store? During that drought? Be the only store in town, as anybody in this courtroom could tell you."

No response.

"Now let's see, where was I? Oh yes, Mr. Hale was moving around the store."

DeBekker: "Objection!"

"Now after you handed Mrs. Dillon the tea you said you did what . . . you 'hovered' there?"

"I was concerned about her."

"You were. They continued to talk?"

"Yes."

"Could you hear what they were saying?"

"No."

"This period of time you were unsuccessfully trying to eavesdrop, how long did it last?"

"I wasn't eavesdropping!"

"How long till Mr. Hale left?"

"A minute. Maybe less."

"And you had your eyes fixed on him and Mrs. Dillon all the time?"

"Yes."

"Had your head forward maybe? Like this? So you could really see them?"

"Yes."

"But you weren't trying to hear the conversation?"

IT WENT WITH the trade sometimes, of course, turning truth into a pack of lies. All for the greater good. At the end of the day Padgett sat at the prosecution table while the courtroom emptied and the crowd went spilling out into the early dark. Whatever self-reproach he felt merely gave a subtle flavor to his thoughts, no stronger than a twist of lemon. He was analyzing the state of play. How effectively had he discredited Miss Kane? He couldn't tell. As for Maggie's lying, he could only hope it wasn't as clear to the jury as it was to him.

Well, he would gallop all the harder and blow his bugle all the louder. Maggie Dillon wasn't going to ruin his crusade for him, not at this late date.

28

EVEN DENTON wound up testifying for the defense. Clagg shanghaied him during one of the recesses—for the boy, spurred in some obscure way by his public humiliation there, had been doggedly returning to court—and all three of his father's lawyers then spirited him into an anteroom to see if he knew anything helpful. He did. The memory had been preying on him. It was of something that happened that summer of 1907, when his father was up visiting from Kentucky. One evening Allie had carted baby Albert off to visit the Dillons, and not long after, by the reading lamp at the kitchen table, Link had startled the children by suddenly crushing his newspaper in his fists.

"I feel like I'm going to lose my mind," he whispered.

What could be better? So they put Denton on the stand to tell that story. He didn't make much of a witness, though. His voice was so weak his words were often lost in the rafters, and Padgett easily neutralized him on cross. ("People use expressions like that all the time, don't they? 'This is driving me crazy . . .'") In fact, the prosecutor turned him to good advantage by bringing out how much Denton missed his uncle. It was at the mention of Ham, not his father, that the boy started to cry.

Afterward Denton slipped out of the courtroom alone and went down to the railroad yards at the west end of town. It was becoming a favorite haunt of his. He was drawn to the wheels, tools, gears, to the grating of the huge mechanized turntable as it shuttled engines in and out of the roundhouse, to the intricate surgeries in the service bays. Once upon a time he'd built his own bicycle. And in the Dillons' barn last summer, with Ham's help, he had been trying to make his own car. First they had taken the wooden wheels off a buggy and fitted it with rubber ones from a couple of secondhand bikes. Then together they'd mounted a boat engine, one cylinder, over the rear axle. . . .

It was probably still there.

The rest of the afternoon he loitered about the rail yards, chilled to the bone but dully happy. In the tin-and-pipe shop, he learned, they were looking for apprentices. Seven cents an hour. Court went on without him, and thus he missed the explosive testimony of his sister Louise.

Presenting a criminal case requires a touch of the vaudeville impresario, or so deBekker had always believed. For him, the overarching logic of an argument was no more important than offering the witnesses in a lively order. He was counting on eighteen-year-old Louise Hale to deliver the wrenching sentimental ballad.

She sat in the witness box in a high-throated dress of dove gray, with her Pre-Raphaelite glow and a plaited shawl about her shoulders ("a pretty young woman," the *Herald* said, "who bears about her face the marks of suffering"). Waiting to begin, she looked out over the courtroom a little above the heads of the audience with the unseeing eyes of the visionary or the blind.

She started with a tender testimonial to her father's many virtues. "He was kind and affectionate to all of us," she told deBekker, and offered illustrations.

"Was he a good provider?"

"Oh yes. Always. Even while he was away he never sent Mother less than fifty dollars a month."

Coaxed by deBekker, she went on to detail the rapid intertwining of the Dillons and the Hales.

"Did there come a time when you suspected there might be something improper afoot between your mother and your uncle?"

The girl's eyes, dreamy before, found focus for the first time. She looked at deBekker.

"Yes," she said.

"When was that?"

"One day I came home from school early . . ." Louise described seeing her mother and Uncle Ham come out of the upstairs bedroom together at the Hales' house. "After that, I couldn't help wondering," she said.

"Did anything else happen to harden your suspicions?"

"I saw them hugging sometimes when my father wasn't there. He kissed her once, sort of. . . . Two or three times they went riding in the buggy with the baby."

"Which baby?"

She paused. "My half brother. Albert."

"Tell us, child, did you say anything to your mother about this?"

"No."

"Why not?"

"I was her daughter. It wasn't my place."

"So these terrible fears of yours, you confided them to no one? Your brother Denton, perhaps? Arthur?"

"No, nobody."

At last she recounted the late-summer visit of the Dillons to Nicholasville—for Louise, a week of wary watching broken by gusts of suspicion. She hadn't actually seen the discovery of the lovers, but that's not what deBekker wanted her for: he wanted her long and poignant description of the four weeks following, when she was her father's only confidante and support. "We talked more than we ever had in our lives before," she said, pausing to pluck a handkerchief from her sleeve and daub the underside of one eye.

"Did he ever vow vengeance against Mr. Dillon?"

"No," she said. "He was firm about that. Adamant. There were times I thought I was more angry than he."

"Your father was resigned, then? Stoical?"

"Oh no." Louise glanced at her father. "He was eating almost nothing but medicine. And he kept saying he wished he were dead. It was . . . I would hold his hand and kiss it and weep and beg him not to say such things. Sometimes we just sat crying together."

She had the whole court in her melancholy spell. Knitting fingers fell quiet. A mother in the audience, rubbing the gums of her colicky baby with whiskey, slowly came to a stop. Padgett was eyeing the jury.

When the time came, he opened his cross-examination as delicately as if he were opening a flower.

"We're all of us deeply sorry for your trouble, Miss Hale. I hope you know that." He mused at the ceiling. "Now, you were saying that in this last month before the shooting, you were closer to your father than anyone?"

"I think so, yes."

"It's a fine thing for a young woman and her father to be so free and open together."

Nothing.

"Did you see any signs of mental disease in him at the time?"

"I could see he was very, very upset."

"And you comforted him."

"Yes."

"Did you urge him to get help? Maybe check into a sanitarium?"

"No."

"So you didn't fear for his reason."

"Of course I did."

"Yet you said nothing?"

"It wasn't my place."

After letting that dangle in the air, Padgett moved on. "Is it safe to say you've sided with your father in the wake of these sorry events?"

"I suppose so. Yes, of course."

"Against your mother?"

No answer.

"Do you hate your mother?"

"No, I don't."

"You don't? After causing you and the rest of the family all this pain and misery?"

"I'm angry with my mother. I don't hate her. There's a difference."

"Tell us frankly. Is there anything you wouldn't say to try to save your father?"

"The only person I hate," said Louise suddenly, "is my uncle."

Padgett could have brushed past this. But he didn't. He made the mistake of saying, "Oh?"

"Everybody thinks he was such a fine man." Her flare of rage jarred the room. "Once, while my father was living in Kentucky . . ." She stopped, then pushed on. "Uncle Ham drove to our house. He told the boys to put his buggy in the barn, and then he came inside. Mama wasn't home, I don't remember why, but he and I were alone there in the house, and when he realized that . . . He embraced me. Put his arms around me and wouldn't let me go. He put his lips . . . I was hitting him, pushing at him. I told him I'd scream for help. Finally he let go."

The courtroom was dead quiet. Padgett licked his lips.

"He was your uncle. Isn't it possible you misunderstood his intentions?"

"I didn't misunderstand anything."

"You said nothing about this to anybody?" said Padgett. He was suddenly on the attack. "Your mother, your father, no one?"

"No. I didn't want to cause more trouble."

"So there's no way to confirm what you're telling us?"

"Confirm?"

"It's your habit to keep silent about everything, isn't it? Whatever happens or doesn't happen, you remain as silent as the tomb. Unless and until it suits your purposes. . . ."

It was full dark when court ended that day. Allie, fighting her way through the eddying crowd, dodged a licorice vendor and finally caught up with her daughter in the street. She yanked Louise around by the arm.

"Is it true?" Allie cried hoarsely, heedless of who heard. "Tell me right now! Is it true what you said in there?"

Louise's eyes, lingering on her mother, were grave and opaque. Then she turned away.

T HAT NIGHT Padgett stayed in his office in town. The monkey stove in the corner was going full blast against the bitter cold outside. Eberhardt had hurled himself disconsolately onto the other sofa and lay wrapped in his coat, snoring lightly.

They were keeping close to the courthouse tonight because the storm, the one everyone had been smelling on the wind all week, had finally struck. Too wound up to sleep, Padgett stood at the bay window watching the snow outside as it whipped and whirled. There were bits of sleet mixed up in it too that snapped against the panes. If this keeps up, he thought, at least it'll keep the goddamn workmen off the roof.

He was brooding over Louise's testimony, of course. Wondering if the highly respected dead man could really have been such a predator. It was certainly possible, Padgett had to admit. Maybe more than possible. The odd thing was, whether it was true or not mattered less to him at this exact moment than the tide of despair he was fighting. Every day this one-man war of his, this campaign to uphold the marmoreal right, became more problematic, more of a bog and a sinkhole. The harder he fought, the deeper he sank. This had been his great mistake, he saw now, trying to pin his own personal salvation on public vengeance. The case was far from lost, he thought. He had delivered many smart strokes along the way, and in a professional way he was keenly looking forward to his shot at the last two witnesses—Allie Hale, then her husband. Padgett had tremendous faith in his abilities still, but that's what concerned him: the dawning fear that if he won, it would be ashes in his mouth and blood on his hands.

The other day he'd noticed one of those out-of-town reporters showing bits of rope to some of his brethren. Souvenirs, the fellow was saying, from hangings he'd covered. He was working a jawload of tobacco while he ticked them off. How, Padgett wondered, had he and this scavenger wound up on the same side?

29

WEDNESDAY, DECEMBER 2. It was past 8:30 A.M., and three of the jurors still hadn't shown up. Judge Houghton was fuming on the bench. Allie sat in her usual corner in the front row, waiting to be called to the stand. To her mourning dress and black bonnet she had added a pair of spectacles. She rarely wore them ordinarily. But at the margin of her mind she knew that everyone in court this morning, certainly every man, would be vividly picturing her in the act of love. The glasses provided her with a scrap of cover for her appearance today at this slave auction.

She heard angry noises behind her, coming from the seating section. After the hoopla of the opening couple of days, the courtroom hadn't been packed to the walls every day, only full. But with Allie scheduled, the hordes had returned. Regulars working their way in, stamping the weather off their boots, were shocked to find their usual spots taken by brand-new faces. This kicked up a lot of ill feeling and hard words, and Sheriff Colbert and Deputy Wallace had their hands full dealing with all the arguments.

Allie leaned her head to the side and looked out the window. The storm had swept away swiftly, leaving low drifts diamonded with ice, and the crawling fog that filled the open spaces made it seem as if the snow were on fire. The sky was still cobbled with clouds. Allie studied them. Not enough blue to make a Dutchman's underpants.

She wondered, in a distant sort of way, how baby Albert was getting on. He was harbored back in Nicholasville for the duration with a neighbor woman—one of the few left who would speak to her.

A smile burst upon her.

It seemed like forever she'd been steeling herself for this day. The whole time marinating in guilt. That's what had brought her here, of course, to testify on Link's behalf. Little as she loved him, Allie owed it to him now to try as hard as she could to save his life. She didn't want the death of two men on her conscience. Besides, Link alive was her penance, her albatross.

A grim brief, all in all, yet now that the moment was upon her at last, she almost felt like laughing. Living under the heat lamp of such phenomenal public displeasure, it finally got to be ludicrous.

She noticed a paper-thin dowager, as ancient as she was determined, making her three-pronged way down the center aisle. At the front row the old lady revolved a careful ninety degrees, like a figurine in a fancy clock, and, resting her hands on her cane, fixed a look of hypnotized pathos upon the gentleman in the aisle seat. Allie laughed at last.

"Alice Thompson Hale." She started.

Here we go, she thought. *Gaily she stepped to the block.*

The direct examination was taken by William Gardiner, the eldest defense attorney. The defense hoped, apparently, that his impeccably gray manner would help tone down her scarlet reputation, at least in the eyes of the jury. If so, it was a doomed attempt.

His first questions, all straightforward, seemed to pass as in a dream; Allie barely registered the sound of her own voice. She came alert, though, when Gardiner asked her about the evening she and Ham were unmasked.

"Just prior, I believe, there was an incident involving pancakes?"

"Not really an incident," Allie said. "Mr. Dillon asked me if I would make him pancakes the next morning."

"He asked this with everyone else present?"

"Yes."

"Do you know why?"

Allie pictured Ham at the table. Her mouth budded. "Just to devil me, I suppose."

"He had the devil in him, did he?"

"Objection."

"What happened next?"

"My husband left the table soon after. To go do some gardening, I think. Mr. Dillon went into the parlor. I followed."

"And?"

"We embraced and . . . my husband stepped through the back doorway and discovered us."

"What did he say?"

"Something at first, I don't remember what, I was too taken aback. Then he came and took hold of my arm, like this"—Allie had rehearsed this particular speech many times—"and he said, 'Now it's out. You two haven't been fooling me as much as you thought.' And then he said to me, kind of whispering, 'That baby is Dillon's, isn't it?' "

"And what did Mr. Dillon say?"

"He didn't say anything. He wasn't there."

"Not there?"

"He went out the front door when Mr. Hale came in."

"Leaving you alone with your enraged husband?" Mr. Gardiner clucked his tongue. Something reared in Allie, a rebel impulse to defend Ham. She had to fight it down.

"So your husband accused you of being the mother of this . . . What was the baby's name, by the way?"

"Albert. Albert Dillon Hale."

"Named after Mr. Dillon, was it?"

"That's right."

Murmurs in the crowd.

"A child you had nursed, caressed, and passed off as your husband's own for nearly eighteen months?"

"Yes." Again, the wild pride kicked up. Her eyes swept the crowd, the women. Would any of you have that kind of nerve?

"How did you respond to your husband's accusation?"

"About the baby? I told him it was true."

"What was his response?"

"He was . . ." She stopped, remembering Link's face at that moment. He'd looked glad, that was the amazing thing. Not just glad, exhilarated, his eyes filled with an unholy glee. It was true! It was true! He'd been right all along! Absolutely radiating vindication. But you couldn't explain a look like that in a courtroom. What difference did it make anyway?

"He was very upset," she said.

"What did he do?"

"There were some words between us, I said, I don't know, it had been going on a long time, and then he bolted out of the room." Allie still hadn't looked at Link once since she'd taken the stand. She couldn't manage it. What a time to realize that the old rage against her husband, dead (she thought) since the death of her lover, had only been sleeping after all. Now it stirred again. "He, uh . . . he went into a dressing room," she said, fighting to stay on course. "I went after him and found him searching around on the shelves. He pulled down a gun."

"A gun? You mean a pistol? What did you do?"

"Nothing."

"You merely stood before him? Unprotesting? Defenseless?"

"Yes."

"What was in your mind?"

"I thought he was going to shoot me," said Allie quietly. Adding to herself: But he didn't have the courage.

"Still, you did not attempt to flee, did you?"

"No."

"Your conscience was too afflicted, was it?"

"Objection," said Padgett.

"Mr. Gardiner," said the judge, who was supporting his face with one fist.

"What happened then?"

"We kept talking, I don't know about what, it seemed to go on a long time. I remember my husband asked me if Mr. Dillon and I hadn't been intimate since my first visit to Elnora back in 1905. I was very surprised, very struck by how much he had guessed."

"How long were you in that room?"

"About ten minutes."

"Was he weeping?"

"Not weeping but . . . I don't know quite what you'd call it. He was very distressed."

"And he kept pointing the gun at you?"

"He pointed it everywhere, even at his own head. I began to fear he might kill Mr. Dillon—whom I could see through the window out on the porch—or, I don't know, anyone at all. Perhaps the baby." A gross exaggeration, that: but she was up here to try to get him acquitted. That's what she had promised to do, to help convince other people he was pathetic.

She described the scene in the yard, Link threatening Ham with the gun. The pleading pantomime of Ham's outstretched hands—*please don't shoot me*—how well she remembered that. She could never have dreamed of him in such a posture.

Remember, Link, we're both Masons . . .

"That night my husband didn't go to bed. I heard him pacing back and forth in his room all night. He talked to himself sometimes. I could hear that too, through the door."

"What was he saying?"

" 'Oh, God, oh, God, I wish I was dead.' " Finally she met her husband's eyes. "Over and over again."

"Would you describe his condition as desperate?"

"Yes. Yes, it was." She sketched the terrible weeks following the Dillons' departure, Link's wailing, his loss of weight, the frenzied way he pored through the Bible. "Mr. Hale and I often talked of the . . . the offense," she said. "I can't remember most of what we said exactly. He kept asking me how it began."

"Did you tell him?"

"No. No more than I'd said that first night."

"You refused to give him details of your intimacy with Dillon?"

"Yes."

"Did that contribute to his agitation?"

"Yes."

"Then why did you do it?"

"I suppose because . . ." Because it was none of his business, she thought. "Because I believed it would only make him worse." That was also true. "I still loved my husband," she added.

"So you were trying to protect him?"

"I see now I only made things more difficult. So much of all this is my fault."

"What exactly is your fault, Mrs. Hale?"

"Objection."

"I'm sustaining that."

Gardiner mused.

"Mrs. Hale, help all of us here to understand. Why did you succumb to the illicit blandishments of Mr. Dillon?"

She considered. "Weakness." Strength.

The lawyer nodded. Abruptly Allie reached up and pulled off her glasses. She tucked them into a small pocket of her dress.

"Your husband asked you to sign a confession?"

"Yes."

"Did you?"

"Yes."

"This confession?" Catching it up from the defense table, Gardiner introduced it into evidence. Dozens of spellbound faces watched it pass from his hand to the judge's and back again.

"He dictated the text to you, I believe?"

"Yes."

"But the words are substantially true?"

"Yes."

"Why would you sign such a damning document, Mrs. Hale?"

"He seemed so miserable." She wanted to take her bonnet off, shake out her hair. She needed her looks, she thought, to take command. "Again, I believed my signing something might make him feel better."

"And did it?"

"No. It did not. He was still obsessed. He . . ." She felt a fleeting pity for the man she'd married. But she couldn't hold on to it; his endless keening wretchedness defeated her again. "Once he came bursting into my room to tell me of a dream he'd just had, of Mr. Dillon and me riding off together on a white horse. And he and Maggie were watching, and my sister was saying, 'Let them go.'"

Padgett glanced over at Maggie, saw her stiffen at the mention of her own name.

"Your husband was threatening suicide?"

"Often. Every day it seemed he . . . It was unbearable." The truest thing she'd said. "Once he came to me and suggested we jump off a bridge together." She had another impulse to laugh.

"A suicide pact? What did you say?"

"I said I wouldn't on account of the children. He never mentioned it again."

"Was he more peaceful after that?"

"No. He was . . ." Her voice trailed off. *Why were they talking so much about Link? What about her own wrecked life? No one was putting out a hand to her.* She took a breath.

"He wouldn't eat. He was taking different medicines, I don't know what all. He couldn't work. I was so worried about him." *Keep saying that.* "He has some family in Kansas, I was hoping he would go visit them, take a holiday. But he said he wasn't strong enough. Then this sanitarium idea came up."

"When was the last time you saw your husband?"

"Heading off for the train station. He was weeping. 'I may never see you again,' he said . . ."

"Tell me, Mrs. Hale, what is your relationship with your husband like today?"

"We're trying to rebuild our lives together. To reconcile, I suppose you'd say." There was noise, a yelp of open laughter. "It takes time," she added angrily.

"You don't want him to pay for your mistakes, do you?"

"Leading," said Padgett.

"Anything substantive, Mr. Gardiner?"

"I want another chance for our family," Allie blurted, "a chance for us all to get back on the right . . ." She felt weirdly detached, a spectator at her own hypocrisy. "That's why I am here today, to ask—not for myself, of course, but for the others, the innocent victims in this . . ."

"And you would include your husband in that list?"

MRS. HALE ON THE STAND TELLS PITIFUL STORY

MAN'S PASSION AND WOMAN'S FRAILTY—

A HUMAN WRECK AND A BLIGHTED HOME—

ONE OF LIFE'S TRAGEDIES

Gardiner's questioning of Allie Hale went on long past lunch. In fact, early editions of the *Herald* were sprouting in the back of the courtroom when A. J. Padgett finally heaved himself to his feet to begin his cross-examination. He intended to strip the witness of sympathy, wanton allure, credibility: anything that would make her appealing to the jury. As he approached, he noticed a roguish red lock of hair curling from beneath her bonnet. The effect was provokingly handsome.

"Mrs. Hale," he said without preamble, "this mourning costume you're wearing today . . . Have you recently lost a relative?"

DeBekker shot out of his seat.

"Objection!"

Great stir in the room.

"Sustained. Stop that." Houghton glowered at Padgett.

"I gather from your testimony," the prosecutor continued easily, once the carbonation in the crowd had settled, "I gather your husband threatened suicide more or less on a daily basis. Of course he never followed through. After all"—a sweep of the arm—"there he sits. But he sure did his best to scare the daylights out of you, didn't he?"

"Objection."

"Do you think he was trying to scare you?" Padgett persisted.

"Perhaps he was. I don't know."

"Or hurt you. Strike back in some way. Perfectly natural to . . ."

"Perhaps."

"In other words, your husband does have a vengeful streak."

"I didn't say that." Strange, she felt suddenly invigorated.

"Did Mr. Hale describe for you exactly how he intended to commit suicide?"

"He didn't give details."

"But shooting himself, jumping off the bridge—he had various scenarios."

"Yes."

"And you took all these threats seriously?"

"Yes."

"You even feared, on at least one occasion you said, for the life of your own child?"

"Yes," said Allie slowly.

"If you thought he was in such a volatile and dangerous condition, why didn't you call the authorities?"

"I don't know. I didn't want him to be . . ."

"What? Publicly humiliated?" That drew titters. "Did you urge him to go to a sanitarium?"

"No."

"Well, now. That's quite a puzzle, isn't it? You—and your daughter too, from what she told us—didn't believe Mr. Hale needed any unusual help. No professional intervention. So how can you sit there now and claim he was unbalanced?"

"I kept urging him to go away for a while."

"Ah yes. To visit some relatives, isn't that what you said? Desperate times call for desperate measures, eh, Mrs. Hale?"

"Objection," deBekker said.

"And was that for his benefit or yours, Mrs. Hale?"

The lawyers wrangled with the judge while Allie wandered in memory. She'd had no energy to do or wish for anything back then, she thought, unless it was that Link shoot himself and end her persecution.

"Let me ask you this," Padgett resumed in a more temperate guise. "When your husband got on the train to Washington, carrying his Smith & Wesson .32 caliber revolver, his instrument of death, this reconciliation you mentioned between the two of you, it was still imperfect, wasn't it?"

"Yes."

"In fact, I inferred from your testimony that during those last four or five weeks before your husband's departure, you and he were not sleeping in the same room."

"That's true."

"You confined your reconciling to the daylight hours?"

Allie sat up a little straighter. "We were talking."

"He was taking various medicines, was he?"

"Yes."

"Which ones?"

"I don't remember."

"You don't? You were so fearful for your husband's health, his well-being, his sanity, his life, but you don't know what drugs he was putting into his body?"

"Dr. Shoop's Restorative," she said. "That was one."

"You've told us your husband was crying and threatening suicide. But he was angry as well, wasn't he? Angry about everything that had taken place?"

"Sometimes, yes."

"In fact, he was mad as a wet hen."

No answer.

"And why not? You maintain an intimacy with your own brother-in-law lasting three years and more, you conceive and bear his child, you try to foist it off on your husband as his own. That's surely enough to make any man take arms against a sea of troubles."

"My husband isn't like that."

"No? The very night of the discovery, didn't he write a letter to Mr. deBekker here cutting you out of his will?"

"Yes," said Allie. "Yes, he did."

"And on the day he left Kentucky to come here and kill his brother-in-law, he hadn't changed his mind about that, had he? At this very moment, today, you are not a beneficiary of your husband's, are you?"

"No."

"But you say you've reconciled."

"We're trying."

"Still, as of now, if your husband were to die on the gallows, you wouldn't get a thing, would you?"

"No."

"So isn't it in your best interests to keep him alive?"

Allie's cheeks turned rose. "I would never do something like that."

"Why not? Because it's against your principles?" Padgett raised a staying hand. "Can we agree on one thing, Mrs. Hale? When your husband left Nicholasville on the train, there was still a sizable gulf between the two of you, no?"

"Yes." She wanted to slap him with both hands.

"The next day he murders your lover. Shoots him down. Spills his blood on Main Street at high noon in front of fifty witnesses. Would you say this act brought the two of you, you and your husband, closer together?"

"Not at first."

"You've visited him in jail?"

"Yes."

"Often?"

"Several times."

"Were you alone?"

"I don't know what you mean."

"Were guards present?"

"Yes."

"So you weren't alone. Do you suppose any of them would testify to having witnessed this grand and glorious event, the reconciliation of Mr. and Mrs. Hale?"

Silence.

"It's never a pleasure to me, Mrs. Hale, to have to pull the truth out of anybody. But look where we are. Hard as we try we can't seem to pinpoint when you two wounded bluebirds came fluttering back together."

"Do you have a question there?" said Judge Houghton.

"You say you wouldn't testify for your husband for money."

"No."

"How about guilt?"

The skin of her forehead and her temples stung.

"Would you get up and tell us he was wild as the east wind—not out of love, we've pretty well buried that notion, but loyalty, let's say, however grossly belated? Would you try to soften the hard truth about this man you married because you feel you got him into this mess?"

"No!" said Allie. "No, I would not." The air was thinner, the trees were fewer. She felt as if she'd never lied at this altitude before.

"Mrs. Hale . . . Were you in love with the deceased?"

A long silence followed. Many eyes flicked to Maggie.

"Were you in love with the deceased?" Padgett repeated.

Allie still did not speak.

"You'd have walked barefoot to Palestine for him, wouldn't you?" said the prosecutor gently. "You know, quite a few of us in this courtroom today miss him too." He waited till he saw the shine of her tears. "That evening the two of you were discovered," he said, "when your husband ran into the next room and put a gun to his head, what exactly did you do?"

"Do?"

"Did you cry out?"

"No."

"Run for help?"

"No."

"Snatch for the gun?"

"No."

"Plead? . . . Weep? . . . *Nothing?*"

A tear, in check till now, slid down her face. She would never have thought that being cross-questioned by this fat lawyer would bring Ham back to her more vividly than anything in weeks.

"Did you intervene in any way? Mrs. Hale?"

"No."

"Did you hope Mr. Hale would pull the trigger?"

"Objection."

"Overruled."

"Did you hope he would kill himself then and there?"

Allie rallied, fought back. "Of course not."

"Of course not."

Padgett was walking away from her.

"I love my husband!" she cried.

"Mrs. Hale, if that were so, none of us would be here, would we?"

The final witness, the defendant himself, would be called to-morrow. Judge Houghton allowed the jurors to go to their homes, first cautioning them not to talk about the case and not to visit saloons.

3 0

"WHAT WAS YOUR FIRST CLUE?"

"First clue?"

"Your first suspicion that there was, ah, a colored gentleman in the woodpile?" DeBekker was gazing away from the witness, out over the audience.

"When I returned home the fact that the child came much sooner than I'd expected, that kept forcing itself on my mind," Link said. "When I was young I studied medicine some, thinking I might become a doctor. I still had the books. So I did some reading. I was . . . it sounds silly now, but I was hoping to find some way a child could be born so much under the usual time. Two months or so."

"But you could not?" said deBekker.

"Not at such a size."

"Which was?"

"Twelve pounds."

Oohs and aahs.

"Did your suspicions deepen over time?"

"Yes."

"How so?"

After being shuttled in and out of jail for weeks, often half sedated, Link found it very strange to be on the witness stand. He was struggling to focus on the fact that his life was at stake. He missed his cough syrup.

"When I visited Elnora, in the summer of '07, I thought then the child looked like Mr. Dillon. I kept trying to disabuse my mind of it, but . . . And then the baby was named after Ham Dillon. At Ham's suggestion."

"Anything else?"

"My wife had changed toward me. She seemed indifferent. Three or four times she spent the night at the Dillons' and took along the baby. Finally I spoke to her about it."

"Did you accuse her of any specific offense?" DeBekker's voice had acquired the lilt some people use to talk to a child.

"I didn't accuse her of anything! I told her that she was letting Ham and Maggie come in between us, that's all."

"You didn't want to go flinging around a lot of wild charges?"

"I had no proof."

"In other words, as always, you were trying to behave in a sober, responsible manner, weren't you, Mr. Hale?"

"I suppose I was."

Having struck the character note once again, deBekker led his client on a stately progress through the picture gallery of his past. ("All the joys and sorrows of his life were touched upon," the *Democrat* noted. "Sentiment was injected into the evidence.") Every plain fact deBekker supplied with a gilded, rococo frame. It was nearing noon when the testimony finally reached the night of the lovers' discovery.

"I said, 'My God, Allie, how could you do such a thing?' And she said . . . well, nothing. She said she couldn't explain."

"Couldn't explain?"

"She said she couldn't resist him," said Link. He made ugly sounds in his chest which turned into crying. "That was all she would ever say." DeBekker let him sob. Link sat up suddenly, jerking his head like a swimmer. " 'Don't do anything!' That's what she said. 'I'll take the baby and go away.' "

"And what did you tell her?"

"I said, 'What good will that do me? You have already broken my heart.' "

A number of ladies in the audience were tearing up now, pulling handkerchiefs out of their sleeves.

"You tried to work in the weeks following, to put this terrible thing behind you?"

"Yes. But the scene of Dillon and my wife in each other's embrace, heart to heart, lips to lips, I couldn't get it out of my mind."

"Tell us about your hallucinations."

"This embrace, I saw it again, up in the sky. I mean I thought I did. The two of them, this vision in the clouds. The kiss was very . . . It rang in my ears. It was very loud."

"How many times did you come near suicide, Mr. Hale?"

Link didn't answer directly. "After that happened I got a revolver and started out into the field to shoot myself. But at the barn I ran into my daughter Marguerite. She took my hand and was prattling away about some game she'd been playing. . . . Several times," he said, finally answering the question.

DeBekker turned to the fatal trip.

"If your destination was Battle Creek, Michigan, Mr. Hale, why did you stop in Washington, Indiana?"

"I still had business interests in Daviess County. Some papers and cash, an interest in a piece of land. I wanted to get them out of the bank."

"Did you plan to see Mr. Dillon?"

"No. No. I had no intention of seeing Mr. Dillon at all."

"And why were you carrying a gun?"

To shoot myself with, Link thought. But he couldn't keep saying that. He gave up some little piece of himself forever every time he said it out loud.

DeBekker asked again. Link was seized with irrational resentment.

"I'd carried a gun as a storekeeper, a deputy sheriff. I was used to having a gun around."

DeBekker gazed at him, the reproachful uncle.

"But you had no idea, did you, that this great political rally would be taking place here that day, a rally which Mr. Dillon would almost surely attend?"

"Not the least idea in the world."

Dubious muttering from the back.

"Still, you telephoned him when you got to Washington. Asked that pretty little operator to place the call."

"I wanted to see if Mr. Dillon was holding anything else of mine."

"No other reason?"

"No."

"But you never reached the bank, did you?"

"No."

"Because you ran into Mrs. Dillon."

"Well, first I headed off to find a law firm. Hastings & Allen. But I never—"

"A law firm?"

"Oh, I got this idea, sort of all of a sudden," said Link. He gave an awkward shrug. "I was thinking of filing a civil suit. You know, against Ham Dillon."

It was the very first either the prosecution or defense had heard of this. DeBekker's voice slowed to an uneasy drawl: "You were thinking of suing the man?"

"Yes. But I considered the exposure of my family and changed my mind."

Padgett sat forward with a faint and predatory smile.

DeBekker finished up with Link and Maggie in the store: what he had or had not seen through that window.

"I was standing there telling her all about everything," Link said, "thinking to myself, I shouldn't, I swore to myself I wouldn't do this, but once I'd started I couldn't stop. I don't remember seeing a thing in that store except the look on her face. That I'll never forget."

"Mrs. Dillon has—"

He felt a surge of fear that nobody believed him. "I didn't want to see Ham! I did not want to see him! It was bad enough just seeing Maggie!"

DeBekker lifted soothing hands. "We understand that. We know. Nevertheless, Mrs. Dillon has testified she pointed her husband out to you."

Link couldn't contain a look of stricken reproach in the direction of his sister-in-law. "She didn't. I didn't look out the window once."

"She has testified you told her you came to town to kill her husband."

"I did not. I never said so."

"She's lying?"

"She's wrong." Link couldn't bring himself to attack Maggie directly. After all that had happened, he still felt a tattered gallantry toward her. Either that, he thought, or I'm still a coward.

"When I went out the door, I turned right. East. I had no idea if Mr. Dillon was east or west or where he was. I wanted to get my bag, but then I saw all these people coming down the street and I thought, I have to get away from them. That's why I went that direction—I thought there was less chance I'd see Ham if I went against the flow of the crowd. I was weak, I hadn't eaten. I had my head down. Then I saw him. I don't remember taking aim. I don't know how many times I shot. I remember Maggie running across the street."

"And then you were arrested? Taken to the mayor's office?"

"I don't remember any of that."

"How long did this blank in your memory last?"

"Till sometime the next day. Noticing the bars, that I remember. Then I knew I was a prisoner."

"And it's your testimony, is it," deBekker said in big wraparound tones, "that you had no control over your actions that fatal day?"

"No control at all. I didn't even know I was firing the shots." Link felt a thrill of uneasiness through his whole system. As if he had said this before but never admitted it.

"And are you sorry now for what happened?"

"I'm as sorry as I can be," he said. "Words can't tell it."

He glanced at Maggie, who looked back iron-eyed.

"HOW'S YOUR HEALTH, Mr. Hale?" said Padgett, first thing. "Right now. Today."

"Today? It's all right."

"You're perfectly strong, perfectly healthy enough to be here and to answer questions, is that right?"

"Yes," said Link.

"Not suffering from any mental disease today?"

"No."

"You're sound as a dollar."

"I'm all right."

"Glad to hear it." Padgett paused, fingering some notes on the table.

"I have some letters here, Mr. Hale. Why don't we talk about these?" Padgett marked them for exhibit, then passed them along to the witness. They were letters from Hale to Dillon written earlier that year, during the summer of 1908.

"These are business letters, aren't they, Mr. Hale?"

Link leafed through them. "Yes," he said.

"In other words, according to this correspondence you were still transacting business with Mr. Dillon last May, July, and August? Is that right?"

"Yes."

"And this was many, many months after you say you first became suspicious of his conduct with your wife. True?"

"Yes."

"Let's take a look at . . ." Padgett walked up, plucked the pages out of Link's hands, and searched. " 'Yours of the twentieth received . . .' This one." He handed the papers back. "This letter of yours concerns what?"

"A farm."

"The two of you bought shares together in a farm near Elnora, didn't you? Just this past July."

"Ham said it was a good investment."

"How did you pay for your portion?"

"By check."

"What kind of check? What does it say there?"

"A blank check," said Link without looking down.

"A blank check. To a man who was supposedly making you so jealous it haunted your every waking moment."

"I still didn't want to say anything of my suspicions," Link said.

"So in these letters you were dissembling."

"I was not voicing my . . ."

"You were hiding what was in your heart. You were saying what was not the truth."

"I suppose so."

"Indeed. As you had been doing for at least a full year and a half."

"I was hoping—"

"How did you sign that letter, Mr. Hale? Would you read it, please?"

Link read: " 'Affectionately, Brother Link.' "

"And what's the sentence just before that? The final one of the text?"

" 'I have the utmost confidence in you.' "

"Thank you." Padgett took his time retrieving the letters and handing them to the clerk. Figuring his best weapon was to let the witness rattle himself.

"Now, your defense," Padgett resumed, "your defense is that you suffered from irresistible or impulsive insanity. Do you think your wife suffers from the same thing?"

"What?"

"Mrs. Hale told you, I believe, that when she took up with Mr. Dillon, it was because she could not resist his advances. Wasn't that your testimony here? She said she couldn't help herself. My question is, when your wife told you that, did you think *she* was insane?"

"Objection."

"Sustained."

"Now, about this gun you bought for the trip . . ."

Link asked for water. A glass was provided. He took a sip, thinking. What if I crack right here? What if he breaks me? Would that help me get off?

"This gun you bought . . ."

"I said before," Link burst out, "I didn't buy it to use on Mr. Dillon."

"Oh?" Padgett came right after him. "Then what was it for? Was it to protect yourself from the thugs and desperadoes you expected to find at Dr. Kellogg's resort?"

Link was silent.

"You kept the purchase of that gun a secret from your wife, didn't you?"

"I didn't mention it to her."

"You kept the purchase of that gun a secret from your wife, didn't you?"

"Yes."

"You keep an awful lot of secrets, don't you?"

"Objection," from deBekker, half rising.

"Now, about this astonishing visit of yours to the telephone exchange the morning of the murder. When you tried to reach Mr. Dillon eight or ten times within the space of a few minutes. You still maintain you didn't want to see him?"

"Yes."

"Then what was your object?"

"As I said before, I wanted to know if he was holding other papers of mine."

"Evidently a question of tearing urgency. Do your business affairs generally get you this fired up?"

"I wanted it taken care of. I wanted nothing to do with him anymore," said Link with some spirit.

"You didn't. Ah yes. You told us you came to Washington to go to the bank. But first I believe you went to the Meredith House?"

"Yes."

"Then to the telephone exchange?"

"Yes."

"Then off toward Hastings & Allen? To file suit against your imminent victim?"

"Yes."

"Everywhere, it seems, but the bank. The one place you might have actually transacted this amazingly pressing business. Where are these papers now, by the way, the ones you were so anxious to get hold of?"

"They're still at the bank."

"Still at the bank. Mr. Hale, let me ask you this." And suddenly Padgett dropped into another key, amiably thoughtful, as if he were shooting the breeze over the back fence. "On that train ride to Washington . . . You're rolling along, looking out the window. The gun's in your pocket. You remember that ride?"

"Yes."

"You didn't have to get off that train, did you?"

"What?"

"You didn't have to get off the train! You could have ridden it straight on up to Michigan, couldn't you?"

"I said before, I never thought that Ham—"

"But you were tempting fate, weren't you, Mr. Hale? At the very least, you were playing with fire, getting off in Mr. Dillon's own back yard. You must have known it at the time."

"I—"

"Instead of going up to Michigan, for the corn flakes and magic shows, you chose to enter the heart of darkness, didn't you, Mr. Hale? *You* did. *You* chose. *You* decided."

"Yes."

"So how can you claim to be innocent?"

DeBekker stood up. "Your honor, as much as we're all enjoying this seminar in moral philosophy—"

"Back to earth, Mr. Padgett."

"Let's put it this way. While you were sitting aboard that train, Mr. Hale, turning things over in your mind, did any ideas come to you? Any scenes, any fantasies of what you'd do if by some wild chance you *did* run into Ham Dillon? Tell me frankly. Anything like that pass through your mind?"

Link had to answer yes.

"And these fantasies of yours. Did any of them include your committing an act of violence?"

MUCH OF THE REST of Padgett's cross-examination, which lasted all through the afternoon, consisted of short jabs to the body, all aimed at establishing the same thing: Link's sanity.

The prosecutor took him through the morning of the shooting step by step, asking over and over again:

"Were you of unsound mind then?"

"I don't know."

"When you left the hotel and went looking for the telephone exchange, were you of unsound mind then?"

"I don't know."

"At the exchange? Were you of unsound mind?"

"I don't know."

"Afterward? When you went looking for that law firm?"

"I don't know."

"You were never disoriented, were you?"

"No."

"So you knew up from down. Your right hand from your left. You knew a hawk from a handsaw."

"Yes."

"You don't specifically recall some moment when you lost the capacity to distinguish right from wrong?"

"No."

"So in other words, to the best of your recollection, you never lost that capacity, is that right? . . . Is that right?"

"I suppose so. I don't know. This is impossible. I can't say."
Link saw he had drunk all his water.

"You did a good deal of loitering along Main Street that morning, didn't you?"

"Not loitering."

"Weren't you deliberately positioning yourself, lying in wait?"

"No."

"Tell us this. Did you blame your wife for your disgrace and humiliation? Or did you blame Dillon?"

Link hesitated. "I always thought it was Ham's fault," he said quietly.

"I see. You blamed Dillon for ruining your life. All right, you're there on the street . . ."

Padgett drove on like this, through the encounter with Maggie, their conference in the store . . .

"When you finally left your sister-in-law, just before you stepped out onto the street, didn't you tell her you would leave town immediately? Without causing any trouble?"

"Yes."

"And your luggage was still at the Meredith House?"

"Yes."

"So why, Mr. Hale, if your object was to get out of town, did you leave Neal & Eskridge's store and turn *in the opposite direction*—east, in the very direction Ham Dillon was? Why did you walk straight toward him?"

"I told you, I was going that way to avoid the crowd. I was planning to circle back to the hotel another way." Link felt another overwhelming rush of anxiety. He saw himself on the gallows. He saw the artist's sketch in the paper.

"You told your sister-in-law you would do one thing, and you did another, isn't that so?"

"No. No, that's not so."

Padgett paused, testing the air once more with his performer's ear. He knew Link Hale had more people on his side than he'd had at the start of the trial. Too much had come out about Dillon along the way. Even some of Ham's friends had defected. But Padgett was sure he could still win. The more isolated he felt, in fact, the more doubts he'd acquired about the justice of his cause, the more he was lashing himself to prevail.

Padgett was walking toward Maggie Dillon, who sat up front in her implacable grief. The prosecutor stopped and extended an open palm. Maggie took the chain of the locket she wore and slipped it over her head. Padgett carried it back to the witness.

"Take a look," said Padgett, popping open the locket. "You see there's a lock of Ham Dillon's hair enshrined here, worn by the widow ever since he died. At your hand. There's a picture of Ham too, on the other side." Padgett mused upon the photograph, then showed it to Link again. "It looks very like him, doesn't it?"

Link struggled to answer. "It looks like the baby too."

Padgett turned, hard and brisk, and took the locket back to Maggie.

"This embrace, this kiss between Mr. Dillon and your wife. You say you saw it where? In the sky?"

"I saw it in the parlor of my home. Later on, yes, I saw something like it in the sky."

"How big were they?"

"Who?"

"Mr. Dillon and your wife."

"In the sky, you mean? I don't know."

"Twenty feet high?"

"I don't know."

"But you saw them clearly."

"Yes."

"Would you look at the ceiling for me, Mr. Hale?"

"The ceiling?"

"Yes."

Link looked.

"See anything?"

"No."

"Just a ceiling?"

"Yes."

"Not the Sistine Chapel?"

"Objection."

"Sustained."

"Now, this kiss. You say it rang in your ears."

"Yes."

"Rang how? Like a telephone? Like a gong?"

"It echoed."

"When you gave Maggie Dillon a kiss in Neal & Eskridge's store, did that ring in your ears?"

"No."

"But that was two minutes before you shot her husband."

"Yes."

"If there was ever a time for a kiss to ring in your ears, wouldn't that be it? When you're supposed to have been insane?"

"I don't know."

"Mr. Hale, is it possible you have feigned madness in order to wreak your revenge on the man who supplanted you?"

"No."

"It's not possible?"

"No."

"You say you can't remember being arrested? Or taken to the mayor's office?"

"That's right."

"And this memory lapse of yours continued what, into the next day?"

"Yes."

"You gave a long jailhouse interview to the reporter from the *Washington Herald*. You don't deny doing that, do you?"

"I've seen it since. I don't remember giving it."

Padgett had the paper in his hands. He read, skimming: " 'I shot to kill' . . . 'my temper overcame me . . .' Several columns of small type. You say you gave this entire interview in a state of somnambulism?"

"I don't remember it."

"All this forgetting that you've done—you've never forgotten the commandments, have you? Do you recall this from the decalogue: 'Thou shalt not kill?' "

"Yes."

"We've heard so much about what a Bible-reading, God-fearing man you are. So this most basic teaching of our religion, that's never once slipped your mind, has it?"

"No."

"Not now, not then, not ever. Yet you trampled on it anyway, spat on it, defiled it. You killed a man in cold blood and then what did you do, Mr. Hale? You crowed about it! You went cock-a-doodle-doo! In the mayor's office, and later on to this newspaper. *'I shot to kill! I shot to kill!'* "

Padgett ended in a great heat. Rising at once, deBekker spoke as soon as the crowd had settled.

"Mr. Hale, are you not also familiar with that other commandment, 'Thou shalt not commit adultery'?"

"Yes."

Sensation in the audience.

31

THE WOLVERINE sat hunched against the far-left wall, scribbling as fast as he could. His makeshift writing table, dragged up from the courthouse basement for the trial, was nicked and gouged, and more than once he punched a hole in the paper with his pen. But the muse was upon him.

"Half the crowd was composed of ladies," he wrote, "the sex that has been called 'only a little lower than the angels' . . ."

It was Friday morning, the fourth of December. Closing arguments today. Hours of furious note taking lay ahead, so the wolverine was getting a jump on his copy.

". . . They were attracted not just by the oratory," he wrote. He paused, sucking a tooth, then resumed. "This was a case of heart interest involving illicit love and the home, which is the real paradise on earth . . ."

The ink-stained wretch to his left, who wore an eyeshade and armbands, was trying out headlines.

COURTROOM GLADIATORS WRESTLE WITH THE JURY

GREAT CROWDS PRESENT TO HEAR THE ARGUMENT

LAWYERS ENGAGED IN MASTERLY ORATORY

His left elbow was planted on a folded copy of the morning *Herald,* as if he were hoping to draw inspiration from it straight up through his arm. "The outcome of the trial remains in doubt," it declared. "Considerable difference of opinion exists among persons that have listened to most of the evidence as to what the verdict will be. . . . The closing arguments may decide the issue. . . ."

Across from the reporters, the courtroom was full and loud with talk: talk with an angry edge now, for with a verdict approaching people were getting more openly combative. Death, prison, loony bin, let him off: all sides had their champions— though the ever-growing Kentucky contingent was still solidly for acquittal.

By now the principals were all in their accustomed seats: Maggie with Dennis, her sour protector, and Harold and Ruth deposited to her right. Across the way sat Allie and her own children— minus Denton, as usual. Opposing counsel were at their tables, opening their satchels and sorting through papers, Eberhardt and Padgett both still pink in the face from a strategy dispute on the way over. They'd had this fight before, in other cases. Eberhardt liked digging up a lot of precedents. He thought they were great persuaders. But Padgett believed arguing the law too fine only got you in trouble. "You can't Shylock a jury, son," he liked to say. "You've gotta give 'em Henry the Fifth."

There was the rap of the gavel. The crowd murmured with pleasure.

J. D. deBekker rose, preened, cleared his throat.

He began with a rippling arpeggio in honor of the state of Indiana, with which, he said, he had been personally unfamiliar before. He was delighted, however, to have had this yawning gap in his experience closed at last. "I only wish," he said, "I could have come to know it under less melancholy circumstances."

"Melancholy but not abject. For my client does not come as a suppliant," he said, sounding his first trumpet note, "but as one demanding right and justice. We would never ask you to trample down the principles of law to save the life of any man. We would never make appeals to some nonexistent or shadow law, some so-called law of nature, some *unwritten law*, however compelling some might find it and however heartily they might urge us to that course. No, sir. We scorn the least reference to unwritten law—unless, of course, it be to those laws that bear the sacred sanction of Almighty God Himself.

"Likewise, we do not seek to prevail by focusing attention on the pitiful circumstances of the defendant—a man who, it is true, has endured like Job; but we scorn to inject pathos into this case. Sentiment has no place here. On the contrary! This is a case of base deception and illicit hungers, of the darkest, most corrupted corners of the human spirit. And these we must utterly condemn. We must face them down with a contempt which is manly, firm, and clear-eyed. For behold their terrible power, gentlemen! My client, here before you, was so staggered when he came upon the worm of evil in his own wife, his own brother-in-law, that he himself was banished, temporarily, from the throne of reason."

There were sighs in the audience, sounds of settling in. This was what they'd come for. DeBekker continued on slow and mighty wings.

"At its heart," he said, "we must never forget, this case involves the American home—the sacred and beautiful home against which he who strikes a blow is an enemy to all mankind, for it is the most sacred spot this side of the home of God Himself. . . ." With his peninsula of silver hair, his long jaw, his shining eyes, the Kentuckian cut a grandly theatrical figure—thanks in small part, perhaps, to an extra snort from his silver flask, just enough to get the gears greased. "Possibly the appearance of so eminent a champion as Mr. Arnold Padgett," deBekker went on, "for the other side, has clouded the thinking of some individuals on this point. And may I say, as a parenthesis, I had never before had the pleasure, or enjoyed the instruction, of seeing Mr. Padgett in combat. The state has certainly not suffered from his vigorous presentation." Padgett inclined his head. "And yet, gentlemen: Is it not manifest that bringing in a hired attorney of such great reputation to lend dignity to the prosecution's case simply proves how fatally weak that case is, stripped down and unadorned? Let us examine the facts."

This deBekker did at tremendous length. Babies' bottles, once full, became empty; bladders, once empty, grew full, and still the defense attorney stood on his bluff pointing out details of the landscape. He was a good deal too wordy for some people; still, just when he seemed to be all curlicues and bluebirds, he would let go with a shot of hard sense. Link gave up trying to follow him and just sat in a mild daze of hope.

"But to return to the vital question," cried deBekker at last. "Was the defendant, or was he not, responsible for his actions at the time of the shooting?

"This dreadful drama, we know, is stained with blood. But if the slayer was not responsible for his act, then no crime was committed. No matter how sensational the deed, the law must throw about the pitiable actor its protecting arm. It matters not whether the finger of God touching a distracted brain renders the victim permanently or only temporarily deranged. All you must determine, gentlemen, is whether Mr. Hale—*not* when he was working as a clerk at the distillery, *not* when he was riding aboard the train, *not* when he appeared here before you on the witness stand—but *at the time of the shooting,* was this man insane? And can you doubt it? Broken in mind and spirit, struggling toward sanctuary, he suddenly sees before him, once again, that face—the face that has haunted him waking and sleeping, the grinning agent of all his miseries. When he fired, gentlemen, Mr. Hale might have been firing at a phantasm in his own dreams.

"Do you believe that to be true? Do you even suspect it might be true? Then you must vote to acquit, gentlemen. Remember, that is your duty. If you have a reasonable doubt of his sanity at the time of the shooting, my client is entitled to the benefit of that doubt."

Padgett sighed discreetly. DeBekker wasn't missing much. His eyes drifted out over the audience. He had never seen so many women present for a closing argument. Women and other lawyers.

"Now, I know that the man who died was very popular in this community, and with good reason. A man of such zeal and charm, in fact, that it stands as a tribute to every citizen of this community that you let justice take its course even in the awful heat of the event, knowing 'there is no grievance that is a fit object of redress by mob law' . . . to quote that great American hero, our sixteenth President . . . whose name in part my client bears. . . . No, I would never seek to diminish Hamlet Dillon in the eyes of his own friends and neighbors. The actions of his life must be their own testament. Of his fateful entanglement with his sister-in-law you are too well informed; of his lewd trifling with her daughter, Louise Hale, I need not speak."

In the audience Dennis leaned over and began massaging Maggie's shoulders.

"Yes, there were those who loved Dillon. His widow loved him so that in the bitterness of her heart, full of a misplaced vengeance, she even took the witness stand and . . . But let that pass. What need to catalogue all the errors in this sad case? Allie Hale has committed a grave error. But she has had the womanhood to confess it, and the world will say to her, as the Savior said to another woman, 'Go thy way and sin no more.'

"As for my client, gentlemen, he has but one request: Give him his liberty. Or give him death. Let there be no middle ground in your decision, no fainthearted compromise. I have Mr. Hale's consent to say this. What better way to show how confident he feels, placing his precious fate in your just hands?"

DeBekker sat down to an eruption of surprised talk. Link sat, lightly gasping, looking vaguely here and there as if hoping for someone's approval. It was true, he had agreed to let deBekker go for broke. It was his last chance, Link thought, to be a brave man.

WHEN PADGETT arose after the lunch break to deliver his own closing, the coldest eyes upon him weren't at the defense table, or anywhere among the hostile Kentuckians strewn through the crowd. They belonged to Maggie Dillon. Even before deBekker publicly insulted her, she had been brooding over the prosecutor's cross-examination of Link. She had noticed something, if few others did: that in all that heat and thunder Padgett had never mentioned her pointing at her husband through the window.

He must think she was lying too.

The fact that Padgett was tossing anything that might hurt the case, that wouldn't have mattered to Maggie. It didn't even matter that she *had* lied. Once again she'd been abandoned and betrayed.

Padgett began by addressing the court in a low and rueful voice.

"Well, somebody here's crazy," he said. "I know it's not the defendant. I'm starting to think it's me. I have to say it's a compliment to Mr. deBekker here that he can even get an old hand like myself a little mixed up. Listening to him, I actually forgot for a moment the first principle of a case like this: that when the party in the dock has no real defense, no alibi, nothing, then the only thing his attorney can do is go into a fan dance about insanity. Hoping against hope he can make somebody else crazy enough to believe it.

"Trying to disguise the naked truth.

"Now, one thing Mr. deBekker told you is undeniably true. I do come here as a 'hired lawyer,' hired by the Dillon family. But I'll tell you, it's really Mr. Hale there, the defendant, I can do the greatest service for—a greater one than his own lawyers have done, including Mr. deBekker, his very old friend. It's a service that will leave him standing like a man on his own two feet. A man in the eyes of his wife, his children, his community. Not a freak, not a low coward cringing behind this fig leaf of a defense, but a man just like the rest of us!

"If Link Hale was insane, then August was the time to shoot. The first moment he discovered the two of them kissing in his house, that moment he ran for the pistol. If he'd shot Dillon then, if he'd shot them both, then he would have had a case! No matter how much blood he spilled in all that terrible confusion, no matter how dreadful the loss of life, I personally would have held open the door to the courtroom and let Mr. Hale walk free.

"But he did not shoot then.

"He waited. He waited and brooded and planned. Mr. Hale bought a revolver, keeping it a careful secret from his wife. He arranged his affairs, again very carefully, so that if anything were to happen to him, his wife, her character blackened, would be left without a dollar, the doors of respectability closed against her. This model Christian, so called, whose Bible teaches him to forgive, he did all this to his own wife out of vengeance.

"And then he bought a train ticket.

"Mr. Hale was on a hunting trip. He denies it now. But today we can all see plainly enough the implacable line he followed. He traveled almost twenty-four hours, gentlemen, all the way here to Washington, to put himself in Ham Dillon's path. He knew his quarry would be here that day. How could he not? It was in all the papers—papers sold in Nicholasville, Kentucky, sold on the train, sold in Seymour, Indiana, where he spent the night. The biggest political event in the state that weekend. His golden opportunity." Padgett picked up Hale's pistol from the evidence table, turned it over idly in his hands, fondled it. Then suddenly he swung his arm and snapped the trigger. Even the judge jumped. Once, twice, five times Padgett fired.

"And what does he tell the world right after? There wasn't a soapbox tall enough for him then. 'I shot to kill!' There's Dillon, a study in blood, lying there dying, and Hale is proud of it—full of that evil pride of a man who has taken a role that is rightly God's alone. Driven by jealousy, Hale would not rest till his enemy had paid to the uttermost farthing. Can anything be plainer?

"The defendant, remember, was born in a state, that dark and bloody ground, where a personal grievance is held to justify killing a man. But we in Indiana aren't like that. We in Indiana don't have to search men as they enter the courtroom to see if they're carrying revolvers. We uphold a higher standard of civilization." The Kentucky bunch howled like a stuck pig at that, and Houghton had to do some hammering with his gavel.

"Mr. Hale says now he regrets his action. I'm sure he does. Regrets, at least, that he's put his own neck in the noose. How much does he regret it? He takes the stand and says he wasn't himself. A colossal lie! The day Hale gunned down his own brother-in-law he was never more himself. On September 11, 1908, this man came into his own. I'll tell you what, gentlemen, in my thirty-two years of practicing law, this is the first time I ever saw a defendant plead insanity and then take the stand to try to prove it with rational argument."

Link was growing more and more demoralized. The longer he listened to Padgett, the more he couldn't help fearing there might be some truth in his words. Maybe the man was right about him: maybe he did harbor some kernel of evil. It was true, he had chosen to come here that day, carrying a gun. *I shot to kill.* Was he guilty in some deeper way than he'd ever acknowledged to himself? More than he had even believed at the time? It was just another notion, one among many, but it was taking up residence in a corner of his heart. It was moving in for good.

"Was Mr. Hale obsessed? Well, sure he was! Of course he was! Nobody here doubts that for a second. But . . ." Padgett approached the jury rail, leaned down, smoothed it like a tablecloth with both hands: *"Obsession is not insanity."*

"And what," he said, stepping back, "what of all these claims that he wanted to die? Look at him! He's still here! If the death angel were to come into this room right now, Mr. Hale would be the first man to get under the table. Give him liberty or give him death?" Padgett snorted. "Another bluff! Even an honest-to-God founding father in a brass-buttoned coat and white wig couldn't dictate to you, the jury, in this proceeding. Mr. Hale has to take whatever punishment you give him. You are the masters here.

"I admit there's room for sentiment in this case, gentlemen. But be sure you place it where it belongs. Mr. Hale has difficulty sleeping? His murdered victim, dead at age thirty-one, is not troubled that way. Mr. Dillon sleeps well, the eternal sleep that knows no waking on this earth. Counsel has had so much to say about the breaking up of the Hale home. He doesn't mention the vacant chair in the Dillon home—a home where the defendant and his family were always welcome. Where there now lives a young widow with her three helpless babes. While you're thinking about homes, gentlemen, don't forget that one.

"Last thing," said Padgett, "before I let go of your lapels. I want to take this chance to pass along a message. It comes from the widow herself, the noble Mrs. Maggie Dillon, and it's a message of love and forgiveness. A message to Allie Hale. For in spite of the ordeal she has endured, and will be enduring years into the future, Maggie Dillon forgives her sister. Forgives her from her heart. Goes to show, it's in the extremes of suffering that we find out who the true Christians are."

It would have been hard to say which of the sisters was more surprised at the finish. Both gaped as Padgett sat, down.

THAT WAS COURT for the day. The crowd filed out, a little groggy with oratory, leaving the reporters to their scribbling. "There was excellent oratory on both sides," the wolverine wrote. "Padgett sent volleys of scorn and outrage into the ranks of the counsel for the defense, touched with the fire of argument that kept interest at a breathless pitch. Yet ever through it has run the sentiment of the pity of it all." Eventually he and the others packed up and disappeared, and Miss Fish the stenographer was left all alone, polishing her notes while she gnawed at another apple.

3 2

O N SATURDAY MORNING, after ten days of testimony and arguments, Judge Houghton delivered his instructions to the jury. "You've sat through some pretty stiff wind," he told them, "blowing from both sides, and I don't envy you the time it's going to take to pick the chaff out of your hair before you can come to a verdict." (This was seen as a veiled warning from the judge that he didn't want to see them back here in five minutes.) "Just remember one thing in your deliberations," he went on. "Stick to the law. And in case you're wondering, I'm about to explain what that is.

"There's murder in the first degree," he said. "Premeditated murder. That's if you find the defendant meant to do it and set out to do it and did it. The penalty for that is death by hanging.

"Next is murder in the second degree. That's if you decide the defendant didn't start off with the idea of murdering Mr. Dillon, but decided to do it when he realized he had the opportunity. That's life in prison. You know, Mr. Foreman, it might help you later if you took some notes." The foreman hastily scrounged paper and pen while the judge waited, scowling.

"Next, manslaughter. The law says that is a killing committed in sudden passion. Man lost his temper. The penalty there is imprisonment for two years, all the way up to twenty-one years. Or anything in between. It's entirely up to you.

"And finally, there's not guilty by reason of insanity. That's if you decide the defendant plain couldn't help it. The horse just rode away with him. Not a thing he could do.

"That's it. Any questions? Okay. You might as well get started. If you go a while, Mr. Allison there"—he pointed at the bailiff—"will bring you lunch. Chicken okay?"

The twelve men trooped out and retired to deliberate in a back room of the courthouse.

MR. ALLISON did bring the jurors lunch, and later on coffee, and then seltzer water and a snack, and then some more coffee. Loungers crowded the saloons and diners as the afternoon hours crawled by. Barkeeps took down their Free Lunch signs. Meanwhile out on the streets there was the usual flow of Saturday shoppers. Even some of the farmers came in on this day to barter—a case of strawberry preserves, say, for a pair of shoes. A lot of these people were put out to find the town so hard to get around in; all the usual hitching rails were taken, and they had to pay good money for stabling. Even so, a number of them stuck around once their business was done, just for the heck of it, to see what would happen.

The sun sank without a verdict. Mr. Allison brought the jurors supper. Lamps were lit. The late papers appeared, which men passed from table to table in the saloons, and in the game room over at the Masonic Lodge. They were just chewing the cud of the news while they waited. "The most hotly contested murder trial that ever took place in Daviess County." That's what the *Democrat* was calling it.

"Our readers have breakfasted, dined, and supped," that article said, "on the incidents of this terrible tragedy. One of the main actors lies buried in a casket made to his measure; the other lives with blood upon his hands and, if reports can be believed, regrets his rash or irresponsible act and hopes there may be 'rain enough in the sweet heavens to wash them white as snow.' The legal battle will be remembered as a cause célèbre in the criminal annals of the county. What will the verdict be?"

Around seven o'clock there was still another influx into Washington, this time by the Saturday-night crowd. These were young people mostly, here to dance or go bowling. The bakeries and ice cream shops always stayed open late for them. That night the vaudeville theater had a full slate and over at the Opera House, Lyman H. Howe was featuring his travel slides of Egypt, Russia, Italy, and France.

Link sat on his cot by himself. DeBekker, his other lawyers, various Kentucky friends had all offered to keep the vigil with him, but he didn't want the pressure of having to behave well. Now that he was alone, though, he wasn't doing much of anything. The tension had all gone into one nerve that seemed to run from his left leg all the way up to his brain. From time to time he snuck a look at Deputy Wallace, who was snoozing on the other side of the bars. Link had been on suicide watch so long it had become a way of life. He thought of it by now as a sort of night light. He would miss it if they took it away.

Maggie was waiting in the second-story sitting room of a boardinghouse she had commandeered. Dennis was there too. Every time she looked at him, he wore the same mask of encouragement; but she didn't feel like talking. Harold and Ruth both lay asleep on a makeshift bed. Harold's jaw was askew as if he'd been kayoed. Two weeks of trial had left the children exhausted.

Aside from the light flung in from the street, the only illumination came from an amber porcelain table lamp painted with pictures of geese in flight. Maggie thought of that gander—it was years ago now—the one that spent a whole summer out behind the barn, honking for his dead mate. It was the worst sound of mourning she had ever heard. It went on and on.

Ham told her then a goose was the only animal that mates for life.

As badly as she wanted Link convicted, sitting here at this moment Maggie felt almost indifferent, wrung out. She had learned too much about human nature these past few months, including her own.

A T   T H E   M E R E D I T H   H O U S E, Allie was trying to pick out a dress.

She had tossed them on the bed in a fan of colors—brown, dark red, blue. Winter shades. She couldn't decide which to wear. Silly, she thought; still, Allie couldn't help feeling it was a crucial decision, what costume she chose to step back into life.

She knew, of course, she was staying fixed on clothes to keep from thinking of other things. For weeks now she had haunted herself with the thought that Link might be executed, that his blood too might be left on her head. But tonight, for the first time, she had another fear, one scratching like a rodent at the base of her brain. What if he got off?

Going home with him again? God. That would be her own life sentence. It would be horrible of course, a yoke on her conscience forever, if he were convicted. Yet wouldn't it be easier on her maybe in the long run?

What if he just went to jail?

She thought of her children. Either way, they were her last consolation. The ones who were still speaking to her, that is; the younger ones. They would have to carry part of her load as well, all through their lives, and that cut her. She wondered if Albert would stick by her when he was older. He wouldn't always be just a cherished symbol of passion. He would grow up and become a man.

She smiled just thinking of him. Link was right: he looked more like Ham every day.

D EBEKKER HAD RETURNED to the Hyatt, where, after offering the bellboy five dollars if he could locate some mint, he retired to his quarters with a bottle of bourbon. Padgett left word with his office boy to come fetch him the second there was a verdict, if one came in tonight. Then he went to the movies.

Now he was slumped in a folding chair staring at the cloth screen waiting for the film to start. He had no idea what it was about, or even what it was called.

He watched the title cards come and go:

Please Applaud with Hands Only. . . . Ladies Without Escorts Cordially Invited. . . . Ventilated and Disinfected Every Day. . . .

He found his thoughts were wandering, not to Link or Ham Dillon, but to Allie Hale. Men's thoughts often wandered to Allie, he supposed. He realized he admired her. Not just her looks. It was something else she had. He wished he could speak to her somehow. Well, one thing he could do: he could pay her the compliment of not feeling sorry for her.

The movie was running. It must have been for a while. A night scene. Exotic trees. Italy?

A young woman came staggering out of some woods, then stood leaning against a tree, breast heaving, with the back of her hand to her mouth. She looked here, there, a picture of distress, then plunged on.

"All over!" read the card. "Her brief passionate love dream was forever put aside!"

The woman was seen clawing through some underbrush.

"How could he have deserted her after their witching night together on the Grand Canal?"

The girl emerged into a sudden and surprising plaza with a sprouting fountain, everything pearly in the moonlight. Sinking down on the steps, she buried her head and sobbed.

Suddenly she lifted her head like a deer, looking here, there. She heard something.

A gallant in a goatee appeared.

Padgett, snoozing, came awake to the booming of the courthouse bell.

Others were already stumbling up the aisles. He lurched to his feet and joined them, almost trampling his office boy coming the other way. Those still trying to watch the movie swore and protested, and as Padgett fled on toward the door, another card appeared on the screen:

Somebody's Baby Is Crying. Is It Yours?

H E   C O U L D   S E E   I T   N O W, the huge courthouse bell, rocking in its shaft. The bailiff must be clinging to it like the Hunchback himself. Padgett popped open his pocket watch as he hurried along. 9:40. Ten hours. The streets were streaming. He'd seen nothing like it since the day Mr. Marshall came to town to give that speech.

A thousand people flocked to the courthouse that night. Most couldn't get in, of course. The jam-up led to some delay getting the prisoner over from the jail, and forcing clear paths for Maggie, and then the Hale children. Allie wasn't with them. At the sound of the signal bell she had grown weak and sunk to the bed. She was still there.

The jury filed into court. The crowd, packed onto their

benches, sat breathing as if the room contained a very limited amount of oxygen.

Houghton rapped for order, though no one was making any noise. He warned that anyone who cut up after the verdict would go to jail. Then he said: "Gentlemen, have you found a verdict?"

"Yes, sir," said the foreman.

An envelope was passed to the judge, who opened it, scanned it, then passed it to Henry Allison to read aloud.

"We, the jury," Allison piped, "find the defendant not guilty, on the ground that he was insane at the time of the shooting."

Before he could finish, there was a wild yell of approval, coming from many throats. Men came swarming over the guardrails and up onto the platform to pump the defendant's hand and congratulate the defense attorneys. DeBekker, in the act of shaking Link's hand himself, saw his client swept away in a tide of well-wishers.

Padgett sat back in an easy posture, unbuttoning the top button of his pants.

He looked over at Maggie Dillon, the way he'd often done these past two weeks. She might have been playing statues. One hand was partway to her mouth.

She knew that Dennis, at her side, was railing and cursing. But she didn't pay him any heed.

The jury had betrayed her. Her own neighbors.

Groping, she tried to lay hold of another idea: no matter how much he deserved it, at least her lying hadn't helped put a man to death. It struggled up in her, this tiny flame. Then it was crushed under a load of snow.

Even members of the jury were shaking hands with Link and his attorneys. Houghton pounded his gavel to the point of doing himself harm, but the celebration went on. It took a long time before Link was taken back to jail.

.   .   .

ON MONDAY a three-man lunacy commission, appointed by Judge Houghton, met in a side room of the courthouse to give Link a sanity test. If they found he was still mentally unstable, he'd be taken off to an asylum; if not, he was free to go. Link, who had spent the past couple of days opening telegrams, holding court in his cell, and accepting the muted congratulations of his wife, woke up nervous. He had to show up, mentally, in his Sunday best.

Padgett dropped by to watch them give the exam. He felt glad they weren't giving it to him. Some Dillon loyalists had been urging him to fight to have Hale committed, but the prosecutor wouldn't do it. After predicating his whole case on Link's sanity, he wasn't about to turn around now and argue he was crazy.

Still, he hated losing this case. Hated it like poison. He'd even come today thinking there was an off chance the examiners might have been friends of Ham's. But no; either that, or they were the last men in town with integrity. They wiggled their fingers, and asked Link who was President, and then they let him go. DeBekker, who still wore the faint cologne of bourbon he'd been sporting since the verdict, gave him a bear hug when it was all over.

Padgett contemplated the ruins of his moral crusade.

For years he'd been a sort of reluctant cynic; his time in politics had pretty well convinced him that the world was a sinkhole of depravity, stupidity, faithlessness. So he was no worse off than he'd been before. Really, what had he lost?

THE NEXT DAY, Link left Washington on the train accompanied by his family. His belly was full with hotel food. He'd been promised his old job back at the distillery, with a raise. He talked happily, with a trace of fearful hope, to Allie about the things they could buy now. He was always, she thought, afraid of something.

As they rode in the buggy to the station, Allie looked out at the odd gawkers and rag ends of the curious who had turned out to see them go. In her mind she began turning them into a crowd, though they weren't a crowd any longer; her eyes shone upon the multitudes. She wore a dark cape and glossy green dress, set off with a silver pin: an aristocrat riding in her tumbril. One who had sacrificed herself for love. It was enough to get her through today.

One member of the Hale family was staying behind. Denton had gotten himself a job that same week working at the B&O shops. The boy turned up at the station to shake hands with his father, kiss his mother, hug his brothers and sisters. But when they climbed aboard and put their faces to the window, and still the train didn't leave, he began to fidget. Finally Denton gave them a last, stumbling wave and took off up the street. They were playing poker over at the roundhouse, he knew, and if he hurried he could still get in the game.

AFTERWORD

ALMOST A CENTURY LATER, Ham Dillon was still a golden boy in family legend. ("They always used to say he'd have been governor," my cousin Sally said.) But aside from a few books, almost none of his papers or belongings have survived, maybe because Maggie held a yard sale a month after he was killed.

Almost no trace remains of Allie, or at least nothing tangible. After the murder her sister cut her right out of the herd, destroying every photograph and memento connected with her.

Maggie I met. She was a very old lady at the time, and I was a very little boy, but I remember the hushed tones in which she was introduced to me—*This is your great-grandmother*—as if I were being presented to Queen Victoria. Maggie was forever warped and embittered by the betrayals of her husband and sister. "She wore black for a long time after his death," my Aunt

Ruth told me. "In the late afternoons she would walk out toward the orchard and stand there, not weeping, just looking." In 1910 she married Ham's brother Dennis, her way of trying to recapture the past. But as Aunt Ruth said, "Uncle Den was just enough like my father to keep reminding her of what had happened." All the way up to her death in the mid-fifties Maggie was famously hard to get along with, though even at a great age she could still turn out a lip-smacking angel food cake.

As for Link and Allie, they returned to Nicholasville together after the trial, but putting the marriage back together was hopeless. According to court records, Link filed for divorce in 1911, claiming his wife had absconded with their children. He withdrew the motion when Allie returned home, apparently out of fear she could lose custody. The two existed side by side till 1917, when Link died. After that Allie took what was left of her brood, including Ham's son Albert Dillon Hale, and moved to Illinois. She married again, a man named Reese.

Albert, the love child, grew up to serve in World War II. Later he worked as a garage manager in Detroit. On November 4, 1951, aged forty-four, he committed suicide by shooting himself through the head.

Maggie's husband, Dennis, managed to hang on to the Dillon farm through the early years of the Depression. In the spring of 1935, while out walking in a field near the house, he was stung to death by a cloud of yellow jackets.

They're buried together, the three of them—Ham, Maggie, and Dennis—on that high knoll in the Walnut Hill Cemetery near Odon. One of the very few real hills in that part of the country. You can stand there and look north across cattle and cropland a good long way.

ACKNOWLEDGMENTS

It's a pleasure to finally be able to thank my agent, Elizabeth Kaplan, who kept the faith of Oscar Hammerstein through some trying times. My gratitude as well to Nan Talese, for spying the possibilities in this project, and for cutting the bar scene; to Jesse Cohen, whose sharp eye and delicate touch made the editing process a rare pleasure; and to Ellen Stern, whose shrewd comments on some early chapters made me realize I wasn't as far along as I thought I was.

Some of the current residents of Daviess County helped me more than I can say—in particular Rex and Linda Sue Myers, whose boundless kindness and energy during my research trips turned up leads I never expected. Lenore Overholser and her sister, Leola Rohrer, also went far out of their way to assist me; so did Don Spillman and Ronnie Donaldson. Of all the period research I did, it was Mr. Donaldson who provided the cream: the marvelous diary of Oscar Hackler, who was Elnora's real-life rural mail carrier at the time of the murder. Stashed away in a leaky attic in Plainville, a nearby town, these volumes gave me a grand sense of the texture and detail of life there and then.

My appreciation as well to Elizabeth Dowling and the staff of the Carnegie Library in Washington, Indiana; Leo Vertrees; Owen Rader; Bonnie Ruth Gress; Marietta McKee; Eleanor Waggoner; and Carol Cabel. In Kentucky I had the aid of Mary Brown Byrd and Howard Teater. Hamp Clark, of Nicholasville, Kentucky, took me on a tour of the ruins of the old distillery where Link Hale once worked, and showed me the bridge Link almost jumped off.

My thanks to Eleanor Arnold for allowing me free access to her oral history project on Indiana farm life; that was an especially valuable resource. Thanks as well to the enterprising staff of the Indiana Historical Society in Indianapolis, including Ellen Crosby, Carolyn Autrey, and Alexandra Gressitt.

From several members of my family came help I consider gallant under the circumstances: my mother, Ruth Brock; my sister, Alice; Sally Rogers; Norma Kralik; and of course Michal Yanson. Ruth and Gale Tomey were presiding spirits.

Thanks to Kevin Dowling, who saw a dam where I only saw a wall, to Jeff Seal, for vital technical support, and to Sarah Wright, Chris Hansen, David Fichter, Chris Behrens, and Dr. Aryeh Maidenbaum. Also to Omar Shapli, Peter Kass, Ron Van Lieu, and my former classmates at the NYU School of the Arts.

Most of all I'm grateful to my wife, Susan, for her unfailing love, patience, and smarts. In more ways than one, she made it possible for me to write this book. (I've never heard of a support group for the spouses of authors, but there probably ought to be one.)

Confidential to Molly and Hannah: The next one's for you.

About the Author

POPE BROCK was born in Atlanta, Georgia, raised primarily in Baltimore, and graduated from Harvard University in 1971. After training in New York as an actor (still a secondary career), he became a freelance journalist, and has written for *Esquire, GQ, Rolling Stone, Life,* and many other magazines. He lives in Chappaqua, New York, with his wife and twin daughters, and is currently at work on a novel.